Python

This book includes

Python for beginners

Python data analytics

Python machine learning

Python for data science

the ultimate guide step by step learn in 7 days

Tony F. Charles

Python for beginners

Introduction

Python is a great language to start your programming journey. It has an easy syntax that makes sense to non-programming professionals. In the background, it's based on the C language which makes it extremely powerful. Since created by Van Rossum in 1991, Python has remained an open source project. It is for this reason you will find a lot of online tutorials and resources about Python.

Today, more fields than ever before are replying on computers to achieve results. Whether you are an aspiring social worker or a game designer, you require a particular degree of computer knowledge to get employment. Even if it's not a requirement, you can increase your productivity by automating your daily tasks. Consider you are a social worker who has to send regular email updates to your boss about the cases you work everyday. Since you already record notes on your computer, you might be able to write a script to extract information from your notes and send emails to your boss automatically at the end of your day. This is just one example, and I am sure you can think about a dozen similar tasks that you do that can be automated.

If you are starting with programming and have no knowledge about computers and programming, this book is written for you. You will find initial chapters easier to understand and as you progress to later chapters, you will have better skills and we will cover more advanced topics. This book is written in one flow and it's better to not skip any topic, let alone an entire chapter.

The software industry is changing rapidly and by the time you are finished with this book, there might be better techniques or tools available. This book focuses on using multiple tools to get the same results so the following can be instilled in your mind: "It doesn't matter what tools you use, the only thing that makes headlines is the end-product." I have high hopes this book will make your programming journey easier.

Chapter 1: Computer Science and Mathematics

Computers were developed by scientists to solve problems. Mathematics is the scientific language to solve problems. Therefore, computers and mathematics are inseparable. Computers utilize mathematical concepts to identify and solve problems. They are much better in sequential processing and more recently in multitasking different processes. Take the example of a french fries seller. He peels and cuts 50 potatoes all by himself. With time, more people start to buy fries from him and he needs to peel and cut more potatoes. He can hire helpers who he will have to pay per hour and also afford their medical and accommodate for their availability. The other option is to get a computer aided automated machine that takes the potatoes, washes, peels and then cuts them according to given criteria. The initial setup cost might be high but due to low operational cost, this is the better option. Not only the cost, the machine will be able to process more potatoes much quicker compared to human helpers.

This is how computers are changing everyone's lives. The cellphone you use all the time is also a computer, a small yet very sophisticated and powerful computer. Let's look at the history of computers.

History of Computers

In the 1880 US census, the population was determined to be a little over 50 million, 50,189,209 to be exact. It took 7 years for the US government to compile the census results and come up with the total number. There was definitely a need to process the census data faster. This need resulted in the invention of punch card computers that were gigantic machines. But, the concept of computers even predates this era.

Abacus

Not a computer but a counting tool, Abacus has been used for centuries by many ancient civilizations to count. How the tool came into existence is a complete mystery. It is still used today to teach children and visually impaired persons how to count.

Abacus is based upon the concept of coding - representing values with symbols. In the case of abacus, numbers are represented by beads and their values are determined by their positions.

1801: To automate the weaving process of different fabric

designs, Joseph Marie Jacquard invented a punch card reading loom. This punch card reading technology was later used by electronic computers in the early 20th century.

1822: People have hated memorizing multiplication tables for ages. Want proof? Charles Babbage, an English mathematician, invented a steam-powered machine to calculate the number tables. The English government funded project ultimately failed, but laid the foundation for computers developed later on.

1890: Remember when we said it took US government seven years to process the 1880 census? In the 1890 census, Herman Hollerith solved the issue by designing a system based on punch cards. It saved $5 million for the government and completed the process in only three years. The company Herman founded later became IBM.

1936: The modern computer is a good example of a Turing machine, a concept coined by Alan Turing in 1936 about a machine that can compute anything that's possible to compute.

1937: Up till this year, computers were electro-mechanical machines. A physics and mathematics professor at Iowa State, J.V. Atanasoff, attempted to build a computer without moving mechanical parts. Did he succeed? Time to do some Googling!

1939: The now globally recognized tech-giant, manufacturers of computer systems and peripherals, the "hp" company was founded by Bill Hewlett and David Packard in a garage of the city of Palo Alto, California.

1941: With the help of his graduate student Clifford Berry, J.V. Atanasoff one ups his previous achievement by designing a computer that could simultaneously solve 29 equations. The computer was the first of its kind because it could hold information in its memory.

1943-44: Two University of Pennsylvania professors, J.P. Eckert and John Mauchly, invent the Electronic Numerical Integrator and Calculator (ENIAC). A precursor to digital computers, it was physically enormous comprising of more than 17,500 vacuum tubes in a 20ft by 40ft assembly.

1946: The United States Census Bureau funded a contract for Mauchly and Eckert to build Universal Automatic Computer (UNIVAC). UNIVAC became the first commercially available computer and was widely used by government departments and research, financial and aviation institutions.

1947: The era of electronic computers started with the invention of the solid state transistor by William Shockley, Walter Brattain and John Bardeen of Bell laboratories. The transistor worked as a virtual switch that could either be off or on to store information. It was much smaller in size, consumed much less power and generated much less heat compared to vacuum tubes.

1953: COmmon Business-Oriented Language (COBOL), the first programming language, was invented by Grace Hooper. Thomas Watson Jr. invents the IBM 701 EDPM for the sole purpose of enabling the United Nations to monitor the Korean region during the Korean War.

1954: With computers becoming more commonly used by various companies, the need for a better programming language became apparent. A team of IBM programmers headed by John Backus developed a programming language named FORMula TRANslation (FORTRAN).

1958: Thanks to rapid advancements in the field of electronics, Jack Kilby and Robert Noyce developed the first integrated circuit to be used as a computer chip. The Nobel Prize in the field of Physics was awarded to Kilby in 2000, more than 40 years after his incredible feat.

1964: A computer with a mouse and Graphical User Interface

(GUI) is demonstrated by Douglas Engelbert as a modern computer prototype. The purpose was to introduce a highly accessible computer model that the general public could feel comfortable with. Computers were no longer just a scientist's play toy.

1962: There was no compatibility and standardization as different manufacturers independently designed computer systems. The issue was addressed by a team of Bell Labs programmers who created UNIX, a C language based operating system. The operating system could be run on various computer systems of that time. The era of system independent software was kickstarted even though UNIX was mostly deployed on mainframe systems by corporations instead of personal computers due to slow performance.

1970: Intel joined the computer race by launching the first temporary memory chips known as Intel 1103 Dynamic Random Access Memory (DRAM).

1973: Connecting multiple computers and/or hardware to combine computational power became easy when one of the research staff members at Xerox, Robert Metcalfe, invented the Ethernet protocol.

1974-77: Personal computers became more popular which led to the unveiling of several different models in the market including IBM 5100, Scelbi & Mark-8 Altair and the Radio Shack's "Trash 80", model TRS-80. Another popular personal computer from that era is the Commodore PET.

1975: The Altair 8080 got featured in the Popular Electronics (PE) magazine as the first true minicomputer for personal use that provide the same computational power of commercial computers. It inspires two computer enthusiasts Paul Allen and Bill Gates to write software for the popular minicomputer. Both later start a software firm on the back of this successful endeavour, called Microsoft.

1976: Apple Computers went operational led by the Two Steves, Steve Jobs and Steve Wozniak. Their first computer Apple 1 was launched on April Fool's day and was the first computer that used a single circuit board.

1977: The Trash 80 demand rose so high among the general public that Radio Shack had to manufacture more than the initial 3,000 unit production. The multipurpose nature of the computer made it hugely popular. In the same year, the Two Steves incorporated Apple and launched the Apple II during the West Coast Computer Fair. The computer offered color graphics and better storage via a drive for audio cassettes.

1978: The first spreadsheet software, called VisiCalc, got introduced. No one knows that name today!

1979: The first word processing software WordStar was launched by MicroPro International headed by Rob Barnaby. The software had various editing and formatting options including the ability to add margins, word wrap and print documents. The company went with a modernistic approach with the software and did not include a command mode which was usually a feature in software of that era. Another great software of that era that did not make it through the years.

1981: The first personal computer made of IBM's Intel hardware and Microsoft's MS DOS operating system, named "Acorn" was launched. Even today, the majority of personal computers have the combination of IBM and Microsoft products. Acorn offered two floppy disk drives and supported a color monitor. For the first time, the computer was sold through third party distributors and was popularly referred to as the PC.

1983: Apple introduced the first personal computer with a true GUI, named Lisa. The computer interface featured graphical icons and dropdown menus. The product flopped but paved the way for the future Apple computer system line of Macintosh. The same year, Gavilan Computer Corp. unveiled the Gavilan SC, the first widely recognized portable personal computer (laptop).

1985: To counter Apple's Lida, Microsoft introduced Windows which became the most widely used operating system in personal computers. In the same year, Commodore launched the Amiga 1000 that had enhanced audio and video abilities. In the same year, a Massachusetts based computer manufacturer Symbolics, purchased the first dot com website domain in the world: "symbolics.com". At this time, there wasn't even a concept of Internet history.

1986: Compaq launched the Deskpro 386 that had a 32bit architecture offering better performance than the competition to the extent it rivalled the mainframes of that era.

1990: In any organization of this era there were several hundred computers, and there was also a protocol to connect them (ethernet), but there was no good way to present information. A European Organization for Nuclear Research (commonly known as CERN, which is short for the french "Conseil européen pour la recherche nucléaire") researcher, Tim Berners-Lee, developed the HyperText Markup Language (HTML) which later became the language of the World Wide Web.

1993: Intel introduced the revolutionary Pentium processors that enabled high quality graphics and audio services to be offered in personal computers.

1994: The launch of hit video games including "Descent", "Alone in the Dark 2", "Magic Carpet", "Command & Conquer", "Little Big Adventure" and "Theme Park" meant the computers were not just for work, people were actively using them for entertainment. There was a demand for better performing computers.

1996: The search engine most people use today, Google, went live developed by Larry Page and Sergey Brin.

1997: Apple was struggling and in a legal dispute with Microsoft with the allegation that Microsoft copied the design and feel of its operating system. Apple took back the case after Microsoft invested an amount of $150 million in Apple.

1999: More mobility freedom became possible for the personal computer users after WiFi was introduced which meant internet and local connections could be made without the need for physical wires.

2001: The rivalry between Apple and Microsoft intensified after Apple released the newly designed Mac OS X. It was an instant hit as it offered secured memory architecture, as well as superior and faster multitasking by preserving software states. As a response, Microsoft released the Windows XP with a distinct GUI and advanced features.

2003: Albeit having a much smaller market share, AMD one ups Intel this time by launching the first ever 64bit system known as Athlon 64 which became an instant hit.

2004: Mozilla launches Firefox browser to rival the widely used Internet Explorer by Microsoft. Although not very intuitive, Internet Explorer was widely used because it was bundled with the popular Windows operating system. Mark Zuckerberg launched Facebook which was a social media platform.

2005: YouTube, the biggest video sharing platform today, was designed and launched by three PayPal employees, Jawed Karim, Steve Chen and Chad Hurley. Google acquired the Linux-based operating system for mobile devices known as Android.

2006: Apple designed the first mobile computer (laptop) MacBook Pro and the desktop computer iMac both of which used an Intel-based dual core system. Nintendo Wii gaming console became available in the market that had games based on motion and gesture detection.

2007: Apple released the groundbreaking smartphone with the brand name iPhone which remained the best-selling cell phone for a long time.

2009: Windows 7 was launched by Microsoft which became widely popular and had advanced capabilities including touch and speech recognition.

2010: Apple reignited consumer interest in tablets by launching the iPad.

2011: Google released the Chrome OS based laptop with the brand name Chromebook.

2012: Facebook gained 1 billion users, becoming the most significant social media platform.

2015: Apple released another technically advanced device: the Apple Watch. Microsoft released the final version of Windows, Windows 10, but still kept support for Windows 7 for years due to its wide use.

2016: Not the first quantum computer, but the first reprogrammable quantum computer was created. Before this, quantum computers were manufactured for specific purposes.

2017: Big improvements were made in the field of "molecular informatics", the science of creating computers using molecules as processing units.

The advancements in computer systems grow everyday. The silicon based electronics have almost reached their limits.

There are various researches going on to find a better base for electronic devices, but they are still far from commercial use.

Computer Architecture

The science of joining computer hardware and software to create unique computational systems is called computer architecture. It has evolved many times during the years as the applications of computers changed. Von Neumann architecture is the most famous computer architecture that relates to modern digital computers. According to this architecture, all computer systems are more or less comprised of following main parts.

Central Processing Unit (CPU)

The brain of a computer, the central processing unit, processes the given input and generates the desired output. The CPU itself is comprised of various parts.

Control Unit

Control Unit controls all the aspects of the CPU so the latter can process data according to set instructions. The supported set of instructions are stored in the permanent memory (Read Only Memory - ROM). It also controls the flow of data within the computer and provides signals for timing operations. If you are a gamer or a professional who has to deal with high quality graphics, you might have tweaked the clock speed of your computer's graphics unit. This is direct interaction with the computer's control unit.

Processor

The processor performs the actual computations. It houses the logic circuits and onboard caches, known as registers, for fast temporary data storage. Registers, which should not be confused with the main memory (RAM), enable the processor to store intermediate data generated during complex computations. The logic circuitry has electronic gates that operate on given data in different ways as told by the given instructions.

Main Memory

The Random Access Memory (RAM) is referred to as the main memory of a computer. Why? Because all the currently running applications are kept here until something is no longer needed. Modern computers have very large RAMs which enables them to hold many dormant applications for a longer time which makes multitasking and application boot up time very fast. Failure of power usually erases the contents of the RAM.

Input Systems

There are various input peripherals that have been developed for different purposes. The most common is the keyboard and the mouse. We have now touch screens, touch pads, voice (microphones) and image recognition (cameras) built into the computer. You can also use a scanner to scan hardcopy documents for easy processing and transmission.

Output Systems

Just like input devices, there are several output peripherals, the most common being the monitor and speaker. The other commonly known output device is the printer. It's interesting to note that the output devices are very few as compared to the input devices. It shows that the focus of computer architecture has always been to enable computers to take input so they can process it in the desired way.

More Components in A Modern Computer

A modern computer has a lot of different components added for enhanced processing capabilities.

External Memory

If you look at the computer architecture, you would notice there's no storage available for the user to store any information. The ROM is read only and houses the instructions and the RAM is temporary. In earlier computers, there were floppy disk drives that acted as an external memory so the computer user could save any information. In later computers, a hard disk was introduced as a permanent part of the computer system that was used to store all the information. With the advancement in memory storage, more devices were introduced such as CDs, DVDs and now the most common, USB flash drives.

Graphics Processing Unit (GPU)

Modern computers are frequently used in applications that demand high quality graphics. Video games have become very common, professionals have to deal with creation and editing of high quality graphics. Even watching high definition movies takes a lot of processing power. To remove excessive load from the CPU of a computer, a standalone processing unit is added to handle all graphics related tasks. Not only does it divide the load, it also divides the heat generation so one part of the computer doesn't get too hot.

<u>Virtual Memory (Paging)</u>

Applications these days take a lot of memory. What happens if your computer runs out of available RAM? Does it hang the system? Not so! Every computer has active memory management that monitors the amount of storage required for uninterrupted operation of the computer. If the RAM is full, the computer declares a portion of the hard disk as a virtual memory section and uses it as extended RAM (or virtual cache). The process is called pagination. Of course, this section is slower than the actual RAM, but helps keep applications ready for access. The user can control how much hard disk space can be used for virtual memory.

Mathematical Concepts

As we have stated before, computers are physical manifestations of several mathematical concepts. Mathematics are the scientific language of solving problems. Over the centuries, mathematicians have theoretically solved many complex issues. Mathematics includes concepts like algebra and geometry.

Number Systems

Mathematics is a game of number manipulation which makes number systems at the center stage of mathematical concepts. There are several different types of number systems. Before we take a look at the number systems, we have to understand the concept of coding.

Coding

A way to represent values using symbols is called coding. Coding is as old as humans. Before the number systems we use today, there were other systems to represent values and messages. An example of coding from ancient times is the Egyptian hieroglyphs.

Number systems are also examples of coding because values are represented using special symbols.

There are different types of number systems, and we are going to discuss a few relevant ones.

Binary System

A binary system has only two symbols, 1 and 0 which are referred to as bits. All the numbers are represented by combining these two symbols. Binary systems are ideal for electronic devices because they also have only two states, on or off. In fact, all electronic devices are based on the binary number system. The number system is positional which means the position of symbols determines the final value. Since there are two symbols in this system, the system has a base of 2.

The sole purpose of input and output systems is to convert data to and from binary system to a form that makes better sense to the user. The first bit from the left side is called Most Significant Bit (MSB) while the first bit from the right is called the Least Significant Bit (LSB).

Here is the binary equivalent code of "this is a message":

01110100 01101000 01101001 01110011 00100000
01101001 01110011 00100000 01100001 00100000
01101101 01100101 01110011 01110011 01100001
01100111 01100101

Decimal System

The decimal system has ten symbols, the numbers 0 through 9. This is also a positional number system where the position of symbols changes the value it represents. All the numbers in this system are created with different combinations of the initial ten symbols. This system has a base 10.

This is also called the Hindu-Arabic number system. Decimals make more sense to humans and are used in daily life. There are two reasons for that.

1. Creating large numbers from the base symbols follows a consistent pattern
2. Performing arithmetic operations in a decimal system is easier compared to other systems

Hexadecimal System

The hexadecimal number system is the only one that has letters as symbols. It has the 10 symbols of the decimal system plus the six alphabets A, B, C, D, E and F. This is also a positional number system with a base 16.

Hexadecimal system is extensively used to code instructions in assembly language.

Number System Conversion

We can convert the numbers from one system to another. There are various online tools to do that. Python also offers number conversion, but it is better to learn how it is done manually.

Binary to Decimal

Here's a binary number 01101001, let's convert it to a decimal number.

$(01101001)_2 = 0 \times 2^7 + 1 \times 2^6 + 1 \times 2^5 + 0 \times 2^4 + 1 \times 2^3 + 0 \times 2^2 + 0 \times 2^1 + 1 \times 2^0$

$(01101001)_2 = 0 + 64 + 32 + 0 + 8 + 0 + 0 + 1$

$(01101001)_2 = (105)_{10}$

Decimal to Binary

To convert a decimal number to binary, we have to repeatedly divide the number by two until the quotient becomes one. Recording the remainder generated at each division step gives us the binary equivalent of the decimal number.

2	105	
2	52	1
2	26	0
2	13	0
2	6	1
2	3	0
	1	1

$$(105)_{10} = (1101001)_2$$

An interesting thing to note here is that $(01101001)_2$ and $(1101001)_2$ represent the same decimal number $(105)_{10}$. It means that just like decimal number system, leading zeros can be ignored in the binary number system.

Binary to Hexadecimal

Binary numbers can be converted to hexadecimal equivalents using two methods.

1. Convert the binary number to decimal, then decimal to hexadecimal number
2. Break binary number in groups of four bits and convert each to its hexadecimal equivalent, keeping the groups' positions in the original binary number intact.

Let's convert $(1101001)_2$ to a hexadecimal number using the second method. The first step is to break the binary number into different groups each of four bits. If the MSB group has less than four bits, make it four by adding leading zeros. Grouping starts from the LSB. So, $(1101001)_2$ will give us $(1001)_2$ and $(0110)_2$. Now, remembering their position in the original binary number, we are going to convert each group to a hexadecimal equivalent.

Here is the table of hexadecimal equivalents of four-bit binary numbers.

Binary	Hexadecimal
0000	0
0001	1
0010	2
0011	3
0100	4
0101	5
0110	6
0111	7
1000	8
1001	9
1010	A
1011	B

1100	C
1101	D
1110	E
1111	F

From the table, we can see (1001)$_2$ is (9)$_{16}$ and (0110)$_2$,the MSB group, is (6)$_{16}$.

Therefore, (1101001)$_2$ = (01101001)$_2$ = (69)$_{16}$

Hexadecimal to binary

We can use the above given table to quickly convert hexadecimal numbers to binary equivalents. Let's convert (4EA9)$_{16}$ to binary.

(4)$_{16}$ = (0100)$_2$

(E)$_{16}$ = (1110)$_2$

(A)$_{16}$ = (1010)$_2$

(9)$_{16}$ = (1001)$_2$

So, (4EA9)$_{16}$ = (0100111010101001)$_2$ = (100111010101001)$_2$

Decimal to Hexadecimal

You can say hexadecimal is an extended version of decimals. Let's convert (45781)$_{10}$ to decimal. But, first, we have to remember this table.

Decimal	Hexadecimal
0	0
1	1
2	2
3	3
4	4
5	5
6	6
7	7
8	8
9	9
10	A
11	B
12	C

13	D
14	E
15	F

We are going to divide the decimal number repeatedly by 16 and record the remainders. The final hexadecimal equivalent is formed by replacing remainder decimals with their correct hexadecimal symbols.

16	45781	
16	2861	5
16	178	13
	11	2

$$(45781)_{10} = (B2D5)_2$$

Hexadecimal to Decimal

Let's convert (4EA9)$_{16}$ to its decimal equivalent.

$(4EA9)_{16} = 4 \times 16^3 + 14 \times 16^2 + 10 \times 16^1 + 9 \times 16^0$

$(4EA9)_{16} = 16384 + 3584 + 160 + 9$

$(4EA9)_{16} = (20137)_{10}$

There's another number system, the octal system, where the number of unique symbols include 0, 1, 2, 3, 4, 5, 6, along with 7. These were developed for small scale devices that worked on small values with limited resources. With the rapid advancements in storage and other computer resources, octal system became insufficient and thus was discarded in favor of hexadecimal number system. You might still find an old octal based computer system.

Fractions (Floating Points)

Decimal number system supports a decimal point '.' to represent portion/slices of a value. For example, if we want to say half of milk bag is empty using numbers, we can write 0.5 or ½ of milk bag is empty. Do other number systems support decimal point? Yes, they do. Let's see how to convert (0.75 $)_{10}$ or (¾ $)_{10}$ to binary.

¾ x 2 = 6/4 = 1 . (2/4)

2/4 x 2 = 4/4 = 1

(0.75 $)_{10}$ = (¾ $)_{10}$ = (.11 $)_2$

Negatives

In the decimal system, a dash or hyphen '-' is placed before a number to declare it as a negative. There are different ways to denote negative numbers in the binary system. The easiest is to consider the MSB as a sign bit, which means if MSB is 1, the number is negative and if the MSB is 0, the number is positive. Determining if a hexadecimal number is negative or positive is a bit tricky. The easiest way is to convert the number into binary and perform the checks for negatives in binary system.

Linear Algebra

Did you hate algebra in school? I have some bad news for you! Linear algebra is heavily involved in programming because it's one of the best mathematical ways to solve problems. According to Wikipedia, algebra is the study of mathematical symbols and the rules for manipulating these symbols. The field advanced thanks to the works of Muhammad ibn Musa al-Khwarizmi who introduced the reduction and balancing methods and treated algebra as an independent field of mathematics. Algebra comes from (*al-jabr*) in the name of the book *al-Kitāb al-mukhtaṣar fī ḥisāb al-jabr wal-muqābala* (The Compendious Book on Calculation by Completion (*al-jabr*) and Balancing (*al-muqābala*)) Khwarizmi wrote on the subject. During that era, the concept of 'x' and 'y' etc. variable notation wasn't widespread but during the Islamic Golden Age, Arabs had a fondness of lengthy "layman terms" descriptions of problems and solutions and that is what Khwarizmi explained algebra concepts in his book. The book dealt with many practical real-life problems including the fields of finance, planning, and legal.

So, we know what algebra is. But, where does "linear" comes from? For that, we have to understand what a linear system is. It is a mathematical model where the system attributes (variables) have a linear relation among themselves. The easiest way to explain this is if the plot between system attributes is a straight line, the system is linear. Linear systems are much simpler than the nonlinear systems. The set of algebraic concepts that relate to linear systems is referred to as linear algebra. Linear algebra helps resolve system problems such as missing attribute values. The first step is to create linear equations to establish the relationship between the system variables.

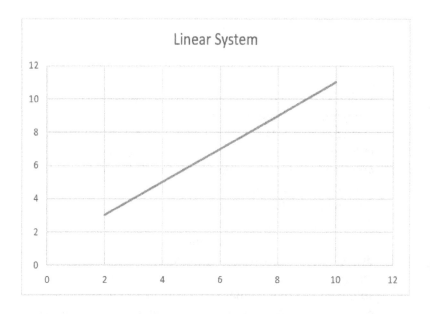

Statistics

Another important field of mathematics that is crucial in various computer science applications. Data analysis and machine learning wouldn't be what they are without the advancements made in statistical concepts during the 20th century. Let's see some concepts related to statistics.

Outlier

Outlier detection is very important in statistical analysis. It helps in homogenizing the sample data. After detecting the outliers, what to do with them is crucial because they directly affect the analysis results. There are many possibilities including:

Discarding Outlier

Sometimes it's better to discard outliers because they have

been recorded due to some error. This usually happens where the behaviour of the system is already known.

System Malfunction

But, outliers can also indicate a system malfunction. It is always better to investigate the outliers instead of discarding them straightaway.

Average

Finding the center of a data sample is crucial in statistical analysis because it reveals a lot of system characteristics. There are different types of averages, each signifying something important.

Mean

Mean is the most common average. All the data values are added and divided by the number of data values added together. For example, you sell shopping bags to a well-renowned grocery store and they want to know how much each shopping bag can carry. You completely fill 5 shopping bags with random grocery items and weigh them. Here are the readings in pounds.

5.5, 6.0, 4.95, 7.1, 5.0

You calculate the mean as (5.5 + 6 + 4.95 + 7.1 + 5) / 5 = 5.71. You can tell the grocery store your grocery bags hold 5.71 lbs on average.

Median

Median is the center value with respect to the position of data in a sample data when it's sorted in ascending order. If sample data has odd members, the median is the value with an equal number of values on both flanks. If sample data has an even number of values, the median is calculated by finding the mean of two values in the middle with equal number of items on both sides.

Mode

Mode is the most recurring value in a dataset. If there is no recurring value in the sample data, there is no mode.

Variance

To find how much each data value in a sample data changes with respect to the average of the sample data, we calculate the variance. Here is a general formula to calculate variance.

sum of (each data point - mean of sample points $)^2$ / number of data points in the sample.

If the variance is low in a sample data, it means there are no outliers in the data.

Standard Deviation

We take the square root of variance to find standard deviation. This relates the mean of sample data to the whole of sample data.

Probability

No one can accurately tell what will happen in the future. We can only predict what is going to happen with some degree of certainty. The probability of an event is written mathematically as,

Probability = number of possible ways an event can happen / total number of possibilities

A few points:

1. Probability can never be negative
2. Probability ranges between one and zero
3. To calculate probability, we assume that the set of events we are working with occur independently without any interference.

Finding the probability of an event can change the probability of something happening in a subsequent event. It depends upon how we are interacting with the system to find event probabilities.

Distribution

There are many types of distributions. In this book, whenever we talk about distribution, we refer to probability distribution unless explicitly stated otherwise. Let's take an example of flipping coins and see what is the distribution of such events.

H H H	T H H
H H T	H T T
H T H	T H T
T T T	TTH

This is a very simple event with only a handful of possible outcomes. We can easily determine the probability of different outcomes. But, this is almost impossible in complex systems with thousands or millions of possible outcomes. Distributions work much better in such cases by visually representing the probability curve. It makes more sense than looking at a huge table of fractions or small decimal numbers.

We call a probability distribution discrete if we know all the possible outcomes beforehand.

Chapter 2: Introduction to Python

Before doing anything else, visit https://www.python.org/. The website contains all Python standard packages and comprehensive documentation. Here's a problem: official documentations are written for professional programmers and it doesn't make sense for beginners. This is where Python beats the competition: the huge community of volunteers and contributors who have created so much learning material that's ideal for beginners. This book is also part of that learning material.

Why Python?

Almost everyone who starts learning programming questions the choices they made before, like why did I pick this language? Why I am learning programming? If you went with Python because it's the trend, we can assure you that you have made a correct decision. Python is a high-level language built for beginners. From the start, the language instils the concept of arranged, clean code in the minds of a programmer. In other languages, you spend considerable time learning the syntax. But with Python, you learn how to program without worrying too much about the specific syntax. It doesn't mean there is no specific syntax to follow, it means there are less things to worry about.

The programming language is open-source which means more people have access to it. You will find tutorials on almost everything there is to do in Python. I still remember the last few months of my college days when I was stuck with my final project. I had tried everything I could think of for days but there was no progress. I started searching on the Internet and after some more worryful hours, I stumbled upon the work of another student who had solved a similar issue. I modified his approach to my requirements and voila, my project was complete! I am very sure that if I had been working with a proprietary platform, I would have failed that course.

Remembering this, I should tell you an important skill that you should master before you start learning programming. The skill is to become an advanced user of search engines. No matter which search engine you use, Google, Bing, Yahoo, etc., you must know all or most of the tips and tricks on how to find something online. There is a high chance someone has already gone through what you are trying to do, or has done something similar. You will feel like a hacker once you master the art of using search engines!

Basic Stuff

Constants

Constants are symbols that already have fixed value in the programming language. As the name suggests, you cannot change constants. Constants have specific data type. For example, number 21 is a constant.

Expressions

Expressions will most frequently appear on the right hand side of an operator and can be a combination of constants, variables, and more operators. When writing a script, an expression will not result in any output unless the result of expression is either stored in a variable or used to make a decision.

Operators

A wide range of operators are supported by Python. Operators are commands/instructions that perform specific operation on the data supplied with the operators which are themselves called operands. Here's a list of some important operators in Python.

Arithmetic Operators

Arithmetics is another vital part of mathematics and Python supports a long list of arithmetic operations. Here are some examples.

Operator   **Meaning**

+ Perform addition of operands - order of operands

doesn't matter

-     Perform subtraction of one operand
from the other (right

side from the left side)

- Multiply operands and their order doesn't affect the output

  / Divide one operand from the other (

  left side by the right side) and returns the quotient

%   Divides one operand from the other(left side by the right side)but the returns the remainder

**   returns exponents of an operand

Comparative Operators

These operators are vital for conditional statements. The below table contains some examples.

Operator	Meaning
==	Check if two operands are equal
!=	Check if two operands are not equal
>	Check if the left side operand is greater

than the right side operand

< Check if the left side operand

is less than the right side operand

Logical Operators

We can perform multiple operations

together and see the combined effect.

Operator	Meaning
and	performs logical AND
	operation - only true if all operands are true
or	performs logical OR operation –
	only false if all operands are false
not	reverse the result of a logical operation

Assignment Operator

The only operator that lets you store information,

the '=' operator, is very crucial to Python

programming. On the left side is always

the variable name, and on the right

side is a constant, expression,

or a function that returns a value.

Python executes operators according to the

PEMDAS rule of precedence. Here is the summary.

1 Anything wrapped with parentheses

will be executed first. If you want

to execute an operation first

by ignoring its precedence, put them inside parentheses.

2 Exponent operator has the next highest precedence.

3 The next precedence is shared by

multiplication and division operations

4 Last but not least, addition

and subtraction have the

same precedence and are executed at the very end

If more than one operators have

the same precedence, Python

will execute the operator that's

at the leftmost side of the expression.

 Here are a few practical examples.

>>>4+(8*(3-1))+(12*2)

44

>>>9183 % 21

6

>>>mon=767

>>>mon*(mon/mon)

767.0

Variables

You can store constants or results gathered

through a function return or expression

 result in a variable. In Python, we do not

have to pre-declare the type of variable.

The type of data stored in the variable determines its type.

A=4

Print= a

We stored the integer '4' in the variable 'a'.

It makes the variable 'a' of the integer type.

There are different rules you need to follow

when creating a variable name.

1. The first character of a variable name must be an alphabet

2. Numbers can be used in a variable name
3. You can capitalize the first name of a variable name but it's not considered good practice

4   Both uppercase and lowercase alphabets can be used in a variable name

Underscore '_' is the only special character

allowed in a variable name

Python has 31 keywords in total that you cannot use

as a variable name. Here's the complete list for reference .

1. global
2. if
3. import
4. in
5. is
6. lambda
7. not
8. or
9. pass
10. print
11. raise
12. return
13. try
14. while
15. with
16. global
17. if
18. import
19. in
20. is
21. lambda
22. not
23. or
24. pass
25. print
26. raise
27. return
28. try
29. while
30. with

31. yield
32. and
33. as
34. assert
35. break
36. class
37. continue
38. def
39. del
40. elif
41. else
42. except
43. exec
44. finally
45. for
46. from

A few examples of assigning variables are below

sTr = "Howdy partner!" #string variable

fLt = 3.14 # floating variable

sTRng = "3.14" #double quotes mean its a string

To check the type of variable, we can use the type() method.

type(sTRng)

You will see the following output.

<type 'str'>

Statements

All the instructions that you give to Python are called statements. Statements may or may not produce an output. When you write a script, you are sequencing a number of statements for the Python interpreter to execute one by one.

Test the following lines of code using Python.

i = 411

i = i + 27

print i

We are doing something unique here. We know that in Python, the right side of the operator '=', which is "i + 27" is calculated first and the result is assigned to the variable name 'i' on the left. Using this knowledge, we have overwritten the value of variable 'i' with a new value.

End of statements

Most programming languages were inspired from the C language, hence use the semicolon ';' to mark the end of a statement. Python, although based on the C language, deviated from this practice and used newlines and tabs to demarcate code blocks. It increased readability but creates problem when copy pasting codes.

If you want to write a single line of code to take two lines on your screen, you can use a backward slash '\'. Here's an example.

```
>>> breKK = \
... 971 + \
... 412
```

The three dots indicate the Python interpreter is waiting for the next part of the code. You will see this when writing a loop, conditional or function code block. Checking the value of variable "breKK" will tell if the program ran correctly. The returned value should be 1383.

```
>>> breKK
1383
```

Conditionals

We use conditionals to check a condition and direct the flow of the program execution. These statements are integral to deploying the concept of control flow in Python.

The if statement

If the given condition is true, execute the next block of code otherwise ignore it.

```
>>> num = 77

>>> if num == 18:

...        print("Execute this")

...

>>>
```

There's no output because the print statement never got executed because the condition "if num == 18" returned false. The indented blocks are referred to as suites. In case the if condition is true, the print statement will be executed. The following code gives the output of "Execute this".

```
>>> num = 77

>>> if num == 77:

...        print("Execute this")

...

Execute this

>>>
```

We can combine the "if" statement with the "else" statement to execute codes in case the "if" condition returns false.

```
>>> vaRa = 47
```

```
>>> if vaRa < 23:

...        print("vaRa is less")

... else:

...        print("vaRa is more")

...

vaRa is more

>>>
```

The variable "vaRA" is assigned the value of 47. The "if" condition returns false which directs the control flow to the code block under "else" statement for execution. We can use elif to check a condition before executing a code block.

```
>>> vaRa = 47

>>> if vaRa < 23:

...        print("vaRa is less")

... elif xcon > 33:

...        print("vaRa is more")

... else:

...        print("undetermined")

...

vaRa is more

>>>
```

Here's an example of nesting multiple "if" statements.

```
>>> ynst = 991

>>> znet = "Tssp"

>>> if znet == "Tssp":

...         if ynst > 200:

...                 print("ynst out of range")

...         elif ynst < 100:

...                 print("ynst too low")

...         else:

...                 print("ynst within range")

... else:

...         print("out of scope")

...

ynst within range
```

As stated earlier, we can combine multiple checks inside an "if" statement using logical operators.

```
>>> ynst = 147

>>> znet = "Test"

>>> if znet == "Result" and ynst == 147:

...         print("Sweet!")
```

... else:

...   print("Bummer!")

...

Bummer!

The "znet == "Result"" check will always return false because znet is assigned the value "Tssp". The "and" operator returns true only if all operations return true which was not the case this time.

Here is another thing that makes Python stand out from other programming languages: it has no switch-case statement. Truth be told, if you properly master if-else-elif, you will never miss the switch-case statement.

Loops

Humans hate repetitive work. It's boring. However, computers excel at performing the same task over and over again. There are two major types of loops in Python: the "for" and "while" loops.

The for loop

The "for" loop is ideal if you know how many times the loop needs to be executed. Let's discuss the things you must know before working with "for" loops.

Iterable

These loops require an entity that offers multiple attributes that the loop can use to iterate over.

Iterator

The loop also requires a pointer like entity that will go over the iterable. Depending upon the iterable, the iterator stores iterable entity's data while iterating.

A simple "for" loop example is below.

>>> for itr in range(190,200):

...   print i

...

190

191

192

193

194

195

196

197

198

199

A simple program, but it highlights a few very important things.

1. range() creates a sequence of numbers starting and ending in the limits given to the method

2. The "for" loop executes as soon as the maximum limit is reached and not when it's crossed. This is evident from the program output as the loop execution stopped as soon as the value of "itr" became 100.

The range() method has a default increment of one but you can change that. But, a point to remember, only integers can be given to the range().

>>> for xyz in range(22,33,2):

...   print(xyz)

...

22

24

26

28

20

32

The range() will work even if we omit the lower limit but we can't pass a step also. For example:

>>> for nUm in range(7):

...   print(nUm)

...

0

1

2

3

4

5

6

7

An important observation here is the number started from zero which is very valuable when using range() to output indices for data structures.

Here's a question: will we get an error if we use a lower limit less than the upper limit? Let's test it out.

```
>>> for per in range(100, 50):
...     print(per)
...
>>>
```

Interestingly, no errors were given. The loop just didn't execute.

The while loop

When we do not know how many times a loop needs to iterate, we use the "while" loop. At the start of each iteration, the condition is checked and the loop block is executed if the condition is still true. This property makes it ideal to create infinite loops which are very important in various applications such as game development.

```
>>> itr = 91

>>> while (itr < 95):

...        print("Executing this statement")

...        itr = itr + 1 # can also write as itr += 1

...

Executing this statement

Executing this statement

Executing this statement

Executing this statement
```

As you can see, we have to explicitly update the "itr" variable because "while" only checks the condition. If we comment out the itr = itr + 1, we will end up with an infinite loop because value of "itr" will never become greater than 95.

"While" loops should be used with extreme care and only when you are confident with your programming skills.

Data Structures in Python

Lists

Up till now, we have seen variables that can hold one value at a time. In many cases, this is insufficient. For example, you want to store the hour marks and the task you need to do in a list.

tasklist = ['8.00','wake up', '9.00', 'work', '13.00', 'lunch', '17.00', 'off to home']

All the values in the "tasklist" are strings but we can combine different types of data in a list. The first item index of a list is always zero. Let's test that theory.

>>> tasklist[0]

'8.00'

The len() function provides the number of items in a list.

>>> len(tasklist)

8

Lists are iterables hence we can use loops to go over them. Let's use a "for" loop to access all the items in our "tasklist".

>>> for tsk in tasklist:

...   print tsk

...

8.00

wake up

9.00

work

13.00

lunch

17.00

off to home

The operator "in" is used to get one item from the list at every loop iteration. We can use an index to get a list item. Can we know the index if we have an item value? Yes we can, and here's an example.

```
>>> for tsk in tasklist:
...     print("Value:",tsk,"- Position:",tasklist.index(tsk))
...
Value: 8.00 - Position: 0
Value: wake up - Position: 1
Value: 9.00 - Position: 2
Value: work - Position: 3
Value: 13.00 - Position: 4
Value: lunch - Position: 5
Value: 17.00 - Position: 6
Value: off to home - Position: 7
```

Lists support negative values as index. For example, to get the last value of a list, we can use a negative one as index.

```
>>> print(implist[-1])
off to home
```

It is possible to replace data in a list.

```
>>> tasklist[2] = "Now it's 9am"
```

```
>>> print(tasklist)
```

['8.00','wake up', 'Now it's 9am', 'work', '13.00', 'lunch', '17.00', 'off to home']

We can verify the membership of an item in a list.

```
>>> if "sleep" not in implist:

...        print("sleep is for the weak")

...
```

sleep is for the weak

The list method of append() can be used to add new items to the list. The new item is added at the end of the list.

```
>>>tasklist.append("dinner")

>>> tasklist
```

['8.00','wake up', 'Now it's 9am', 'work', '13.00', 'lunch', '17.00', 'off to home', 'dinner']

We can use the insert() method to add an item at a specific index position.

```
>>> tasklist.insert(8,"19.00")

>>> tasklist
```

['8.00','wake up', 'Now it's 9am', 'work', '13.00', 'lunch', '17.00', 'off to home', '19.00', 'dinner']

We can remove a specific item using its value through the remove() method.

```
>>> tasklist.remove("19.00")
```

>>> tasklist

['8.00','wake up', 'Now it's 9am', 'work', '13.00', 'lunch',
'17.00', 'off to home', 'dinner']

We can remove a specific item using its position with the
pop() method.

>>> tasklist.pop(8)

"dinner"

>>> tasklist

['8.00','wake up', 'Now it's 9am', 'work', '13.00', 'lunch',
'17.00', 'off to home']

In case no index is provided, pop() removes the last item in
the list. So, in the above code we could have gotten the same
result by not providing the index '8' in the pop().

The extend() method is one of the many ways to join two
lists.

>>> funlist = ["weekend","24/7 fun", "no work"]

>>> tasklist.extend(funlist)

>>> tasklist

['8.00','wake up', 'Now it's 9am', 'work', '13.00', 'lunch',
'17.00', 'off to home', "weekend","24/7 fun", "no work"]

All the items from "funlist" are added at the end of "tasklist".

You can nest lists as well which means a list can contain other
lists.

>>> newlist = [tasklist, funlist]

Dictionaries

A dictionary is an advanced form of arrays because we can set custom index (called key) for each item (called value) in it. The key and value can be of any data type.

You can change the contents of a dictionary. A dictionary can hold another dictionary.

Let's rewrite our tasklist as a dictionary. You will immediately see the data make more sense.

>>> taskDict = {

... "8.00": "wake up",

... "9.00": "work",

... "13.00": "lunch",

... "17.00": "off to home"

... }

Instead of a numerical index, we use the key to retrieve a value.

>>> taskDict["9.00"]

work

To know how many key-value pairs are present in a dictionary, we can use the len().

>>> len(taskDict)

4

We can also get all the keys in a dictionary using the method keys() which returns a list containing all the keys.

```
>>> taskDict.keys()
```

['8.00', '9.00', '13.00', '17.00']

In a similar way, the values() method returns all the values in a dictionary as a list.

```
>>> taskDict.values()
```

['wake up', 'work', 'lunch', 'off to home']

Let's add a list to this dictionary.

```
>>> taskDict["Fun List"] = ["weekend","24/7 fun", "no work"]
```

"Fun List" is the key. Dictionaries have become ordered in Python 3.0+ that make them even faster and newly added items are always added at the end of a dictionary.

The pop() method is also supported by dictionaries.

```
>>> taskDict.pop("Fun List")
```

["weekend","24/7 fun", "no work"]

The operator "in" is applicable to dictionaries too but it works slightly different. For dictionaries, the "in" operator retrieves the keys. We can use it with a loop to retrieve the keys and values of any dictionary.

```
>>> for timeMarc in taskDict:

...        print("Time:", timeMarc,"- Task:",taskDict[timeMarc])

...
```

Time: 8.00 - Task: wake up

Time: 9.00 - Task: work

Time: 13.00 - Task: lunch

Time: 17.00 - Task: off to home

The "in" operator along with the conditional "if" statement can be used to check if certain data is present as a key in a dictionary.

```
>>> if "22.00" in taskDict:
...        print("you should be asleep by now!")
... else:
...        print("good boy")
...

good boy
```

To find something in the values, we can replace taskDict() with taskDict().values()

```
>>> if "sleep" in taskDict.values():
...        print("sleep is good!")
... else:
...        print("sleep is for the weak!")
...

sleep is for the weak!
```

We can add a dictionary inside another dictionary.

>>> newDict = {

... "a": "apple",

... "b": "ball",

... "c": "cat",

... "d": "door",

... "vowels": {'one': 'a', 'two': 'e', 'three': 'i', 'four': 'o', 'five': 'u'},

... }

Tuples

Tuples don't serve any purpose other than to provide a medium when we are required to pass information between system layers or components without the chance of change.

Here's our first tuple.

>>> tasktup = ('8.00','wake up', '9.00', 'work', '13.00', 'lunch', '17.00', 'off to home')

>>> print(tasktup)

('8.00','wake up', '9.00', 'work', '13.00', 'lunch', '17.00', 'off to home')

Python allows you to change the type of a variable. For example str(64) will convert it into '64'. We can use the same concept to change a tuple. We first convert the tuple to a list, make the edits, and convert the updated list back to a tuple.

```
>>> templist = list(tasktup )
```

```
>>> templist.pop()
```

'off to home'

```
>>> templist.insert(8,"overtime")
```

```
>>> tasktupnew = tuple(templist)
```

```
>>> tasktupnew
```

('8.00','wake up', '9.00', 'work', '13.00', 'lunch', '17.00', 'overtime')

Sets

Python has maintained the rules of mathematical set theory when creating its "sets" data structure.

```
>>> taskset = set(['8.00','wake up', '9.00', 'work', '13.00', 'lunch', '17.00', 'off to home'])
```

Since the sets are unordered, there's no index. Therefore, you cannot change items in a set using an index value, but you can add new items or remove existing ones.

We can use all the other methods we have learned so far and also some more such as add() and update(). Both add new elements at the end of the set. You are already familiar with the remove() and discard() and both are supported by sets.

Chapter 3: Shifting Gears

Python is very extendable, thanks to the hundreds of external libraries written by volunteer contributors. In this chapter, we are going to work with some of the external libraries, how to install and import them, and use the methods available in those libraries.

External Libraries

We are going to use the popular chart creation "matplotlib" library as a means of demonstrating how to install and import an external library.

We can use pip to install matplotlib. Open the Windows command prompt and run the following command. A note here: If you are using an advanced interpreter like PyCharm, the command prompt is accessible from the interpreter. You do not have to open command prompt separately.

pip install matplotlib

Python will download and install the library and all the required resources. Once it is setup, we can import the library to start using it.

import matplotlib.pyplot as plt

When we ask Python to import a library or your own written module, there is a path registry that Python searches to find that resource. The following code will give you all the paths registered in the registry.

>>> import sys

```
>>> for resourcePath in sys.path:

...        print(resourcePath)

...
```

You can import your own script in another script. Place your script in one of the paths the above code outputs and you will be able to use "import" to use it in another script.

The import process takes a lot of resources and can make your interpreter or entire computer become unresponsive. Do not worry, just give it a minute, the process will finish and everything will be back to normal. If you are running in interactive mode and there's no output, it means the import was a success. Otherwise, there will be an error.

Because the import process takes too many resources, it's only run once for each resource. Duplicate import for the same library/module is ignored.

import datetime

import datetime

In the above two import statements, only the first one will run. Python will not execute the second statement. It means you cannot recursively call your module just like you can recursively call a function to do something. If the module/library has various functions (methods), we can import a specific one just like we did with the matplotlib.pyplot. Once imported, we can start using it.

```
>>> plt.plot([10, 13, 15, 17])
```

[<matplotlib.lines.Line2D object at 0x000001905095FF88>]

The pyplot is a simple line chart or line graph. If you look closely, we have given coordinates using the plot() function.

>>> plt.ylabel("Y Coordinates")

Text(0,0.5,u'Y Coordinates')

>>> plt.xlabel("X Coordinates")

Text(0.5,0,u'X Coordinates')

>>> plt.style.use('grayscale')

The "Text" outputs are just a confirmation that the axes labels are updated to the new values. To view the plot, we use the show() method.

>>> plt.show()

The plot is shown in a new window. It looks like below.

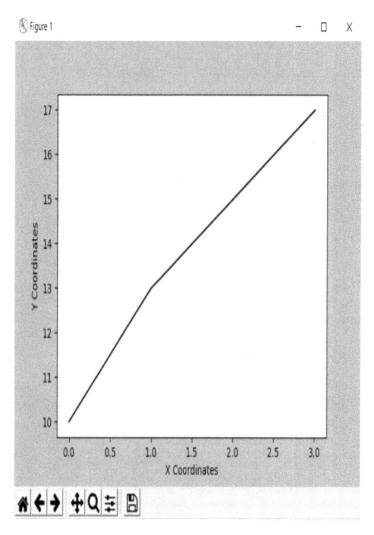

We set the plot style as grayscale otherwise the line would have been colored. There are different tools available to edit or save this plot. The plot remains open until you close it using the close button. This is important because the interactive mode might be unresponsive until you close the graph.

The matplotlib library is a huge resource to visualize data in many different ways. It's not possible to cover it completely in this book. We used it as an example for importing and using an external library. Later on, we will use another library to create graphs and plots.

Strings

Python supports extreme string manipulation. The language considers strings as a data structure, specifically a list of characters. This enables the programmer to manipulate strings in ways not possible in other programming languages. The advanced methods make Python also better for data analysis where the data is string most of the time. Data type conversion is also very straightforward. Python handles all string operations faster than the competition.

```
>>> op = "974"
```

```
>>> type(op)
```

```
<class 'str'>
```

```
>>> pp = 'this is string'
```

```
>>> type(op)
```

```
<class 'str'>
```

Enclose anything in single or double quotes for Python to consider it as string type. Notice how Python returned "class". This has changed in recent Python versions so the language has become more uniform with the statement "Everything in Python is a class."

```
>>> strJ = op + pp
```

```
>>> print(strJ)
```

974this is string

The '+' operator acts as a concatenator for strings. We can also use the join() method to concatenate strings.

```
>>> strJ = op.join(pp)
```

```
>>> print(strJ)
```

t974h974i974s974 974i974s974 974s974t974r974i974n974g

The output is a little weird and unexpected but this is just how join() method works. The result looks more like a multiplication of both strings. The join() method breaks the argument string into individual elements and joins the string the method is applied to with those individual elements.

```
>>> str(00457)
```

```
  File "<stdin>", line 1
    xx = 00457

         ^
```

SyntaxError: invalid token

In newer Python versions, we cannot put leading zeros, it gives a syntax error. There's a work around though: the zfill() method.

```
>>> str(457).zfill(6)
```

'000457'

The zfill() method is only applicable on strings, so we need to convert the number to string before adding the leading zeroes. There are already three digits in 457 so we gave six as zfill() argument because we want to add three leading zeros making the total characters in the string six.

The len() works on the string the same way it works on other data structures - it gives the number of elements.

>>> exStr = "139 characters"

>>> len(exStr)

13

Combine len() with range() and we can dissect the string to access each character individually.

>>> for chr in range(len(exStr)):

...   print(exStr[chr], end=' ')

...

1 3 9   c h a r a c t e r s

Some observations.

1. Just like lists, we can access the string using its index
2. To stop Python from adding a newline after the print output, we have added a comma ',' which adds a space instead of a newline

There are several ways to access the elements of a string. Let's try another method that uses the 'in' operator.

>>> for chr in exStr:

...   print(chr)

...

139 c h a r a c t e r s

Fewer characters to get the exact same output. The first character has the index zero, as proven by the example below.

```
>>> exStr[0]
```

```
'1'
```

The last element has an index which is one less than the length of the string.

```
>>> exStr[len(exStr)-1]
```

```
's'
```

All this information can be used to utilize a while() loop.

```
>>> ind = 0
```

```
>>> while ind <= len(exStr) - 1:
```

```
...        print(exStr[ind])
```

```
...        ind = ind + 1
```

```
...
```

139 c h a r a c t e r s

In the while loop, we could have wrapped "len(exStr) - 1" within parentheses but it isn't required for our current example.

Slice and Dice Strings

Slicing a string is very easy using the indices. Slicing creates a new string from the string.

string[start index:optional stop index:optional step amount]

Let us have this slicing technique applied to the exStr string.

>>> exStr[4:]

'haracters'

Since we did not provide a stopping index, the returned string has all the characters from the starting index to the end of the original string. The easiest way to reverse a string is to use slicing without the start and stop indices and use a step value of negative one.

>>> longstr[::-1]

'sretcarahc 31'

Extraction and Replacement of Substrings

The creators of Python have tried their best to have Python make sense in every way possible. The method names almost always closely resemble their application. Let's focus on the string method split(), which splits the string according to the given substring.

>>> exStr.split()

['13', 'characters']

Since we didn't provide any argument to split(), the default value of space ' ' was used. This is apparent from the example below.

>>> 'kajhskjdha'.split()

['kajhskjdha']

Let's provide a substring.

>>> 'kajhskjdha'.split('a')

['k', 'jhskjdh', '']

The returned list of strings do not have the argument we used to split the string. We can also replace a portion of a string with something else.

>>> exStr.replace("13","some")

'some characters'

Note that replace() doesn't change the real string. We can definitely check the contents of exStr.

>>> exStr

'13 characters'

The replace() by default replaces all the instances of a specific substring with the required substring.

>>> exStr.replace('a','e', 1)

'13 cheracters'

Not just a single character, replace can be used to replace entire words or phrases with something new. You might have used the find and replace tool on many software applications that deal with text such as word processors. Notice how easy it is to implement such as feature using the replace() method. Maybe a future challenge could be to develop a word processing application using Python?

Exceptional Handling

Error Types

There are two main categories of errors in Python.

Syntax errors

When you do not follow the rules of script writing in Python, you will get a syntax error, also called parsing error. We have already seen an example of syntax/parsing error.

>>> str(00457)

  File "<stdin>", line 1

  xx = 00457

       ^

SyntaxError: invalid token

Whenever an error occurs, Python tries to provide an explanation so the programmer knows what needs to be fixed. The explanation and hints are sometimes not very easy to understand but most of the time, you should consider the hints carefully.

Exceptions

If you make no mistakes in syntax during the program writing, you might still end up having the wrong output or breaking program flow with an error. Let us discuss some more errors.

Index error

Using an index that is not present in a data structure will lead to an index error.

```
>>> listrand = ["python","the","best", "programming", "language"]

>>> listrand[100]

IndexError: list index out of range
```

Name error

If we use a resource without assigning a value to it first, we get an error.

```
>>> listrand = ["python","the","best", "programming", "language"]

>>> print(listrandom)

NameError: name 'listrandom' is not defined
```

Type error

When we try to perform an operation that is not supported by the given data, it leads to a type error.

```
>>> intpp = 741

>>> strpp = "007"

>>> strpp + intpp
```

TypeError: can only concatenate str (not "int") to str

If you apply the arithmetic operator '+' but the position operands is reversed, the explanation of type error becomes different.

>>> intpp + strpp

TypeError: unsupported operand type(s) for +: 'int' and 'str'

Import error

If you import a library/module that Python is not able to find in the directories listed in the path directory, you will get an import error.

>>> import custmod

ModuleNotFoundError: No module named 'custmod'

>>> from math import triag

ImportError: cannot import name 'triag' from 'math' (unknown location)

We see two different descriptions for the same error because the error happened due to different reasons.

Logical error

When you make an error that's not an error for Python but we still don't get the output we were expecting, then we have encountered a logical error. Logical errors are very difficult to find and fix because you do not get any hint as to what's causing it.

Let's write a script with a logical error to illustrate how a logical error can occur. Even with this simple example, it would be a serious task to find the cause of error because it's really not apparent.

```
import math

num1 = 200

num2 = num1 / 5 * math.pi

print num2
```

The following output is generated after saving and executing the above script.

```
125.66370614359172
```

The result is wrong because we were expecting an output of 12.732395447351628. We know that there is something wrong with the program, but we have no idea where the issue is. We will have to deploy troubleshooting techniques to find the problem. We know that Python always follows PEMDAS when calculating the result of an expression containing arithmetic operators. Since multiplication and division have the same priority, Python is going from left to right with the execution. The "num1" is divided by "5" and that result is multiplied by the pi value. We have to use brackets to force Python to executing the problem.

```
num2 = num1 / ( 5 * math.pi )
```

The correct output will be shown now.

```
12.732395447351628
```

Exceptional Handling

All errors, except logical ones, break the execution flow. This is unacceptable if you are creating an application. In earlier days, it used to be very common that an unexpected situation would break the application or system. Thanks to better programming practices now, exceptional handling is now part of all high-level programming languages and all programmers utilize it to create distributable applications. What is exception handling? The technique to handle errors so they don't break the program execution. For example, we know users will enter bad data even though we have given all the instructions. It is always a good idea to wrap the input() statement inside a try-except pair. Even if the data provided by the user is correct, it is very easy to forget that input() takes the input as string. Applying any method or operation on this input that is not compatible with strings will result in an error.

```
>>> try:

...     capT = input('Enter a number: ')

...     res = capT / 2

...     print(res)

... except:

...     print("There is an error in the try block")

...

There is an error in the try block
```

We tried to divide a string and strings do not support division. An error has occurred but because it's in a code that's wrapped with "try", execution flow doesn't break. However, the entire code block is ignored and the code block wrapped with "except" is executed. Hence, the output that we see is "There is an error in the try block".

There is also the "else" wrapper that we can use to execute code block in case the "try" block code doesn't raise an exception. Remember that if there's no error, the "try" also gets executed. Here's an example proof.

```
>>> centRy = 113

>>> try:

...        print(centRy)

... except:

...        print("No exceptions this time")

... else:

...        print(centRy)

...

113

113
```

There's another option, "finally", code wrapped with it which will be executed no matter what the result of the code block inside "try" was.

```
>>> chk = "This value is safely stored."

>>> try:

...        print(chk)

... except:

...        print("Something is wrong")
```

... finally:

...   print("I will persevere")

...

This value is safely stored.

I will persevere.

Best Troubleshooting Practices

In the above section, we saw the simplest possible examples for each type of error. Sometimes even with the Python hint, we do not know what the cause of the error is or how to fix it. This happens because the explanation provided by Python doesn't make sense to us. Let's see our previous example again.

```
>>> str(00457)
```

File "<stdin>", line 1

xx = 00457

        ^

SyntaxError: invalid token

We know we have made a mistake, and we also know there is a syntax error. But, we don't know that Python doesn't support leading zeros and that's what is causing the error. "Invalid token" doesn't make sense unless you already know what it means. If you are seeing this error for the first time, you will have to research to understand what has happened and what needs to be changed. As stated before, logical errors are even harder to fix because we have no idea what and where things went wrong. Imagine a script of thousands of lines of code and you are not getting the expected output. What to do next? Where do you start? How do you track the issue smartly so you do not waste more time in troubleshooting than you did coding? There are some best practices when it comes to debugging and troubleshooting.

Planning before execution

There is a reason companies spend more budget and time at planning a particular business venture than actually doing it. All the aspects are carefully analyzed and discussed to remove any loopholes. There are various tools that help here. In programming, we have algorithms (textual) and flowcharts (visual). Both tools should be deployed, but algorithms are usually used before flowcharts because algorithms are system independent. They are used to roughly estimate the process. Flowcharts are much more detailed and easier to understand as they not only show the flow of execution but also the different requirements.

Leave breadcrumbs

Programming is like exploring a huge cave or walking a labyrinth. If you did not leave breadcrumbs to help you back track, you will be lost forever! Comments are useful because most of the time there are multiple people working on the same project and everyone needs to understand what you have written. It also helps you remember what you did when you were coding because, believe me, no one remembers what they did. If you don't remember how you resolved a problem or why you coded a specific way, it's very difficult to update it or correct it.

Dry run

A lost art - this used to the the main troubleshooting method. There are now better tools such as live trackers that you can utilize to see all the changes happening in a program. But, this tradition of using the pen and paper and doing it the hard way has lead to great discoveries. I still prefer that method. There's just something about it that helps me visualize the links between different things and find the problem. Of course, that doesn't work in a script that has thousands of line. For those projects, you definitely need the latest debugging tools.

Test unexpected behaviour

Programmers are problem solvers. They think in a specific mindset but that might not always be how the end user would think or use the product. The best way to make sure your program does not break because the user entered "one" instead of '1' is to unit test the script with millions of different inputs and analyze the result. If the script breaks in certain situations, you can program to fix them.

Debugging in Python

The "pdb" tool is the standard debugging tool in Python and works the same way debuggers work on other platforms. You can add a marker so the debugger would start from there and then execute your code step by step, monitoring all the changes your script makes. Here's a script that we are going to examine with the "pdb" debugger.

```
import pdb


pdb.set_trace()

num = input("Enter a number: ")

try:
```

```
        numAct = inp(num)

except:

        print(type(num))

print('Multiplication table of %d', %num)

for mult in range(1, 21):

        print("%d x %d = %d" % (num, mult, num*mult))
```

A simple multiplication table generator script where the first line has the "pdb.set_trace()" set. Before we could use the tracer, we have to import the "pdb" library. The debugger will start from the very first line. A small window will appear that belongs to the debugger and can take various commands. You can start debugging by passing many commands including the following.

1. (s)tep - execute the line of code debugger is currently positioned at
2. (c)ontinue - execute the remaining code unless a breakpoint is met, in that case stop the execution there
3. (n)ext - works well on functions and executes until a newline is met or until a return is encountered

Use the commands to see how your program changes with the execution of each line.

Functions

Python supports object-oriented programming as well as functional programming. In the latter, programmers can name some lines of code and use that name to run those lines of code as many times as needed. The lines of code defined by a name are called functions. You can also make the function take on arguments which can be passed when calling the function.

```
>>> def prntseq(num):
...     # print sequence of numbers from 1 up till the given number
...     cnt = 1
...     while (cnt <= num):
...         print(cnt, end=", ")
...         cnt = cnt + 1 # can also write as cnt += 1
...
```

We have created a simple function using the "def" keyword. The function, named "prntseq" prints a sequence of numbers from one to the ending limit passed during the function call. The "num" function variable takes on the passing argument so we can use it in the function *definition*. Let's run the function with an argument of 10.

```
>>> prntseq(11)
1, 2, 3, 4, 5, 6, 7, 8, 9, 10, 11
```

We can also give an expression as an argument and Python will pass the result to the function. Here is a simple example.

```
>>> prntseq(5*3)
1, 2, 3, 4, 5, 6, 7, 8, 9, 10, 11, 12, 13, 14, 15
```

A function can take an unlimited number of arguments, but

it's good practice to limit arguments of every function to a maximum of two. We should divide our function into smaller functions if there is a need to use more than two arguments. We created a multiplication generator script a couple of pages ago. Let's create a function to get the same output.

```
>>> def mlt_tbl(mul, timz):

...        print('Multiplication table of %d' % mul )

...        for seq in range(1,timz+1):

...                print("%d x %d = %d" % (mul, timz, mul*timz))

...

>>> mlt_tbl(9,12)

Multiplication table of 9

9 x 1 = 9

9 x 2 = 18

9 x 3 = 27

9 x 4 = 36

9 x 5 = 45

9 x 6 = 54

9 x 7 = 63

9 x 8 = 72

9 x 9 = 81
```

9 x 10 = 90

9 x 11 = 99

9 x 12 = 108

When there are hundreds of functions in your script there are few things to keep in mind.

1. Add exception handling whenever using arguments in expressions because the wrong data type can break execution
2. Create a function template and stick to it for all functions. This will help you have better expectations. A function definition should be divided into smaller chunks such as imports, variable assignments including all input(), actual work on the data, and in the end the return or other form of output such as print().
3. Use operators and methods that return the same output for all or most of the data types.

```
>>> def dosum(numx, numy):

...      print numx+numy

...

>>> dosum(7845, "this a string")

TypeError: unsupported operand type(s) for +: 'int' and 'str'
```

This shows how important it is to deploy exception handling and type conversion together when creating functions.

The Concept of Recursion

You can call a function inside its own definition creating a sort of loop to perform the same action consecutively on a data. It's like using a hammer to put up a nail on the wall. A lot of times, especially when dealing with numbers, we perform an operation that gives us a result and we have to perform the operation on that result again. Here's a simple example of recursion to find the factorial of an integer. Factorial of a number is the product of all numbers from one to that number. For example, the factorial of 4 is 1*2*3*4 = 24.

```
def get_fact(num):

    if x == 1:

        return 1

    else:

        return (num * get_fact(num - 1))
```

When we test the above function with "print(get_fact(6))", we get the output as 720, which is correct because 1*2*3*4*5*6 = 720. Note that we have declared a base condition, a condition that once met will stop the recursion. In the above code, "x == 1" is that base condition. We are using the knowledge that when a function is called from another function, the execution of the latter function is suspended until execution of the former function ends.

Variable Scope

In Python, variables have local scope by default. What does local scope mean? It means if you define a variable inside a function definition, it is not accessible in another function's definition. If we want a variable to be available in all function definitions, we can declare them outside of all function definitions. Another method is to use the "global" keyword.

```
x = 123 # this is a global variable
```

```
def tstFun():

    y = 789 # this is a global variable

    print(x + y)
```

```
tstFun()
```

Class and Objects

When we build something in real-life, we need a blueprint or schematic so we know what to put where. Classes are the blueprints of programming languages that are used to construct objects. They are the basis of object-oriented programming and help program complex concepts by replicating the same features multiple times.

```
>>> class frstcls:

...     prp = 554

...
```

Variable "prp" is known as a class property. We can create new objects once the class has been defined.

```
>>> obj1 = frstcls()
```

```
>>> obj1.prp
```

554

Every object created using the frstcls() class will inherit the property "prp". We can also create functions to the class that will become object methods. In fact, every class must have the __init__() function which is sort of an initiation function. The __init__() function is used to declare all properties of the class and optionally set their values, it can also be used to declare dependencies. Classes and objects are much more prevalent in video games where these concepts are used to create non-player characters to enrich the gaming experience. Most non-player characters share the same design and mechanics with cosmetic changes.

```
>>> class npc:

...     def __init__(instance,type,id,health,armor,mechanics):

...             instance.type = type

...             instance.id = id

...             instance.health = health

...             instance.armor = armor

...             instance.mechanics = mechanics

...
```

Every object created by the class is its "instance" which is what is passed to the __init__() function. Let's use our class to create an npc player.

```
>>> npc1 = npc("Mercenary", "Sailor", 75, 0, [2, 'walk', 'shoot'])
```

We can access individual object parameters easily like below.

>>> npc1.armor

25

>>> npc100 = npc("Level Boss","Pirate King",1000,500,[5, 'fast move', 'double 'jump', 'move tracker', 'slasher', 'unlit revolver''])

If you think that's a tough one, wait for the final level boss!

All object parameters are mutable unless we have an immutable data structure like a tuple.

>>> plyratk = 80

>>> if plyratk >= 75:

...   npc1.hp = 0

... else:

...   npc1.hp = npc1.hp - plyratk

...

>>> npc1.hp

0

We can perform all other methods that we have used for data structures and variables up till now, and then some on objects.

>>> del npc1.specialmoves

>>> del npc2

Scheduling and Automating Python Scripts

We can use the "Task Scheduler" that comes standard with all Windows installations to schedule and automate any tasks including execution of Python scripts.

Search "Task Scheduler" in Windows 10 start menu. An application with the same name will appear in the search results, select it. Currently, the application looks like the following screenshot.

A new window "Create Basic Task Wizard" will popup when "Create Basic Task" is clicked.

The step by step process is detailed below:

1. Enter a memorable and recognizable name so identifying different tasks later would become easier. It is also recommended to add a concise description. Click "Next".
2. We have to set a trigger which can be a specific time or an event in another Windows application or system. Whenever the trigger would occur, Windows will run the scheduled task. Select "Daily" for now.

3. Let us set 11:59pm "everyday" and whatever the current date is as the starting point. Keep one in the recur field because we are going for a daily schedule. Click "Next".

4. We want to run a Python script so we will keep the option "Start a program" selected. Click "Next".

5. In the final step, we have to direct Windows which program we want to schedule. To schedule a Python script, we should first run Python interpreter and then load the script as an argument. For example, if the Python interpreter is located at "C:\Python\python.exe" and the script you want to run is located at "D:\myscript.py".

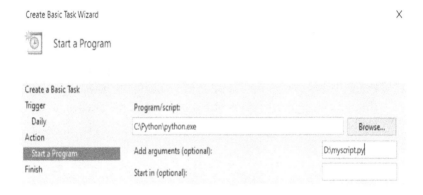

Click "Next" and you will see a summary of the task you have setup. Click on "Finish" to create the scheduled task you have setup that will run everyday at 11:59 pm.

It is such a good way to automate your daily tasks!

If you do not want to pass an argument or if the above process does not work for you, you can also schedule a Python script through the Windows Batch (.bat) file that are basically Windows script files. To schedule this way, we can add the following instruction to a batch file.

C:\Python\python.exe "D:\myscript.py"

Make sure to save the file. Now, we can schedule the batch file using the Windows "Task Scheduler" and Windows will execute the Python script.

This was a tutorial on how to create a very simple scheduled task. The "Task Scheduler" also offers many advanced options that are out of the scope of this book but you should explore them. There are a lot of similar tools available in Windows that an average user does not know about. It's always fun to explore new things!

Chapter 4: Basic Data Analysis

Everything in this world is constantly generating data. If we can record that data, we can process it to find the hidden meanings. It can help in making important decisions regarding your business or life. In this chapter, we will take a look at the basic data analysis concepts.

Data Parsing

There are many different ways to access data from the same file type. There are several libraries and depending upon the Python installation for the operating system in use (Windows in our case), there are even more options available.

Excel

MS Excel is the most widely used spreadsheet software in both personal and commercial domain. Due to this reason, there are several options to get data from MS Excel spreadsheets. In the below example, we are leveraging the Windows client for Python to get data from an excel sheet. Note that this Windows client method can be used to integrate with any application running on Windows operating system.

import win32com.client as win32

exc=win32.gencache.EnsureDispatch('Excel.Application')

```
exc.Visible=True
```

```
filepath = "" # set the file path here
```

```
wrkbk = exc.Workbooks.Open(filepath)
```

```
wrksht = wrkbk.Worksheets('Sheet1') # get the sheet with the
name "Sheet1"
```

```
wrksht.Name = 'Python Created' # change the name of that
sheet
```

```
wrksht.Cells(1, 1).Value = "Hello" # set the value of the first
cell in the worksheet
```

As you can notice, the first cell in the worksheet has row and column values of one.

An alternate approach

An alternative is to use another library specifically made to read data from an Excel file. We are going to use "xlrd" library.

```
wrkbk = xlrd.open_workbook(filepath)
```

One issue with "xlrd", which is not an issue but an inconvenience when you are developing a script, and actually an improvement from the user-side perspective, is that the Excel file is not visible so you have no idea what the Excel file looks like.

Once we have the workbook, we can access any sheet using its name or index.

```
wrksht = workbook.sheet_by_name('Sheet1') # access the
sheet by the title of 'Sheet1'
```

```
wrksht = workbook.sheet_by_index(0) # access sheet with its
position
```

In an Excel workbook, the position of a sheet can be changed so it's better to get sheets using their name and not the index.

```
print wrksht.cell(0, 0).value
```

In the "xlrd" library, the first cell of a sheet has a row and column indices of zero. To get all the values in a spreadsheet, we can use nested for loop to access each sheet and all the cells in it. One problem though, if we accidentally try to access a cell that is empty, we will get an error. For example, consider that the cell(100, 100) is empty. The following will result in an error.

```
print wrksht.cell(100, 100).value
```

To avoid this issue, we can read the number of rows and columns with data in an Excel sheet like below.

```
print("number of rows:", wrksht.nrows) # get number of rows
with data
```

```
print("number of columns:", wrksht.ncols) # get number of
columns with data
```

Using the above information, we can correctly set the limits on our "for" loops.

CSV

Comma Separated Values (CSV) files are a common method to distribute data over the internet due to its low file size. In data analysis, most of the times you will be reading and writing data in this format. They are essentially a text file where every data value is separated by a comma. For example, here is an example of some CSV data.

name,department,designation

Sinclair,IT,network engineer

Jones,Sales,inside salesperson

Sasha,HR,hiring manager

Alexa,Admin,VP secretary

The code to read the comma separated data from a CSV file saved in the same directory as the script file.

```
import csv

import os, sys


curdir=os.path.dirname(sys.argv[0]) # gets the directory where the script file is located

filep = os.path.join(curdir,"employee_data.csv")


with open(filep, mode='r') as csv_file:

        csv_read = csv.DictReader(csv_file)

        line_cnt = 0

        for row in csv_read:

                if line_cnt == 0:
```

```
        print('Column names are',row.keys())

        line_cnt += 1

        print(row['name'],"works in
",row['department'],"as a/an ",row['designation'])

        line_cnt += 1

        print('Processed',line_cnt,"lines")
```

This will output:

>>> Column names are ['name', 'department', 'designation']

Sinclair works in IT as a/an network engineer

Jones works in Sales as a/an inside salesperson

Sasha works in HR as a/an hiring manager

Alexa works in Admin as a/an VP secretary

Processed 5 lines

The first line of output that has the column names might not have the column names in this order because we are reading data by storing in a dictionary and we already know dictionaries are unordered data structures. When reading as a dictionary, the key is set as the first row header value of that column and the data from the relevant row. But, what would happen if there are no column headers? We might have to add a column header before we use this method.

To write a csv file, we can store all our data in a dictionary and that dictionary content is written to a csv formatted text file.

import csv

```
import os, sys


curdir=os.path.dirname(sys.argv[0])

filep = os.path.join(curdir,"join_date.csv")


with open(filep, mode='w') as csv_write:

        col_hdr = ['Name', 'Join Date', 'Salary']

        fin_file = csv.DictWriter(csv_write,
fieldnames=col_hdr)


        fin_file.writeheader()

        fin_file.writerow({'Name': 'Sinclair', 'Join Date': '12-
Mar-13', 'Salary': '45,000'})

        fin_file.writerow({'Name': 'Jones', 'Join Date': '07-Jun-
09', 'Salary': '58,500'})

        fin_file.writerow({'Name': 'Sasha', 'Join Date': '07-Jun-
09', 'Salary': '85,000'})

        fin_file.writerow({'Name': 'Alexa', 'Join Date': '07-Jun-
09', 'Salary': '65,500'})
```

Websites

Everything you do online is recorded by someone with the chief purpose of knowing about you and marketing you relevant ads. It sounds cool but, personally, I think it pushes humans to become too much of a habitual animal. If you keep getting bombarded with things you like, not only its frustrating, it also affects your behaviour. For example, I like sushi but that doesn't mean wherever I go I only want to eat sushi! Where's the fun of exploring new food and places and experiencing the adventure of trying the unknown? I do not want everything I do recorded and analyzed. Or, if I do, I want to be compensated for it!

But, truth be told, there are various other applications of data recording and analysis besides shoving ads in your face. There have been huge strides in technology, especially in the fields of medicine and agriculture by knowing more about the environment and all the other factors involved. Precise predictions are regularly made about the weather which help the general public in planning different aspects of their daily lives.

The world wide web is a huge resource of free and paid data. You can tap into this resource to create applications to make lives better for the people. But, the rules of ethics should not be broken in any case. It's the weight of the world on the shoulders of data analysts and scientists - if you stumble upon information that is true but too dangerous, do you show it to the world or forward it to the global stakeholders? As Spiderman once said, power comes with responsibility!

Python has several libraries for web scraping as well. We are going to use "scrapy" now. Note that "scrapy" is usually used for large projects. For simpler web scraping projects, we can use libraries such as "BeautifulSoup".

Using Scrapy

You have to install the "scrapy" library before you use it.

pip install scrapy

After the installation is finished, we have to setup a project. This is done for every website we have to scrap. In the "scrapy" library, each scraper we build is called a spider, because spiders crawl. Using the Windows command prompt, navigate to the directory where we want to create the project and then run the following command.

scrapy startproject frstspydr

You do not have to name your crawler spider, especially if they give you the heebie jeebies! A new folder with the name "frstspydr" will be created in the directory that we navigated to.

The first step is to update the "\frstspydr\frstspydr\settings.py". In the "settings.py" file, two changes need to be made. We have to uncomment the "ITEMS_PIPELINE" tuple in case it's commented out and make edits so the file content looks as below.

#Export as CSV Feed

FEED_FORMAT = "csv"

FEED_URI = "reddit.csv"

The above lines indicate we are going to save the scraped information in a CSV formatted life. We are using a Reddit name because we are going to scrap a Reddit thread.

Going back to the command prompt, run the following command.

scrapy genspider redditcrawl
www.reddit.com/r/breakingbad/

The above command will create a new spider inside the "\frstspydr\frstspydr\spiders\" folder using a standard template. We are going to use this newly created spider to get all the text and images from theBreaking Bad show Reddit thread.

If you open the "\frstspydr\frstspydr\spiders\redditcrawl.py" file, the below code is visible.

```
import scrapy


class RedditbotSpider(scrapy.Spider):

    name = 'redditcrawl'

    allowed_domains = ['www.reddit.com/r/breakingbad']

    start_urls = ['http://www.reddit.com/r/breakingbad']


    def parse(self, response):

        pass
```

Some observations:

1. The spider can be named anything
2. The allowed_domains adds security by setting the domain that can be crawled using this crawler. This is entirely optional
3. Upon successful crawl, the parse function is called and executed

Next step is to update the start_urls argument in the RedditcrawlSpider class so it has the correct HTTPS format

URL. Most websites nowadays have the secured HTTPS and we cannot access data from those sites using the unsecured URL version.

start_urls = ['https://www.reddit.com/r/breakingbad/']

See the "pass" inside the parse() function. Replace that with the following code block.

```
def parse(self, response):

                        # Extract the html text with the css class selector

                        title = response.css('h3._eYtD2XCVieq6emjKBH3m::text').extract()

                        images_url = response.css("img::attr(src)").extract()

                        # Gather the data for every row

                        for item in zip(titles,images_url):

                                # store all the data in a dictionary

                                scraped_info = {

                                        'title' : item[0],

                                        'images_url': item[1],

                                }


        # Send all the scraped info to scrapy
```

```
yield scraped_info
```

We have used the html class selector. We are going to use the css class values of html to get the text content (the post titles) and featured image URLs. Let's save the file and start using the crawler. The following command starts the crawler bot.

```
scrapy crawl redditcrawl
```

Before running the scrapper, make sure to change the working directory using the command prompt to the directory where the redditcrawl scraper resides. Not changing the directory and running the above command will result in an error.

While the crawler is running, it will output a lot of lines on the screen, but you can ignore all of them. After the crawl process is finished, you can navigate to the folder where you saved the crawler and find the reddit.csv file. The file will have all the post titles and direct URLs to the featured images, one in a row.

We can also download the images by creating a pipeline

```
ITEM_PIPELINES = {

    'scrapy.pipelines.images.ImagesPipeline': 1

}

IMAGES_STORE = '' # add the folder path where the images should be stored
```

If you are going to download the image files, make sure to comment out the CSV creation code we added earlier because sometimes performing both together leads to conflicts.

You can customize the crawler to get anything from any website. The "scrapy" framework supports multithreading which means you can deal with tons of online data without any compromise on performance. Still, be careful because this framework uses a lot of processing power. Smart programming goes a long way here.

Using BeautifulSoup

Beautiful Soup is a web scraping library in Python better suited for simpler tasks. It is way faster and easier to use to extract specific information from a website. First we install the library.

pip install BeautifulSoup4

Beautiful Soup extracts data from a website but is not able to make a connection with it. We need another library such as "urllib.request" to establish a secure connection with the website so Beautiful Soup can work.

We will scrape data from "example.webscraping.com" which has 25 pages containing the names and flags of all the countries in the world. The homepage URL is:

http://example.webscraping.com/

The URI of the last page is:

http://example.webscraping.com/places/default/index/25

This website is unsecured and the URLs share a common structure. Utilizing the inspection tool of Google Chrome, we inspect the html markup of the website. We notice that individual html elements do not have unique attributes, therefore we will extract accordingly by filtering through specific html elements.

The complete code is presented below along with comments for easier understanding.

```python
from bs4 import BeautifulSoup

import time

import urllib.request


webURL = "http://example.webscraping.com/"


for pag in range(0, 26): # 0-26 because we have 25 pages where second page is '1'

    if pag == 0:

        lnk = webURL

    else:

        lnk = webURL + "places/default/index/" + str(pag)

    try:

        time.sleep(1)

'''
```

Beautiful Soup reads data very quickly, too quickly for most servers' liking. If they see your script sending several requests to the site very quickly, they will think you are trying to hack or DDoS the site. To prevent that from happening, the server can temporarily block your IP. We are adding a delay of 1 second between consecutive server requests so that situation never happens.

'''

```python
        page = urllib.request.urlopen(lnk)

        soup = BeautifulSoup(page, 'html.parser')

        cntry_names = soup.find_all('td') # get all
country names in a page

        cntry_flags = soup.find_all('img') #get all
flag's image URL in a page

    except:

        print("Something bad happened while trying
to scrap the website.")

    if (cntry_names): # only run the following 'for' loop if
content_id is not empty

        for  name in cntry_names:

            print(name.text.lstrip()) #lstrip()
removes any unwanted spaces from the text

    if (cntry_flags): # only run the following 'for' loop if
content_img is not empty

        for itr in cntry_flags:

            print(webURL + itr['src'].lstrip('/'))
#lstrip() removes extra forward slashes from the URL
```

The above code opens each website page and gets the
country name and the country flag. We can also store this
gathered data in a CSV file so we can access it later without
having to scrap the website another time.

```
f = open('scrapData.csv','w')

if (content_td): # only run the following 'for' loop if
content_id is not empty

        for itm in content_td:

                f.write(itm.text.lstrip())

if (content_img): # only run the following 'for' loop if
content_img is not empty

        for itr in content_img:

                f.write(webURL + itr['src'].lstrip('/'))
```

Working with NumPy

The "numpy" library provides us with one more data structure: the numpy arrays. These arrays closely resemble the mathematical matrices. In fact, all the matrix concepts can be applied on the numpy arrays. We have to install the array before using it.

pip install numpy

Once installed, we can start using the library.

import numpy as np

arr = np.array([36, 69])

brr = np.array([[75, 53],

        [95, 51]])

print(arr.ndim) #get dimension of array which is returns the number of rows in the array

The number of elements in each row must be the same in a multidimensional array. The output of the above script is:

1

To get the number of rows and columns, we have to use the "shape" property.

print(arr.shape) # for a multidimensional array, returns a tuple containing number of rows then number of columns, for a single dimensional array, the number of columns is returned

print(brr.shape)

The output is:

(2,)

(2, 2)

The numpy arrays look very similar to nested lists, but support many methods that we cannot apply on nested lists. To see how many items are in an array, we use the "size" property.

print(brr.size) # returns 6 because total 6 elements are present in the "brr" array

Individual elements in the array can be accessed using the indices just like in a list, but the syntax is a little different. In a numpy array, the first row - first column position has 0, 0 index.

print(arr[1,1]) #outputs 53 because 1, 1 means second row and second column

As the name suggests, *numpy* arrays are geared towards number types. But, we can also store strings with the requirement that all elements in an array must be of same data type.

crr = np.array([111, "is called", " a Nelson", True])

print(crr)

The output will be.

['111' 'is called' ' a Nelson' 'True']

The numpy library converted all the data to the string type. We have to be careful because during data analysis, if we program our script to find the boolean "True" value in this array, the script will always return null because the boolean "True" has been converted to the string "True". Another observation is that the commas are missing but that's just what printing a numpy array looks like. We can print another array just to be sure.

print(bArr)

[[75 53]

 [95 51]]

What if we have an array that has only numbers and Boolean values? Here is an example:

drr = np.array([183, True, False])

print(drr)

The output is:

[183 1 0]

The numbers one and zero are numerical equivalents of Boolean "True" and "False".

Numpy arrays cannot be changed once created. Although, new arrays can be made by manipulating the existing array.

err = np.append(arr, 3347)

print(err)

The output is:

[36   69   3347]

Reminder: leading zeros are not allowed in Python numbers anymore.

frr = np.array([14.7, 3.00])

print(frr)

Which gives us the output of:

[14.7 3.]

Appending data in a multidimensional array creates a new one-dimensional array.

grr = np.append(brr[0], 4) #new one dimensional array

print(grr)

The output is:

[75 53 95 51   4]

Removing an element from an array also leads to creation of a new array.

hrr = np.delete(grr, 3) #this method removes an element by finding it through its index. 3 has index of 4 in grr

print(hrr)

The output is:

[75 53 95 51]

There are many standard arrays that are used in various applications. The numpy library has special methods to create such arrays quickly.

zrr = np.zeros((2, 3)) #this will create an array with all elements zero in floating type

print(zrr)

zrrint = np.zeros((2, 3), dtype=int) # if we want to create an array of integer zeros

print(zrrint)

The outputs are.

[[0. 0. 0.]

 [0. 0. 0.]]

[[0 0 0]

 [0 0 0]]

We can also create a three-dimensional (3D) array.

threDrr = np.ones((2, 3, 3)) #this is taken as a multidimensional (3D) array consisting of two 2D arrays each of 3 rows and 3 columns

print(threDrr)

The output is:

[[[1. 1. 1.]

 [1. 1. 1.]

 [1. 1. 1.]]

 [[1. 1. 1.]

 [1. 1. 1.]

 [1. 1. 1.]]]

If you want the elements of an array to follow a specific sequence, we can do that with a couple of methods.

seqrr = np.arange(0, 101, 10) #create an array with elements in a sequence by setting how much interval should be added between each element

print(seqrr)

linrr = np.linspace(0, 100, 11, dtype=int) #create an array with elements in a sequence by setting how many elements are needed in the array. Python automatically sets the appropriate step value

print(linArr)

The outputs is:

[0 10 20 30 40 50 60 70 80 90 100]

[0 10 20 30 40 50 60 70 80 90 100]

A few things to remember:

1. linspace() includes the maximum value in the sequence unlike the arange() which works like the range()
2. linspace() creates sequence in floating type numbers unless instructed otherwise just like in our example ("dtype=int").

To create an array with all element positions taken by the same number, we use the full() method.

fillrr = np.full((2,2), 7)

print(fillrr)

The code outputs the following:

[[7 7]

 [7 7]]

As stated earlier, the numpy arrays are the closest implementation of matrices in Python. As such, there are various methods available in numpy library to perform matrix operations. Identity matrix are used frequently in matrix operations and we can create an identity matrix as a numpy array with a single line of code.

idrr = np.eye(2, dtype=int) #identity matrix always has the same number of rows and columns (i.e they are square matrices) and one of the diagonals has all elements set as '1' print(idrr)

The output is:

[[1 0]

 [0 1]]

The numpy library has randomizer methods that generate random integer or float numbers to fill in an array. This is particularly useful when you want to create several arrays to test a script.

randIrr = np.random.randint(1, 15, size=(4, 4)) #1 and 15 are minimum and maximum limits so numpy will generate random numbers that lie within this range. (4, 4) will be the size of new array created

print(randIrr)

randFrr = np.random.random((3, 3)) #this time we didn't give any limits and the returned array will have a size of 3 rows and 3 columns

print(randFrr)

The output of the above code is below. You will see different output when you run the code because randomizer will output different numbers.

[[7 8 9 9]

 [5 14 7 2]

 [3 2 9 13]

 [1 3 8 8]]

[[0.29457456 0.83468151 0.35160973]

[0.29059067 0.896374607 0.38657756]

[0.5831767 0.54060431 0.94441115]]

Below are some examples of operations you can perform on numpy arrays.

arr = np.array([

    [7, 8, 9],

    [9, 8, 7]

])

brr = np.array([

    [1, 2, 3],

    [3, 2, 1]

])

#addition

print(np.add(arr, brr)) # this is a scalar addition which we can also do with '+' operator like arr + brr

#subtraction

print(np.subtract(arr, brr)) #again a scalar operation hence aArr - bArr also gives same output

#multiplication

print(np.multiply(arr, brr)) # element by element (scalar) which is also arr * brr

#division

print(np.divide(arr, brr)) #also aArr / bArr because a scalar operation

The output of the above script is:

[[8 10 12]

 [12 10 8]]

[[6 6 6]

 [6 6 6]]

[[7 16 27]

 [27 16 7]]

[[7. 4.   3.]

 [3. 4.   7.]]

We can also perform dot and cross products on arrays.

drr = np.array([

         [7, 8, 9],

         [9, 8, 7],

```
        [4, 5, 6]
])
err = np.array([
        [1, 2, 3],
        [3, 2, 1],
        [4, 5, 6]
])
#dot product
print(np.dot(drr, err))


#cross product
print(np.cross(drr, err))
```

The outputs are:

```
[[67 75 83]
 [61 69 77]
 [43 48 53]]
[[6 -12 6]
 [-6 12 -6]
 [ 0  0  0]]
```

Dot and cross products play a significant role in vector theory.

You can read about it online. To transpose an array, we have the property 'T'.

print(drr.T)

The output is:

[[7 9 4]

 [8 8 5]

 [9 7 6]]

Finding different kind of sums results in many interesting values.

print(np.sum(drr)) #sum all elements in an array, returns a single value

#sum the elements in either the rows or columns

print(np.sum(drr, axis=0)) # axis = 0 means we sum all elements in the rows

print(np.sum(drr, axis=1)) # axis = 1 means we sum all elements in the columns

Here are the outputs:

63

[20 21 22]

[24 24 15]

Chapter 5: Advanced Data Analysis

Chapter 4 has a lot of information on data analysis, but Python supports much more advanced data analysis tools.

Using pandas Framework

When it comes to data analysis, Python has another ace up its sleeve: the "pandas" framework. The framework provides two new data structures, "series" and "dataframe". The framework also provides out of the box data acquisition techniques for all popular data sources such as spreadsheets and CSV files. Without wasting another minute, let us dive into the concepts and working of this library.

pandas Series

The "pandas" Series data structure has features combined from both dictionaries and numpy arrays. It is an advanced way of declaring and manipulating a group of numbers with a specific sequence.

from pandas import Series

import pandas as pd

asr = Series([1, 7, 9]) # the syntax closely resembles that of a numpy array

```python
print(asr)

print(asr.values)  # get all values as a list just like a dictionary

print(asr.index)  # get all indices as a list, we can say they are
# the "keys" of this data structure - another resemblance with a
# dictionary. Since we didn't set specific keys, the values were
# assigned number indices


kes = ['1st', '2nd', '3rd']

bsr = Series([3, 9, 7], index=kes) # we can set custom "keys"
# for the data structure


print(bsr)

print(bsr['1st'])  # get element using key just like a dictionary

print(bsr[0])  # get element using index just like any other
# data structure in Python


adic = {

        '1st': 245,

        '2nd': 265,

        '3rd': 888

}
```

```
csr = Series(adic)  # creating a series from a dictionary is very
easy
```

```
print(csr)
```

```
ind = ['1st', '2nd', '4th']
```

```
dsr = Series(adic, index=ind)  # if a key isn't in the original
dictionary (4th isn't present in this case), "NaN" is added as
value for that key
```

```
print(dsr)
```

```
print(pd.isnull(dsr['4th']))  # check if an element has "NaN"
value, in this case the output will be Boolean True
```

```
dsr.name = 'Info' # give name to entire series
```

```
dSer.index.name = 'Key' # give name to the index/key column
```

```
print(dsr)
```

```
dsr.index = ['un', 'deux', 'nul']  # we can change the keys of a
series, this is a major upgrade from a dictionary where the
keys are immutable. Changing the indices/keys removes any
```

name we have given to the index column

print(dsr)

The outputs of the above "print" statements are.

0	1
1	7
2	9

dtype: int64

[1 7 9]

RangeIndex(start=0, stop=3, step=1)

1st	3
2nd	9
3rd	7

dtype: int64

3

3

1st	245
2nd	265
3rd	888

dtype: int64

1st   245.0

2nd   265.0

4th   NaN

dtype: float64

True

Key

1st   245.0

2nd   265.0

4th   NaN

Name: Info, dtype: float64

un   245.0

deux 265.0

nul   NaN

Name: Info, dtype: float64

Time series

A quantity that can be measured with respect to time can be represented as a time series - a special type of pandas Series where the index column has time values. If you take a look at any log file, you will notice how each entry is preceded by a timestamp showing when that particular log entry was made. The logs are sorted according to time, either latest to earliest or vice versa.

The pandas framework provides a lot of methods to

manipulate time series that are beneficial in various applications. All the rules of pandas series work on time series but we need to understand how Python works with dates before we can move on to the next topic. The below script shows different manipulation techniques of time.

```python
from datetime import datetime

from datetime import timedelta

from dateutil.parser import parse


nowTime = datetime.now()  # get the current date and time value


print(now)  # the returned data has the current date and time including the year, month, day, hour, minutes, seconds, milliseconds, and microseconds values


nxT = nowTime + timedelta(12)  # timedelta() creates time object that can be used to jump time according to the arguments provided. In this case, we want to get the date and time 12 days from current date and time


print(nxT)


print(str(nxT))  # string looks the same as datatime format
```

```python
print(nxT.strftime('%Y-%m-%d'))  # reformat datetime value
```

```python
impTime = '2016-11-09'
```

```python
print(datetime.strptime(impTime, '%Y-%m-%d'))  # format
```
string as datetime

```python
print(parse(impTime))  # when the string has a format that's
```
the same as a datetime format, we don't need to use strptime() and declare a format. We can use parse() to quickly convert such string to a datetime object

```python
print(parse(ranTime, dayfirst=True))  # the dayfirst argument
```
swaps the position of months with days to follow the international date and time convention.

The respective outputs of the above print statements are:

2019-10-30 08:10:25.841218

2019-11-11 08:10:25.841218

2019-11-11 08:10:25.841218

2019-11-11

2016-11-09 00:00:00

2016-11-09 00:00:00

2016-09-11 00:00:00

pandas DataFrames

The dataframe is the most advanced data structure in Python and can handle gigabytes of data processing without slowing down the computer. Thanks to the process optimizations done behind the scenes, pandas dataframes are ideal for all data analysis and machine learning applications.

Let us take a look at some basic dataframe manipulation.

import pandas as pd

monLst = ['Jan', 'Feb', 'Mar', 'Apr']

quartrStats = {

       "Ad Spending": [12000, 24000, 9000, 11000],

       "Revenue": [55000, 15745, 21000, 47314],

       "Store Manager": ['Jones', 'Joshua', 'Marcus', 'Smith']

}

dfnew = pd.DataFrame(quartrStats, index=monLst) # assigning custom keys/indices to the dataframe

dfalt = pd.DataFrame(quartrStats) # creating a dataframe with default keys/indices

dfalt.set_index('Store Manager', inplace=True) # assign an existing data column as the index column, "inplace" argument makes sure the original dataframe is overwritten with the change. By default, whenever a change is made to a dataframe, the original is kept intact and a new dataframe is created to carry the changes.

print(dfnew)

print(dfalt)

The output is:

	Ad Spending	Revenue	Store Manager
Jan	12000	55000	Jones
Feb	24000	15745	Joshua
Mar	9000	21000	Marcus
Apr	11000	47314	Smith

	Ad Spending	Revenue
Store Manager		
Jones	12000	55000
Joshua	24000	15745
Marcus	9000	21000
Smith	11000	47314

We can extract a single column or a set of columns from a dataframe. Converting a dataframe column to a numpy array is also straightforward, which leads to the million dollar question: can we use a numpy array to create a dataframe?

The code below actually performs all these tasks.

```
print(dfnew['Revenue'])  # a new series is created with the
same index as the source dataframe
```

```
print(dfnew.Revenue)  # this will only work if the column
header has no spaces, therefore it is a good idea to use
underscores '_' or dashes '-' instead of spaces when adding
column header in a dataframe
```

```
print(dfnew[['Ad Spending', 'Revenue']])  # use multiple
columns of a dataframe to create a new dataframe with the
same index as the original one
```

```
print(np.array(dfnew[['Ad Spending', 'Revenue']]))  # convert
the newly extracted dataframe to a numpy array
```

The output of the above script is:

```
Jan    55000

Feb    15745

Mar    21000

Apr    47314

Name: Revenue, dtype: int64

Jan    55000

Feb    15745

Mar    21000
```

Apr   47314

Name: Revenue, dtype: int64

   Ad Spending Revenue

Jan 12000   55000

Feb   24000   15745

Mar 9000   21000

Apr 11000   47314

[[12000   55000]

[24000 15745]

[9000 21000]

[11000 47314]]

Parsing Data

"pandas" framework supports easy and fast data retrieval from various resources without the need of another library. Search the Internet for "AAPL", which is the stock price data of the global tech giant Apple Inc.. You can use a data aggregator service like Quandl. Let's download the data to the Python folder in the "csv" format. The following code will read all the downloaded data.

```
import pandas as pd


# read local CSV data

datF = pd.read_csv('EOD-AAPL.csv') # this is the downloaded
```

CSV file, replace it with the name of your file

```
datF.set_index('Date', inplace=True) # making date column
the index of the dataframe

datF.to_csv("newF.csv")  # create a new CSV file and transfer
all the dataframe data
```

```
print(datF.head()) # print the first five rows of the dataframe
```

```
datF = pd.read_csv('newF.csv', index_col=0)  # this is how to
set a specific data column as an index column during data
read using the column index. Zero index means the first
column
```

```
print(datF.head())
```

```
datF.rename(columns={'Open': 'Open_Price'}, inplace=True)
# we can rename a single or multiple columns by passing the
values as key-value pairs of a dictionary to the rename()
method
```

```
print(datF.head())
```

```
datF.to_csv("newFn.csv", header=False)  # save data to a CSV
```

file while ignoring the column header

datF = pd.read_csv('newFn.csv', names=['Date', 'Open', 'High', 'Low', 'Close', 'Volume', 'Dividend', 'Split', 'Adj_Open', 'Adj_High', 'Adj_Low', 'Adj_Close', 'Adj_Volume'], index_col=0) # we can also set the column names when reading data from a CSV file

print(datF.head())

The output of the above script is:

```
         Open        High    Low  ...       Adj_Low
Adj_Close  Adj_Volume

Date                          ...

2017-12-28 171.00 171.850 170.480 ... 165.957609
166.541693 16480187.0

2017-12-27 170.10 170.780 169.710 ... 165.208036
166.074426 21498213.0

2017-12-26 170.80 171.470 169.679 ... 165.177858
166.045222 33185536.0

2017-12-22 174.68 175.424 174.500 ... 169.870969
170.367440 16349444.0

2017-12-21 174.17 176.020 174.100 ... 169.481580
170.367440 20949896.0


[5 rows x 12 columns]

         Open High    Low  ...       Adj_Low  Adj_Close
```

Adj_Volume

Date   ...

2017-12-28 171.00 171.850 170.480 ... 165.957609
166.541693 16480187.0

2017-12-27 170.10 170.780 169.710 ... 165.208036
166.074426 21498213.0

2017-12-26 170.80 171.470 169.679 ... 165.177858
166.045222 33185536.0

2017-12-22 174.68 175.424 174.500 ... 169.870969
170.367440 16349444.0

2017-12-21 174.17 176.020 174.100 ... 169.481580
170.367440 20949896.0

[5 rows x 12 columns]

             Open_Price High   Low ...
        Adj_Low Adj_Close Adj_Volume

Date   ...

2017-12-28 171.00 171.850 170.480 ... 165.957609
166.541693 16480187.0

2017-12-27 170.10 170.780 169.710 ... 165.208036
166.074426 21498213.0

2017-12-26 170.80 171.470 169.679 ... 165.177858
166.045222 33185536.0

2017-12-22 174.68 175.424 174.500 ... 169.870969
170.367440 16349444.0

```
2017-12-21    174.17 176.020 174.100 ... 169.481580
170.367440 20949896.0
```

[5 rows x 12 columns]

```
          Open High    Low ...         Adj_Low  Adj_Close
Adj_Volume

Date                       ...

2017-12-28 171.00 171.850 170.480 ... 165.957609
166.541693 16480187.0

2017-12-27 170.10 170.780 169.710 ... 165.208036
166.074426 21498213.0

2017-12-26 170.80 171.470 169.679 ... 165.177858
166.045222 33185536.0

2017-12-22 174.68 175.424 174.500 ... 169.870969
170.367440 16349444.0

2017-12-21 174.17 176.020 174.100 ... 169.481580
170.367440 20949896.0
```

[5 rows x 12 columns]

Write data

We can use pandas framework to write data in various common formats. Let's look at an example where we write data to an HTML file.

datF.to_html('datF.html') # such as simple implementation

You can view this new HTML file by opening it up in any browser. To view the markup of this page, you can open it using any text editor. You can also use the inspection tool of the browser to view the markup.

Internet Scraping using pandas

We can scrape websites using the pandas special library "pandas_datareader". We need to install it using pip before we can use it.

pip install pandas_datareader

Run the following script after the installation has completed.

import pandas_datareader.data as web

rngstrt = '1/1/2009'

rngstp = '5/5/2015'

dfnew = web.get_data_yahoo('GOOG', rngstrt, rngstp)

print(dfnew.head()) #output first five rows of the dataframe

The output will be:

       High   Low ...   Volume Adj Close

Date   ...

2009-01-02 160.309128 152.179596 ... 7248000.0 160.060059

```
2009-01-05  165.001541  156.911850  ...  9814500.0
163.412491

2009-01-06  169.763687  162.585587  ...  12898500.0
166.406265

2009-01-07  164.837143  158.779861  ...  9022600.0
160.403763

2009-01-08  161.987823  158.077484  ...  7228300.0
161.987823
```

[5 rows x 6 columns]

Visualize Data

It is very difficult to even read thousands of lines of data, let alone find a relationship in the data. But, this becomes easier when we plot charts using the data. Many trends and system behaviours becomes instantly recognizable.

Plot a Chart

There are several libraries to create graphs using Python. We have already seen matplotlib in action. Let's work with pygal now. We can install this library using pip.

pip install pygal

All the codes in this section are inspired from the Pygal official documentation available at http://www.pygal.org/en/stable/documentation/. Here's a simple line chart generating code.

```python
import pygal

from pygal.style import LightenStyle

dark_lighten_style = LightenStyle('#000000')

bar_chart = pygal.Bar(style=dark_lighten_style)

bar_chart.add('Fibonacci', [0, 1, 1, 2, 3, 5, 8, 13, 21, 34, 55])

bar_chart.add('Padovan', [1, 1, 1, 2, 2, 3, 4, 5, 7, 9, 12])

bar_chart.render() # show the chart

bar_chart.render_to_file('bar_chart.svg') # save the chart as
svg image file
```

Here is the output chart:

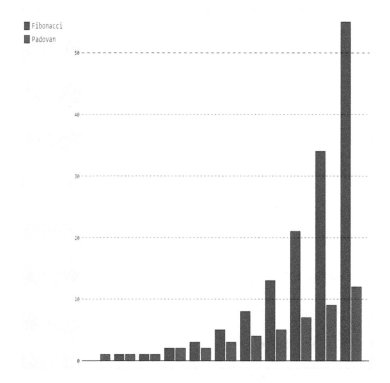

We are using the LightenStyle() to create a grayscale color scheme with the base color of black (hex code: #000000). We pass that custom color scheme as the style to be used for the chart. Pygal smartly chooses the best grayscale shades to plot the chart.

Let's create a pie chart.

import pygal

from pygal.style import LightenStyle

dark_lighten_style = LightenStyle('#000000')

```
pie_chart = pygal.Pie(style=dark_lighten_style)

pie_chart.title = 'Browser usage in February 2012 (in %)'

pie_chart.add('IE', 19.5)

pie_chart.add('Firefox', 36.6)

pie_chart.add('Chrome', 36.3)

pie_chart.add('Safari', 4.5)

pie_chart.add('Opera', 2.3)

pie_chart.render() # show the pie chart

pie_chart.render_to_file('pie_chart.svg') # save the chart as
svg image file
```

The output chart looks like the following:

Browser usage in February 2012 (in %)

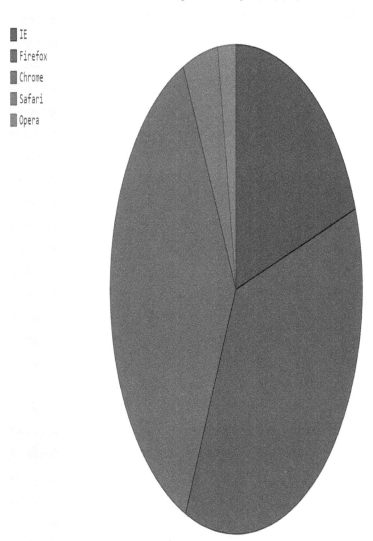

Notice how the Pygal is taking care of styling the chart legend and title. If we had used "matplotlib", we would have had to set all these things ourselves.

There are so many options available with Pygal and you

should explore the library further. One last example we are going to cover is to create a box chart, which is a very common sight in financial applications, especially trading. Here's the complete code.

```
import pygal

from pygal.style import LightenStyle


dark_lighten_style = LightenStyle('#000000')


box_plot = pygal.Box(style=dark_lighten_style)

box_plot.title = 'V8 benchmark results'

box_plot.add('Chrome', [6395, 8212, 7520, 7218, 12464, 1660, 2123, 8607])

box_plot.add('Firefox', [7473, 8099, 11700, 2651, 6361, 1044, 3797, 9450])

box_plot.add('Opera', [3472, 2933, 4203, 5229, 5810, 1828, 9013, 4669])

box_plot.add('IE', [43, 41, 59, 79, 144, 136, 34, 102])

box_plot.render_to_file('box_chart.svg') # save the chart as svg image file
```

The output:

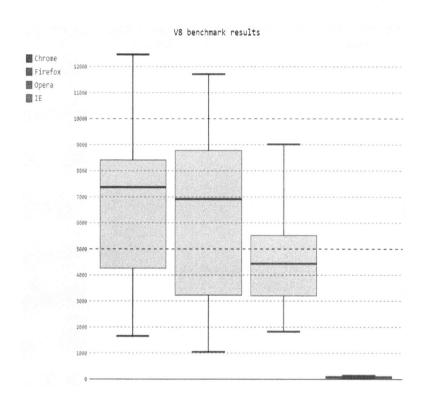

Final note: "svg" format is still a relatively new format and you might not be able to open images with this format on your Windows computer. You can use your Google Chrome browser to view "svg" images.

Chapter 6: Web Applications with Python

Django is an external library widely used to create web applications using Python. It's used by online giants like Instagram and Pinterest. The codes in this chapter are inspired by the work of YouTube channel "techwithtim".

Setup Django

Let's install using pip.

pip install django

Now, let's create our first application. We need to setup the initiation files as a project that will serve as the environment of the application. Using the command prompt, navigate to a folder that will house the application files. To setup the application project, run the following command.

django-admin startproject firstapp

"firstapp" is the name of our first project. To see if the project is setup correctly, run the following command on the command prompt. Make sure you have changed current directory to the correct folder.

python manage.py runserver

To create an application inside this project environment, run the following command.

python manage.py startapp firstapp

Note that the project name and application can be different. To change the different application pages (called views), move to the application folder and change the file named "views.py".

views.py file

```
from django.http import HttpResponse
```

```
def index(request):

    return HttpResponse("This is a brand new web app!")
```

We need to create a URL to access this view. Let's create a new Python file "urls.py" in the application directory. Add the following code to it:

urls.py

```
from django.urls import path
```

```
from . import views
```

```
urlpatterns = [

    path('', views.index, name='index'),

]
```

There is another "urls.py" if you navigate inside the application directory. Modify it so it has the following code.

```
# urls.py

from django.contrib import admin

from django.urls import include, path


urlpatterns = [

    path('', include(firstapp.urls')), # firstapp is the name of our
app

    path('admin/', admin.site.urls),

]
```

You can view this web application by going to the following URL in the browser.

127.0.0.1:8000

First Web Application

Every web application that deals with data usually has a database to store information. We are going to set up an SQLite3 database for our application.

Go to the "settings.py" file inside the web application folder and add one line in the section.

```
# Application definition


INSTALLED_APPS = [
```

'django.contrib.admin',

'django.contrib.auth',

'django.contrib.contenttypes',

'django.contrib.sessions',

'django.contrib.messages',

'django.contrib.staticfiles',

'firstapp.apps.FirstappConfig', # <- add this line, firstapp is the name of our application

]

Now using command prompt, let's move to the directory containing "manage.py" and run the following command.

python manage.py migrate

This command will create an empty database in the application directory. We can add information in the database when needed.

Let's create an admin page. We will first need to setup the database correctly. Run the following command but first make sure you are in the directory that contains "manage.py"

python manage.py createsuperuser

You will now see an admin dashboard created. To view this newly created admin page, go to the following link

127.0.0.1:8000/admin

The admin dashboard is usually created to view the details of the web application. Let's put the database details in the dashboard by adding following block of code in the "admin.py".

```
from django.contrib import admin

from .models import ToDoList, Item

# Register your models here.

admin.site.register(ToDoList)

admin.site.register(Item)
```

Let's get a little fancy and start with HTML templates. Templates are a well-known concept in web designing nowadays. Templates are HTML files that can be shared by different pages that should have the same design and content. Of course, you can overwrite specific details of a template to show different stuff on a specific page. For this project, we are going to create a base HTML template file and then create two more HTML files that share that template. In the main folder, create a base.html and add the following code to it.

```
<html>

<head>

  <title>{% block title %}Tim's Site{% endblock %}</title>

</head>


<body>

  <div id="content" name="content">

                    {% block content %}
```

{% endblock %}

    </div>

</body>

</html>

Notice the places where we have used placeholders wrapped in "{% %}". We must include the closing "{% endblock %}" placeholder. We will insert custom content here when we create specific HTML files. Let's create home.html with the following code. The first line tells Python what parent template to use for this HTML file.

{% extends 'main/base.html' %}

{% block title %}

Home

{% endblock %}

{% block content %}

<h1>Home Page</h1>

{% endblock %}

Let's create the other HTML file that will use some Python conditional statements to generate the code. Variable names are enclosed in double spaces "{{}}".

```
{% extends "main/base.html" %}

{% block title %}View List{% endblock %}


{% block content %}

                                <h1>{{ls.name}}</h1>

                                <ul>

                                {% for item in ls.item_set.all
%}

                                        {% if item.complete
== True %}

                                        <li>{{item.text}} -
COMPLETE</li>

                                        {% else %}

                                        <li>{{item.text}} -
INCOMPLETE</li>

                                        {% endif %}

                                {% endfor %}

                                </ul>

{% endblock %}
```

We have to update the "views.py" and "url.py" to start showing the new HTML files (pages) on the web application.

```
# views.py

from django.shortcuts import render

from django.http import HttpResponse

from .models import ToDoList, Item

# Create your views here.


def index(response, id):

            ls = ToDoList.objects.get(id=id)

                    return render(response, "main/list.html", {"ls":ls})


def home(response):

                    return render(response, "main/home.html", {})
```

The empty {} is used to pass a dictionary containing the variables to the templates.

```
# urls.py

from django.urls import path


from . import views
```

```
urlpatterns = [

path("<int:id>", views.index, name="index"),

path("", views.home, name="home")

]
```

After adding simple HTML page, let's add a simple HTML form. Let's create another template "formCreate.html" with the following code.

```
{% extends 'main/base.html' %}

{% block title %}

Create New List

{% endblock %}


{% block content %}

                         <h3>Create a New To Do
List</h3>

                         <br>

                         <form method="post"
action="/create/" class="form-group">

                         {% csrf_token %}

                         <div class="input-group mb-
3">

                                 <div
class="input-group-prepend">
```

```
                                        <button
name="save" type="submit" class="btn btn-
success">Create</button>

                                        </div>


                        {{form.name}}

                        </div>

                        </form>
```

{% endblock %}

We must use "{% csrf_token %}" in every form we create because it adds necessary security measures to the form. The {{form}} is set when creating a form using this template, you can say it will be the ID of that form.

Let's update "views.py" for this form.

```
def create(response):

    return render(response, "main/formCreate.html", {"form": form}) # goes inside views.py
```

We also have to update the "urls.py".

```
from django.urls import path

from . import views


urlpatterns = [

path("", views.home, name="home"),
```

```
path("home/", views.home, name="home"),

path("create/", views.create, name="index"),

path("<int:id>", views.index, name="index"),

]
```

We have to add the following code block to "views.py" to create a form instance using the formCreate.html

```
...

from .forms import CreateNewList

...

def create(request):

    form = CreateNewList()

    return render(request, "main/formCreate.html", {"form":
form})
```

Now, we have built the form but there's no way to retrieve information from the form. Let's understand some HTML concepts.

POST Request: When information needs to be passed from the front-end (website interface) to the backend (server/database), POST HTML request is used. This is a secured and encrypted request.

GET Request: When information needs to be passed from the backend (server/database) to the front-end (website interface), POST HTML request is used. This is an open and unsecured request.

We have to add the POST and GET requests to the "views.py".

```
def create(response):

  if response.method == "POST":

    form = CreateNewList(response.POST)


    if form.is_valid():

      n = form.cleaned_data["name"]

      t = ToDoList(name=n)

      t.save()


    return HttpResponseRedirect("/%i" %t.id)


  else:

    form = CreateNewList()


  return render(response, "main/formCreate.html",
{"form":form})
```

We can add Bootstrap stylizing and JavaScript customization to the django web application. What's Bootstrap? It's a style library available for free to make web applications responsive. To add these features, we have the change the base.html file. Replace <home> with <!doctype html> and add the following lines between <head> and </head>.

```
<meta charset="utf-8">

<meta name="viewport" content="width=device-width,
initial-scale=1, shrink-to-fit=no">

<link rel="stylesheet"
href="https://stackpath.bootstrapcdn.com/bootstrap/4.3.1/c
ss/bootstrap.min.css">
```

Let's add the following codes just before the </body> tag.

```
<script src="https://code.jquery.com/jquery-
3.3.1.slim.min.js"></script>

<script
src="https://cdnjs.cloudflare.com/ajax/libs/popper.js/1.14.7/
umd/popper.min.js"></script>

<script
src="https://stackpath.bootstrapcdn.com/bootstrap/4.3.1/js/
bootstrap.min.js"></script>
```

Now, we can add Bootstrap classes to the elements to make them better looking without writing our own stylesheet. We can also write JavaScript and jQuery codes for added dynamics.

The possibilities are endless with Django Python framework and there are even more Django extension libraries available. For example, to add the capability of user sign up we can use "django-crispy-forms" external library.

Chapter 7: GUI and Computer Peripheral Control

Working with command prompt might look nerdy cool at first, but it's not a good way to take inputs from users in today's world. Everything requires a visual touch. Python provides considerable resources and tools to create a Graphical User Interface (GUI). Let's create some fun things.

Create GUI for File and Folder Selection

We can give users the ability to visually navigate to a file and folder for various file operations. This is enabled by using Python's standard GUI library, Tkinter, a unique name with powerful GUI capabilities. The code enables a user to select a file so we can extract the file path.

import Tkinter

import tkFileDialog

rut = Tkinter.Tk()

rut.withdraw() #hide the tkinter window

fileAcc = tkFileDialog.askopenfile(parent=root,initialdir="/",mode='rb',title='Pick any file') if fileAcc != None:

print fileAcc.name

We can restrict the file type the user can select through the GUI. Let's pass more arguments to the askopenfile() method.

fileAcc = tkFileDialog.askopenfile(parent=root,initialdir="/",mode='rb',title='Pick any file',filetypes = (("All Excel files","*.xl*"),("All files","*.*")))

Taking Control of Keyboard and Mouse

We are entering the domain of programming that can be attributed to hacking. Taking control of a keyboard and mouse can be used for nefarious purposes. But, there are benefits to teaching this topic.

1. Clients want to test their web applications. You can write a Python program to automatically test their web app in several ways. One script can do the work of an entire QA team.
2. You want to automate some tasks on your computer that will take too much time to directly integrate with Python. For example, instead of using an Excel related library to open an Excel spreadsheet, you can use this technique to achieve the same results.

The external library "pyautogui" helps us in this respect. No other library is required for a Windows system.

pip install pyautogui

When "pyautogui" takes control of either keyboard or mouse, it blocks your access to those devices. If you make an error in the script, you might lose access to the input devices unless you hard reset the computer. Don't worry, "pyautogui" provides pause and failsafe features. "Failsafe" is triggered when the mouse hits the top right corner of the screen and device control is returned to the user. The "pause" creates a delay so you can stop the program execution if need be. Note that once you lose control of your keyboard, you won't be able to use the CTRL+C to break the program execution.

```
import pyautogui

pyautogui.FAILSAFE = True

pyautogui.PAUSE = 1
```

Before we automate the keyboard or mouse, we need to know what is the size of the screen so we would know the limits.

```
pyautogui.size()
```

Mouse automation

```
for xy in range(8):

                pyautogui.moveTo(50, 50,
duration=0.5)

                pyautogui.moveTo(100, 50,
duration=0.5)

                pyautogui.moveTo(100, 100,
duration=0.5)

                pyautogui.moveTo(50, 100,
```

duration=0.5)

The above code moves the mouse cursor in a square shape pattern in the clockwise direction. Each movement will occur in 0.25 seconds so it will be visible for you to see the movement. In the above example, we have used fixed coordinates. We can use relative coordinates also, just like we have used below.

pyautogui.moveRel(50, 50, duration=0.5)

All this wouldn't make sense if we don't know what the current position of the cursor is.

pyautogui.position()

We can also automate mouse click like this.

pyautogui.click(7, 3)

We have to provide fixed coordinates to the click() method, not relative. The click() method mimics the left mouse button being pressed and released. We can use "pyautogui.mouseDown()" and "pyautogui,mouseUp()" to automate either pressing or releasing of the mouse button. The "pyautogui.doubleClick()" simulates a double click. You can use "pyautogui.rightClick()" to simulate a right click and a middle button click with "pyautogui.middleClick()".

There are two methods "pyautogui,dragTo()" and "pyautogui.dragRel()" to automate dragging, both of which work in a similar manner as moveTo() and moveRel() methods we have seen before. The difference is that with drag modules, the mouse button is also left clicked to force a drag instead of just moving the cursor.

Newer mice come with the scrolling wheel and it can be automated too with the scroll() method. You have to pass an integer value that pyatuogui uses to determine how much the screen has to move up or down. The integer values will result in different scroll movement on different screen sizes and computer systems. One important thing to remember: the scroll() method is relative, which means the scrolling will start from the current position of the mouse.

We can also take a screenshot with "pyautogui" library using the screenshot() method.

viewfreeze = pyautogui.screenshot()

Keyboard automation

Keyboard actions can be simulated using the rhe "pyautogui.typewrite()" method. Depending upon the application currently active, the same key presses might result in different actions. Here is an example of typing a string with each keystroke happening after a delay.

pyautogui.typewrite("Dora The Explorer!", 0.71)

We can also automate keyboard actions such as adding a new line by passing a special code in the typewrite(). Here's a table of codes assigned to different keyboard actions.

Key string	Meaning
'a', 'b', 'c', 'A', 'B', 'C', '1', '2', '3', '!', '@', '#', and so on	keys for single characters

'enter' (or 'return'or '\n')	ENTER key
'esc'	ESC key
'shiftleft', 'shiftright'	Left and Right SHIFT keys
'altleft','altright'	Left and Right ALT keys
'ctrlleft','ctrlright'	Left and Right CTRL keys
'tab' or '\t'	TAB key
'backspace','delete'	BACKSPACE and DELETE keys
'pageup','pagedown'	PAGE UP and PAGE DOWN keys
'home','end'	HOME and END keys
'up','down','left','right'	ARROW keys

'f1','f2','f3' and so on...	F1 to F12 keys
'volumeup','volumedown','mute'	VOLUME control keys. Your keyboard might have these keys but your system might still be able to recognize these commands
'pause'	PAUSE key
'capslock','numlock','scrolllock'	LOCK keys
'insert'	INSERT or INS key
'printscreen'	PRINT SCREEN or PRTSC key
'winleft','winright'	Left and Right WIN keys (Windows only)

We can combine different keypresses to type a special character. The following lines of code result in '%' getting typed.

```
pyautogui.keyDown('shift')

pyautogui.press('5')

pyautogui.keyUp('shift')
```

The hotkey() method is very useful because we can perform system operations like copy and paste by mimicking the simultaneous press of CTRL and another key. For example, here is how we can automate a copy command.

```
pyautogui.hotkey('ctrl','c')
```

Chapter 8: Gaming with Python

Gaming is not new, it's as old as the computers. It's one of the biggest industries related to computers and programming in terms of revenue and salaries. With the advent of smartphones, more and more independent developers are launching games in the hope of hitting the jackpot. The codes in the chapter are inspired by the work of Youtube channel "techwithtim".

Python provides a way to create 2D games and we are going to take a look at it now.

PyGame Introduction

The "pygame" is an excellent external library for building games. Let's install "pygame".

pip install pygame

The following code shows the basics of setting up a game environment. Comments are added to explain important points.

import pygame

pygame.init() # start the gaming engine

win = pygame.display.set_mode((500, 500)) # This line creates a window of 500 width, 500 height

pygame.display.set_caption("First Game") # change window name

Initializing the character attributes.

```
x = 50
```

```
y = 50
```

```
width = 40
```

```
height = 60
```

```
vel = 5
```

```
# setting an infinite loop
```

```
run = True
```

```
while run:
    pygame.time.delay(100)

    for event in pygame.event.get():
        if event.type == pygame.QUIT:
            run = False # end game loop only in this condition

    keys = pygame.key.get_pressed() # check if a keyboard key
```
is pressed and which key it is

```
    # move the character wrt to the keyboard key pressed
```

```
    if keys[pygame.K_LEFT]:
```

```
        x -= vel


    if keys[pygame.K_RIGHT]:

        x += vel


    if keys[pygame.K_UP]:

        y -= vel


    if keys[pygame.K_DOWN]:

        y += vel



    win.fill((0,0,0))  # Fills the screen with black so there's no
tail of the character

    pygame.draw.rect(win, (255,0,0), (x, y, width, height)) #
draw the character

    pygame.display.update() # update the display on every loop
execution


pygame.quit() # stop the game when loop is broken
```

Creating a 2D Game

We are going to create the popular Tetris game that will become more difficult over time.

Part #1: Initialization

We have to create the game environment before we can start coding the mechanics and other details. Here's the complete code that initializes the Tetris game environment. Comments are added where necessary to describe certain aspects.

```
import pygame

import random


# creating the data structure for pieces

# setting up global vars

# functions

# - create_grid

# - draw_grid

# - draw_window

# - rotating shape in main

# - setting up the main


"""
```

```
10 x 20 square grid

shapes: S, Z, I, O, J, L, T

represented in order by 0 - 6
"""


pygame.font.init()


# GLOBALS VARS

s_width = 800

s_height = 700

play_width = 300  # meaning 300 // 10 = 30 width per block

play_height = 600  # meaning 600 // 20 = 20 height per block

block_size = 30


top_left_x = (s_width - play_width) // 2

top_left_y = s_height - play_height


# SHAPE FORMATS
```

```
S = [['.....',

      '.....',

      '..OO.',

      '.OO..',

      '.....'],

     ['.....',

      '..O..',

      '..OO.',

      '...O.',

      '.....']]


Z = [['.....',

      '.....',

      '.OO..',

      '..OO.',

      '.....'],

     ['.....',

      '..O..',

      '.OO..',

      '.O...',
```

```
            '.....']]


I = [['..0..',

      '..0..',

      '..0..',

      '..0..',

      '.....'],

     ['.....',

      '0000.',

      '.....',

      '.....',

      '.....']]


O = [['.....',

      '.....',

      '.00..',

      '.00..',

      '.....']]


J = [['.....',
```

```
        '.0...',

        '.000.',

        '.....',

        '.....'],

    ['.....',

        '..00.',

        '..0..',

        '..0..',

        '.....'],

    ['.....',

        '.....',

        '.000.',

        '...0.',

        '.....'],

    ['.....',

        '..0..',

        '..0..',

        '.00..',

        '.....']]
```

```
L = [['.....',

    '...0.',

    '.000.',

    '.....',

    '.....'],

    ['.....',

    '..0..',

    '..0..',

    '..00.',

    '.....'],

    ['.....',

    '.....',

    '.000.',

    '.0...',

    '.....'],

    ['.....',

    '.00..',

    '..0..',

    '..0..',

    '.....']]
```

```
T = [['.....',

      '..0..',

      '.000.',

      '.....',

      '.....'],

     ['.....',

      '..0..',

      '..00.',

      '..0..',

      '.....'],

     ['.....',

      '.....',

      '.000.',

      '..0..',

      '.....'],

     ['.....',

      '..0..',

      '.00..',

      '..0..',
```

```
'.....']]
```

```python
shapes = [S, Z, I, O, J, L, T]

shape_colors = [(0, 255, 0), (255, 0, 0), (0, 255, 255), (255, 255, 0), (255, 165, 0), (0, 0, 255), (128, 0, 128)]

# index 0 - 6 represent shape


class Piece(object):

    pass


def create_grid(locked_positions={}):

    pass


def convert_shape_format(shape):

    pass


def valid_space(shape, grid):

    pass
```

```python
def check_lost(positions):
    pass


def get_shape():
    pass


def draw_text_middle(text, size, color, surface):
    pass


def draw_grid(surface, row, col):
    pass


def clear_rows(grid, locked):
    pass


def draw_next_shape(shape, surface):
    pass


def draw_window(surface):
    pass
```

```python
def main():

    pass


def main_menu():

    pass


main_menu()  # start game
```

Part #2: Game Design

I have divided the code into various sections for easier understanding. You need to keep all this code in one script file.

Class for Piece Shapes

We are going to create different shapes and it's better to create a class for all shapes that defines all the common properties and functions.

```python
class Piece(object):

    rows = 20  # y

    columns = 10  # x


    def __init__(self, column, row, shape):
```

```
        self.x = column

        self.y = row

        self.shape = shape

        self.color = shape_colors[shapes.index(shape)]

        self.rotation = 0  # number from 0-3
```

Create a Game Grid

This piece of code creates the visible gaming area. The randomly generated shapes will occupy this grid according to the user input.

```
def create_grid(locked_positions={}):

  grid = [[(0,0,0) for x in range(10)] for x in range(20)]


  for i in range(len(grid)):

    for j in range(len(grid[i])):

      if (j,i) in locked_positions:

        c = locked_positions[(j,i)]

        grid[i][j] = c

  return grid
```

Randomizing Shape Generation

This code generates different shapes randomly. Note that we already set all the shapes that will be generated during initialization.

```python
def get_shape():

  global shapes, shape_colors


  return Piece(5, 0, random.choice(shapes))
```

Game Grid Build

This part of script builds the grid where the game will be played.

```python
surface.fill((0,0,0))

  # Tetris Title

  font = pygame.font.SysFont(\'comicsans\', 60)

  label = font.render(\'TETRIS\', 1, (255,255,255))


  surface.blit(label, (top_left_x + play_width / 2 -
(label.get_width() / 2), 30))



  for i in range(len(grid)):

    for j in range(len(grid[i])):

      pygame.draw.rect(surface, grid[i][j], (top_left_x + j*
30, top_left_y + i * 30, 30, 30), 0)



  # draw grid and border
```

```
draw_grid(surface, 20, 10)

pygame.draw.rect(surface, (255, 0, 0), (top_left_x,
top_left_y, play_width, play_height), 5)

pygame.display.update()
```

Create Game Loop

This is the main loop that will be constantly running looking for events and invoking necessary actions. The "while" loop helps create an infinite iteration that will only break if we lose or win the game.

```
def main():

    global grid


    locked_positions = {}  # (x,y):(255,0,0)

    grid = create_grid(locked_positions)


    change_piece = False

    run = True

    current_piece = get_shape()

    next_piece = get_shape()

    clock = pygame.time.Clock()

    fall_time = 0
```

```python
while run:

    for event in pygame.event.get():

        if event.type == pygame.QUIT:

            run = False

            pygame.display.quit()

            quit()


        if event.type == pygame.KEYDOWN:

            if event.key == pygame.K_LEFT:

                current_piece.x -= 1

                if not valid_space(current_piece, grid):

                    current_piece.x += 1


            elif event.key == pygame.K_RIGHT:

                current_piece.x += 1

                if not valid_space(current_piece, grid):

                    current_piece.x -= 1

            elif event.key == pygame.K_UP:

                # rotate shape

                current_piece.rotation = current_piece.rotation +
```

```
1 % len(current_piece.shape)

        if not valid_space(current_piece, grid):

            current_piece.rotation = current_piece.rotation
- 1 % len(current_piece.shape)


    if event.key == pygame.K_DOWN:

        # move shape down

        current_piece.y += 1

        if not valid_space(current_piece, grid):

            current_piece.y -= 1



draw_window(win)
```

Part #3: Building the Game

Add Visuals to the Game Grid

We are going to add grid lines so players will know how much space a shape takes and how much the shape can be moved.

```
def draw_grid(surface, row, col):

# This function draws the grey grid lines that we see

    sx = top_left_x

    sy = top_left_y
```

```
for i in range(row):

    pygame.draw.line(surface, (128,128,128), (sx, sy+ i*30),
(sx + play_width, sy + i * 30))  # horizontal lines

    for j in range(col):

        pygame.draw.line(surface, (128,128,128), (sx + j * 30,
sy), (sx + j * 30, sy + play_height))  # vertical lines
```

Track Position of Shape in the Grid

During the game, we must be able to track the position of the shapes. Here's the code to do that.

```
def convert_shape_format(shape):

    positions = []

    format = shape.shape[shape.rotation % len(shape.shape)]


    for i, line in enumerate(format):

        row = list(line)

        for j, column in enumerate(row):

            if column == \'0\':

                positions.append((shape.x + j, shape.y + i))


    for i, pos in enumerate(positions):

        positions[i] = (pos[0] - 2, pos[1] - 4)
```

```
    return positions
```

Check if Certain Grid Space is Valid

To make sure the shape doesn't move into a space that's already taken or is out of the available grid, we have to write a function. Here's the code to check grid space validity.

```
def valid_space(shape, grid):

    accepted_positions = [[(j, i) for j in range(10) if grid[i][j] ==
(0,0,0)] for i in range(20)]

    accepted_positions = [j for sub in accepted_positions for j
in sub]

    formatted = convert_shape_format(shape)


    for pos in formatted:

        if pos not in accepted_positions:

            if pos[1] > -1:

                return False


    return True
```

Check if Game is Lost

We have to constantly check if user has lost the game. Here's the function code to check that.

```
def check_lost(positions):

    for pos in positions:

        x, y = pos

        if y < 1:

            return True

    return False
```

Modify Game Loop

Remember we created the main game loop in Part #2? We need to add more codes to it. Add the following code block right after the "while run:" line.

```
fall_speed = 0.27


    grid = create_grid(locked_positions)

    fall_time += clock.get_rawtime()

    clock.tick()


    # PIECE FALLING CODE

    if fall_time/1000 >= fall_speed:

        fall_time = 0

        current_piece.y += 1

        if not (valid_space(current_piece, grid)) and
```

```
current_piece.y > 0:

    current_piece.y -= 1

    change_piece = True
```

Before the "draw_window(win, grid)" line, add the following lines of code.

```
shape_pos = convert_shape_format(current_piece)


    # add color of piece to the grid for drawing

    for i in range(len(shape_pos)):

      x, y = shape_pos[i]

      if y > -1: # If we are not above the screen

        grid[y][x] = current_piece.color

    # IF PIECE HIT GROUND

    if change_piece:

      for pos in shape_pos:

        p = (pos[0], pos[1])

        locked_positions[p] = current_piece.color

      current_piece = next_piece

      next_piece = get_shape()

      change_piece = False
```

After the "draw_window(win, grid)" line, add the following lines of code.

Check if user lost

```
    if check_lost(locked_positions):

        run = False
```

Part #4: Adding Features to The Game

Show Next Shape on the Side

We want to show the next shape that will enter the grid from the top on the right side of the grid. Here's a function to do that.

```
def draw_next_shape(shape, surface):

    font = pygame.font.SysFont('comicsans', 30)

    label = font.render('Next Shape', 1, (255,255,255))


    sx = top_left_x + play_width + 50

    sy = top_left_y + play_height/2 - 100

    format = shape.shape[shape.rotation % len(shape.shape)]


    for i, line in enumerate(format):

        row = list(line)

        for j, column in enumerate(row):
```

```
        if column == '0':

            pygame.draw.rect(surface, shape.color, (sx + j*30, sy
+ i*30, 30, 30), 0)



    surface.blit(label, (sx + 10, sy- 30))
```

We need to call this function in the main() so it will constantly run.

```
# This should go inside the while loop right BELOW
draw_window()

# Near the end of the loop

draw_next_shape(next_piece, win)

pygame.display.update()
```

Clear Filled Row

When a grid row is completely filled, it must be removed from the grid and all other rows shifted down. Here's the function code to do that.

```
def clear_rows(grid, locked):

    # need to see if row is clear then shift every other row
above down one


    inc = 0

    for i in range(len(grid)-1,-1,-1):

        row = grid[i]
```

```
    if (0, 0, 0) not in row:

        inc += 1

        # add positions to remove from locked

        ind = i

        for j in range(len(row)):

            try:

                del locked[(j, i)]

            except:

                continue

    if inc > 0:

        for key in sorted(list(locked), key=lambda x: x[1])[::-1]:

            x, y = key

            if y < ind:

                newKey = (x, y + inc)

                locked[newKey] = locked.pop(key)
```

We also need to call this function from the main() function. Add the following lines of code at the end of "if change_piece:" block.

```
# call four times to check for multiple clear rows

        clear_rows(grid, locked_positions) # < ---------- GOES
HERE
```

Part #5: Raise Difficulty

In a Tetris game, we can increase the game difficulty by increasing the speed with which the shapes fall down the grid.

In the main() function, just before the "while run:" line, add the following line of code.

level_time = 0

Now, add the following line of code at the start of "while run:" loop.

level_time += clock.get_rawtime()

```
  if level_time/1000 > 5:

    level_time = 0

    if level_time > 0.12:

      level_time -= 0.005
```

Part #6: Game Build

The following lines of code will go at the end of the script.

win = pygame.display.set_mode((s_width, s_height))
pygame.display.set_caption(\'Tetris\')

main()

We can add many more features to the game to offer a better gaming experience. Here are some ideas:

1. Add a scoring system. For example, award 10 points for each filled row cleared from the grid
2. Add a main menu to the game
3. Add an exit screen with score etc. summary after the game stops running

The above example is just the beginning when it comes to creating games with Python. Well-known games including Battlefield 2 and The Sims 4 utilize the power of Python to create a highly immersive gaming experience. If you want to become a game developer and don't have the capital to invest in proprietary platforms, Python can help you become famous!

Creating an Executable Distribution of Software

We have to install an external library to create distributable ".exe" package for any Python script.

pip install pyinstaller

Using the command prompt, navigate to the directory where the Python script is present. Let's say our script file name is "appComp.py". We have to run the following command.

pyinstaller --onefile appComp.py

The process can take a few minutes to complete depending upon your script. It automatically takes care of any libraries you added in the script. Once it's finished, a few new folders and files will be present in the folder where your Python script was present. Open the "dist" folder and you will see the "appComp.exe" file. Easy!

Conclusion

Python has created a revolution in the programming world due to its open source nature. The rise of data analysis and machine learning have also made Python very relevant. It offers easier syntax but doesn't compromise in power or speed. All these qualities have made the language ideal for people who are not programmers but want to create scripts to achieve specific objectives.

Python 2.7 is the most popular version even though the support is going to end very soon. Code written in Python 2.7 is not forward compatible with Python 3.0. It definitely created a dilemma for companies who have relied on Python for years. It's not easy to port millions of lines of code. Due to this reason, Python 2.7 End of Life (EOL) has been extended several times. But, it's certain it will not be extended this time.

There are various books and YouTube channels that you can refer to if you want to build upon the skills learned in this book. Python is a great programming language if you want to freelance or start your own programming firm. I hope your Python journey is fun and full of rewards!

References

Eric Matthes, Python Crash Course, 2nd edition. San Francisco, CA: No Starch Press Inc., 2019.

James R. Parker, Python: An Introduction to Programming. Dulles, VA: Mercury Learning and Information, 2017.

Ryan Turner, Python Programming: 3 Books in 1: Ultimate Beginner's, Intermediate & Advanced Guide to Learn Python Step-by-Step. James C Anderson, 2018.

Steven Samelson, Python Programming: A Step-by-Step Guide From Absolute Beginners to Complete Guide for Intermediates and Advanced. Steven Samelson, 2019.

Python machine learning

circumstances is the author responsible for any losses, direct or indirect, that are incurred as a result of the use of information contained within this document, including, but not limited to, errors, omissions, or inaccuracies.

Introduction

The world continues to advance every day. Every now and then, we find humanity discovering newer realms and expanding the horizon far beyond what we once thought possible. That is the magic of science. However, this entire feat was probably not possible without the invention of computer programming languages. Every major success we have had in terms of technology comes from some form of computer programming.

Today, the world is awash with programming languages such as the R, C# (called C Sharp), JavaScript, the list is just endless. While we continue to search for new languages to further explore new possibilities, one language stands out for its sheer effectiveness, simplicity and exceptional use in the world of today. Created by Guido Van Rossum, Python has become a new benchmark for beginners and experts alike.

Leading platforms around the world are using Python as their core programming language. Whether we speak about social media giants such as Instagram, or the latest radar-guided and satellite-guided self-driven cars, Python is found to be in the heart of the entire success. It is because of Python that the world has now taken an interest in Data Science and Machine learning, the two leading frontiers of technology.

Naturally, it makes great sense for any programmer to seek guidance to learn and master the technicalities involved behind these two, which is where this book will step in.

Unlike many other books, we will jump straight to the good bits and keep it true to the "clean code writing" practice as possible. You will get ample explanation only where they may be required; the rest are self-explanatory by nature.

What exactly is machine learning? While the book talks about the more advanced aspects of machine learning, here's a little explanation for anyone who is thinking about taking up Machine Learning as their choice of field.

Generally speaking, we human beings learn from our past experiences and correct our headings to ensure the results we desire are obtained. Machines, on the other hand, are programmed by us, without the option of allowing them to learn from their past experiences. With Machine Learning, we now have the option to allow the machines to learn from their past experiences. Sure enough, the machine cannot do anything unless we allow it to carry out a specific task. In this case, we will become the trainer and the machines will become the students. We will use this book to have a look into what are some advanced ways to ensure that we train our machine, test out their capabilities, check their accuracy and quite a lot more.

The idea to write a book with practical codes is one that has been taken up by quite a lot of esteemed authors and publishers, however, this book was created to ensure a good chunk of such codes and variations were used. We will encounter quite a few terminologies that may seem daunting at first, but the explanations provided should be easy to understand.

Python Machine Learning is a book that ensures all technicalities are catered and applied to examples to showcase their unique features and differences. Through carefully created codes and snippets, it would be easy to draw a conclusion and learn a thing or two about the various methods used within this book.

While there are quite a few graphs that were omitted, owing to the fact that these were almost identical in nature, readers are encouraged to try to manipulate the data to see the minor yet existing differences.

To get the most out of this book, there is only one thing you can do: Practice. The more you practice your coding skills, the better you learn and understand matters. In the interest of advanced learning, we will not be visiting any basics but instead will be focusing on advanced terminologies, methods, and their usages only.

If you have just started using Python, it is best that you create a good understanding of how to code with Python before embarking on a journey to the world of Machine learning.

Who should read this book?

This book ideally aims to provide a learning experience to professionals who are practicing machine learning tools to investigate real-world issues. This book is an advanced level of learning and requires some basic knowledge of machine learning and artificial intelligence (AI). There is quite a lot of software that can be used for applying machine learning algorithms, but we will focus on using Python along with a few selected software's and libraries. It is understood that by reading this book, you have a basic understanding of what libraries are and how they are used in python for algorithm development. You must be familiar with the basics of NumPy, Matplotlib and Scikit-learn as these will be our primary sources to work with.

If you have yet to come across these libraries and software's, it is probably best to acquire the required knowledge first prior to reading the content within this book. While there is no harm in doing so, there is a good possibility that you might be overwhelmed with commands, functions, libraries, and other methods used within the book if you have never used them before.

There will be times where you might feel overwhelmed by the sheer number of codes used within this book. If you are not sure about some of these, you can always browse the internet to gain a better perspective. These codes were designed with specific datasets and hence some functions, methods and parameters were used that were related to these codes. For a list of complete methods and functions, be sure to visit websites pertaining to said libraries to find a list of these. We will not be going through all of them within this book.

Before you do go ahead and start your journey, it is essential to know that you will need to use the latest version of Python on your system. It does not matter whether you are using Windows, Macintosh OS or any distribution of Linux, the coding will remain universal. However, having Python-2 will surely have a few troubles. Therefore, it is essential that you use Python-3.x.x (whichever is applicable) to follow the book without encountering any errors.

Purpose of this book

There are many books written on python and machine learning. It is only natural that you might be asking how is this book any different. Most of these books either dive deep into theories behind python and machine learning unnecessarily or gave simple generic examples consisting of general problems. This book deals with only real-world problems and applies almost all methods of machine learning to make you gain a better understanding of algorithms and provide you with a practical way to resolve and investigate real-world issues.

At the end of reading this book, you will be able to compare all methods of machine learning and ready to apply these algorithms both efficiently and effectively. This book is to be taken as a reference book and does not necessarily guarantee that the content shown here would work on future versions of the language or software's used. All commands, libraries, coding methods used here were valid at the time of writing this book. If you run into such issues where certain methods, functions or commands no longer work, use the Python community to seek answers.

Python is one of the most well-documented languages in existence that allows you to learn almost everything about the language by scrolling through the community forums. You are encouraged to take advantage of it when and where possible to help you further accelerate your learning.

It is imperative that you understand that we will be using Anaconda as our prime environment for development purposes as it contains all the necessary packages and libraries that we need in order to try out, test, and learn machine learning. The datasets used within the book are predefined and available within Scikit-Learn. Should you find yourself in a spot of trouble, you can always search for those online to find out how to access them.

The Python version in use throughout the book will be 3.x.x as Python 2 is slightly different and will run out of services soon. If you do not have Python 3 installed, head over to www.python.org to download the latest version of Python 3.

Although the book provides various examples and data visualizations, it is not to be taken as the only guide to learn from. This book covers all the bases of Machine Learning and puts various methods to use with numerous scenarios. You can visit online repositories to gain access to all of these datasets and libraries. Use this book as your reference, and aim to learn and develop a sound understanding of matters involved in machine learning. By the end of this book, we aim to allow a student or an aspirant to have enough confidence to carry out various experiments using their own imaginations, scenarios and codes.

If you encounter errors during the process of executing codes or during the installation of any of the libraries, software or plugins, ensure to visit the concerned websites or ask the ever-active community of Python programmers and Machine learners on various platforms.

All the codes written were tried and tested during the writing of this book. All of these were found to be working and result-oriented. However, it is not to be taken for granted that these codes will work perfectly in future releases of any of the components involved.

Lastly, the book was written after thorough research and wishes to provide more practical coding than theory. Should you feel overwhelmed at any point, stop and take a bit of a break. Do not try and pace through the lines. Sometimes, a glass of water and some fresh air might be just what you need to get you back into the productive zone.

Take this book as your ultimate reference book and extract as much knowledge from this book as possible. Always remember that you can and will encounter errors. There is nothing to be alarmed about any of those as these errors will not affect or jeopardize your system as a whole. Upon encountering an error, debug the code and correct the values, parameters or arguments to ensure the code is able to work perfectly.

Chapter 1: Getting Started With Machine Learning

Machine learning is a method that is used to get information from the given data sets. These data sets are then used to train systems using the provided information so that they can be used to provide output of corresponding input when any input is given. It has numerous applications. Although it can be used for both small and sizeable data, usually it is mainly used to process a high quantity of data in quick time and then return the output in relation to the input provided.

Machine learning is what allows AI to gain the ability to self-learn and improve itself through various occurrences and experiences. There is a reason that this field has quickly garnered quite a lot of attention from the rest of the world. More and more people are now willing to learn Python to understand Machine Learning and be able to write and execute programs that can further enable their AIs to become intelligent systems.

We already have an example of how this sublime technology is being used in weather systems. Through carefully designed architectures and programs, the system now has the ability to comprehend, understand and then predict what the weather conditions will be like in the coming days. This is made possible through effective use of AI. Take the machine learning away, and we might be back to computing individual variables and data for hours before realizing that the results are in a little too late.

What is Machine Learning?

By now, you may have already acquired an idea as to what machine learning is. It is an efficient way to process large quantities of data in the smallest amount of time and allow systems to gain the ability to learn from the given data. It is used to provide prediction of future values by training itself with current and old values. It is used in many cases these days such as the automatic recommendation regarding best movies, ordering the best food, and buying the best products.

Similarly, it is used to recognize your friends in photos stored on Facebook and other social platforms through facial recognition. It is also used in platforms such as Amazon and Netflix. Hence, machine learning can be used in many ways, and that is precisely why it is necessary to gain an understanding at an advanced level so that it can be used to solve multiple problems and deliver various services to ease the users further.

In the old days, "if and else" statements were used for processing of data or adjusting user input in order to make intelligent applications. There was a spam filter that was used to transfer specific emails to spam folder. How do you think this was done with emails to categorize them as spam?

Spam filter used a list of blacklisted words that helped the filter to identify spam. This filter can be used as one of the examples of intelligent applications. This problem can be solved by a human as well, but in that case, a person requires enough understanding of processes to come up with such a model. Manual or hand-coded rules can be useful but not in every case, as mentioned above. It can have some disadvantages as follows:

· The code or system will work for a specific problem; any change in the problem can lead to failure of that code or system.

· A human being may not be able to develop such a thorough understanding quickly and might consume quite a lot of time to carry out such work.

Similarly, there is one more example in which the hand-coded method fails, and that is the detection of a face in an image. Although every smartphone these days can detect and identify faces in the pictures, these were not identified successfully in the past. The reason behind failure in detection and identification of faces in an image in the recent past is the difference in perception of pixels between a human and a computer.

Computer perceives images differently as compared to humans. The improvement from failure to success in detection of a face in an image is due to the utilization of machine learning algorithms. The machine learning-based program contains large samples of pictures, which is enough to detect and identify various faces within an image.

Types of learning and their examples

Just a few minutes ago, we discussed the use of spam filters within our emails and how it transfers individual emails to our junk mail folder while retaining the others in the inbox. The machine learning algorithm can perform this work efficiently. All it requires is a sample of spam words or emails for the training of the model, and then that model will categorize spam emails. In reality, that model will predict emails as spam or otherwise.

The model that requires training needs machine learning. Furthermore, the selection of methods depends on the situation of the problem at hand.

If the problem provides the information of categorization as an input, it is known as **supervised learning**. On the other hand, if the problem does not provide the information of categorization as an input, it is known as **unsupervised learning**. Clustering is a perfect example of unsupervised learning, while classification and regression are examples of supervised learning.

The term 'Supervised' learning is recognized from the term supervision, just as a teacher supervises his/her students on a specific task and guides them regarding inputs and outputs. In doing this, they learn the sequence of that particular problem.

Likewise, supervised learning takes inputs and learns its outputs as well, and when other data is given to it, it can predict its output using the trained model.

Supervised learning can further be explained, and to do that, let us assume another example situation. Suppose that you are presented with three similar pills of the same dimensions and all are of the same color.

- Pill A - five grams
- Pill B - six grams
- Pill C - 7 grams

We have the weights. Here, the weight will turn into a component called 'feature,' which we will be using shortly to classify these. Let us assume that we have another data that is already defined in the machine. The machine will cross-check with the data and immediately recognize these pills based on their 'features' and provide them with their names. Names are defined as labels. Your end result may look like this:

- (name of drug) - 5 grams
- (name of drug) - 6 grams
- (name of drug) - 7 grams

Here, the name of the drug can be anything that is predefined. The same can be used to identify coins, metals, ornaments, and objects.

In the above example, we have features and the machine uses labeled data to identify these and provide outputs accordingly.

On the other hand, unsupervised learning has no awareness of outputs to specific inputs, and when a different data set is given, it can just categorize outputs on the basis of some parameters such as Euclidean distance, etc. To put it in plain terms, unsupervised data works on unlabeled data and provides outputs in cluster forms.

We will see some more examples of both supervised learning and unsupervised learning to develop a better understanding of these schemes. One of the most common examples of supervised learning is the identification of zip codes from handwritten digits on an envelope.

In this example, you have scans of handwriting as input, and zip code is the desired output. You need to collect multiple envelopes to create datasets for the training model. Hence, when any handwritten digits are provided to the system as an input, the algorithm will provide the zip codes as output.

Another example of supervised learning is determining whether the tumor is benign in a medical image. Here, you have the medical images as input, and the desired output will inform whether the tumor is benign or not. You would need to collect multiple medical images to make datasets for the training model. Hence, when any medical image is fed to the system as an input, the algorithm will come into play and inform regarding the intensity of the said tumor. Machine learning is used quite often in the field of medical imaging.

To quote yet another example of supervised learning, it is the detection of fraudulent activity in the transactions of credit cards. Following the same pattern as above, you have credit card transactions as input, and the output will determine whether the said transaction is legitimate or fraudulent in nature. Once again, you will need to collect credit card transactions to make datasets for the training model. Hence, when any credit card transactions are fed to the system as inputs, the algorithm will produce the results accordingly.

With a bit of an understanding of how supervised learning works, let us now look at some examples of unsupervised learning. One of the examples of unsupervised learning is the identification of topics in blog posts.

The large number of textual data that you have represents these blog posts as input, and you want to summarize the themes of these posts. Since you don't know about these topics, the outputs are unknown. Hence, without any known corresponding outputs of these inputs, you need to summarize the themes of these posts. This can pose a bit of a challenge as you will need to rely on other methods to gather the related information and categorize them accordingly. See how supervised learning is much more efficient?

Another example of unsupervised learning is the segmentation of customers into groups with similarities. In this example, you have a massive number of customer records as input, and you want to identify which customers have similarities.

Customers can be parents, book buyers or gamers. You don't know about these groups, and naturally the output is unknown. Hence, without any known corresponding outputs of these inputs, you need to identify similarities among customers and then segment them on the basis of those similarities on your own.

Finally, we have an example of unsupervised learning for the detection of abnormal access patterns to websites. Here, you have a large number of website access records as input and you want to identify which access is classified as abnormal. The abnormal accesses will be different from each other. Since you have no idea about these accesses and how they are organized, the outputs are unknown. Therefore, without any known corresponding outputs of these inputs, you now need to identify which access is abnormal on your own.

By no means are we stating that of these two methods only one is usable. There are cases where both can be used, depending on the input and output of the scenario. However, as the book progresses, you will soon learn why the former is favored over the latter.

Now that we have seen a few examples where Machine Learning is applied, let us now shift our attention to the more technical aspects, one where we start setting up our environment, gathering the right tools and starting our own venture.

Installing Machine Libraries in Your System

Before we commence, the readers are reminded that this book is meant for intermediate to advanced users, which is why we will not be explaining the basic terminologies involved in Python and programming in general, such as libraries, classes, arrays, lists, tuples and so on.

There are multiple libraries that are required to be installed in

Python in order to apply Machine learning. Some of them are basic libraries, while some are more advanced in nature. Each library has its own usage. These are usually used for performing specific operations.

First, we have Scikit-learn. Scikit-learn is a free-to-use package, hence it is also known as an open-source package. It is being developed much throughout the world, and it is being used by many programmers. It is quite a great package, and almost every advanced program should be able to recognize it.

It contains many Machine learning-based algorithms. This package relies on other two packages of Python; SciPy and NumPy. Furthermore, you will need to install additional packages of Python, such as matplotlib for plotting, and Jupyter Notebook for development.

There are some distributions of Python that automatically install some packages when installed. Anaconda is one of them. It is used for large-scale processing of data, scientific computing, and analyzing of prediction. It automatically installs Scipy, NumPy, pandas, matplotlib, Jupyter Notebook, IPython, and Scikit-learn.

Enthought Canopy is another distribution of Python, which is usually used for scientific computing. It automatically installs Scipy, NumPy, pandas, matplotlib, IPython, and Jupyter Notebook. However, it does not automatically install the Scikit-learn package, especially with the free version.

Python (x,y) is another distribution of Python, which is also used for scientific computing. It is a free version. It automatically installs Scipy, NumPy, pandas, matplotlib, IPython, and Scikit-learn. If you have installed Python, you need to use pip command to install all of the above mentioned package.

$ pip install scipy numpy matplotlib pandas ipython scikit-learn

Once done, we are ready to proceed to the next step.

How to import libraries

To import libraries and verify their versions, run the following line of codes:

Input:

import sys

print("Version of Python: {}".format(sys.version))

Output:

Version of Python: 3.6.5 |Anaconda, Inc.| (default, Mar 29 2018, 13:32:41) [MSC v.1900 64 bit (AMD64)]

In order to import pandas:

Input:

import pandas as pd

print("Version of pandas: {}".format(pd.__version__))

Version of pandas: 0.23.0

In order to import matplotlib:

Input:

import matplotlib

print("Version of matplotlib: {}".format(matplotlib.__version__))

Output:

Version of matplotlib: 2.2.2

In order to import SciPy:

Input:

import scipy as sp

print("Version of scipy: {}".format(sp.__version__))

Output:

Version of scipy: 1.1.0

And then for the rest:

Input:

import IPython

227

```
print("Version of IPython: {}".format(IPython.__version__))
```

Output:

Version of IPython: 6.4.0

Input:

```
import sklearn

print("Version of sklearn: {}".format(sklearn.__version__))
```

Output:

Version of sklearn: 0.19.1

You may have noticed that we are always demanding the console to print out the version information. This part is to ensure that we know which versions we are using as some of these commands may stop working in future releases.

We are all set to move toward our next chapter. This is where we will learn in detail about supervised learning and how we can apply it in various circumstances.

Chapter 2: Supervised Machine Learning for Discrete Class Label

Supervised learning holds quite a significance in the field of Machine Learning. We can already sense a feeling that the word 'supervised' has something to do with supervision. It is just as a teacher would teach and guide students about which inputs can provide outputs of desired types. But, when we mention supervised learning, you will come across another term that tags along with supervised learning: Classification.

Understanding the Concept of Classification

Supervised machine learning is divided into two types, classification, and regression. Classification is used to predict discrete labels. It is further divided into two categories, binary classification and multi-classification. Binary classification is used to divide two classes while multi-classification is used to separate multiple classes. We can safely say that binary classification yields us either a yes or a no. We discussed the example of classification of emails as either spam or not in the previous chapter as an example. That example relates to the binary classification.

On the other hand, regression is used to predict continuous numbers or floating-point numbers. Its examples are: prediction of an individual's annual income from his/her education, age, and residence. While predicting annual income, the predicted output will be an amount that will be of any value. Similarly, predicting the yield of a cornfield by providing number of features such as previous yields, weather, and the number of employees allocated on that farm is an example of regression. The predicted output can be any number.

It is very important to distinguish between classification and regression. You can distinguish between these two terms by figuring out whether predicted output contains any continuity or not; if yes, then it is an example of regression. In the example of the annual income of individuals, you can see how it is an example of regression.

Suppose you need to translate the language of any website, you can translate that language completely with a single click. This is an example of classification.

Overfitting and underfitting

While training datasets, you need to take care of some of the factors. Assuming that you are training datasets to make a model. You are sure that your dataset or model will work on your test data, but will that model work on a new test data? Are you quite sure about it? Will you need to completely change the model to work for other test data?

To explain further, let us take this statement as an example:

"People older than 40 want to buy a boat."

This statement can explain the behavior of all the customers; you know you just need to create a threshold of 40. Any other person that has an age of less than 40 will be considered as not willing to buy a boat. But on the other hand, you cannot simply tell any simple rule for this problem at first look. If you make a very complex model that will work for that specific problem, and it fills too closely to that specific problem, it is called overfitting. On the flip side, if you make a very simple model that is not taking care of all aspects of data, your model will neither work for the test data nor will it work effectively for the training set as well. This problem is called underfitting.

The reason behind these errors is that with making complex models, you allow your model to perform well on training data. But when you create too complex of a model, you force yourself to think more and more and in return you come up with taking care of each and every data point, and that might be counterproductive. Although that model will work on your training data but it will not work with new data. Similarly, a model that is too simple leads us to failure in prediction. You need to trade-off between overfitting and underfitting to get the right balance and get the optimum output.

Along with these factors, you need to keep in mind the time required in simulation of any algorithm. The more complex you create your algorithms, the more time it will consume for simulation. Sometimes, we are bound by time limits and require quicker results, and in such cases, we need to keep our algorithms simple. We will encounter all these factors while performing classification methods. It is recommended that you try out executing the programs and methods with numerous values. It is a good practice to develop an understanding.

Machine Learning Methods

K-Nearest Neighbors

Suppose you have an individual profile and you have successfully gathered some data pertaining to the liking and disliking of a person for movies. Based on the data we have gathered, let us assume the following situations:

- Mr. A loves to watch horror movies
- Mr. A prefers watching movies based on Science Fiction
- Mr. A dislikes watching romance films
- Mr. A prefers watching movies based on true stories
- Mr. A watches movies that are 90 minutes long

Now we have some general data, and if we map these values on a graph, where the x-axis represents genres and the y-axis represents the runtime of the film, we can easily visualize the data. So far, so good.

Let us bring a little technicality in this mix. Suppose there is a new movie out that is around 100 minutes long, and it is an action movie. This will now pose a problem for us.

In the initial data that has been gathered, there is no mention of the word 'action' and we already have a 90 minutes runtime mark established. Will Mr. A like this movie? This is where the K-Nearest Neighbors method comes into play.

It is the simplest machine learning algorithm to be used for the classification process. It has become a very popular machine learning algorithm for both classification and regression processes. It takes K nearest neighbors (KNN) to calculate a new data point for a given data. If the value of k is one, then it will be in its simplest form, which will take only one nearest neighbor to calculate a new data point from a given data. It will operate the same way for calculating new data points for all the given data.

To put things in the simplest words, the KNN method will take into consideration the nearest data points and gauge the majority. If the model sees that similar items are more in number compared to the ones that Mr. A dislikes, it will end up recommending this movie to Mr. A. Quite similar to how we see recommendations on YouTube, Netflix, and other streaming platforms.

Now, let us dive in a little deeper into the technicalities and see how KNN works with datasets. We will apply KNN on both Iris and Breast cancer datasets to perform classification process and we will then check its performance.

Applying KNN on Breast cancer dataset

Let us see how KNN works with a relatable example, as shown under:

Input:

Importing required libraries

from sklearn.datasets import load_breast_cancer as cancer

from sklearn.neighbors import KNeighborsClassifier as KNN

import matplotlib.pyplot as plt

Loading input data

value = cancer()

Data = value.data

Target = value.target

Splitting input data into training and testing data

ts = len(Data)

trs = round(0.7*ts) #You can change this partition and the remainder will be for testing

Data_trn = Data[0: trs]

Target_trn = Target[0: trs]

Data_tst = Data[trs:]

Target_tst = Target[trs:]

Printing size of training and testing data

print(Data_trn.shape)

print(Data_tst.shape)

Output:

(398, 30)

(171, 30)

Input:

accuracy_trn = []

234

```python
accuracy_tst = []


limit = range(1, 11)

for i in limit:

    # Training the model

    knn = KNN(n_neighbors = 2)

    knn.fit(Data_trn, Target_trn)

    # Calculating accuracy of Training Data

    accuracy_trn.append(knn.score(Data_trn, Target_trn))

    # Calculating accuracy of Testing Data

    accuracy_tst.append(knn.score(Data_tst, Target_tst))


# Plotting accuracy of training and testing data

plt.plot(limit, accuracy_trn, label = "Accuracy of Training Data")

plt.plot(limit, accuracy_tst, label = "Accuracy of Testing Data")

plt.xlabel("Value")

plt.ylabel("Accuracy")

plt.legend()
```

Output:

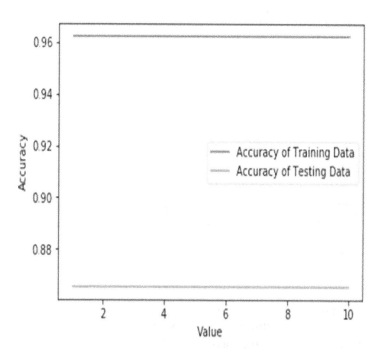

Accuracies of training and testing on Breast cancer dataset using KNN with 2 neighbors without split command

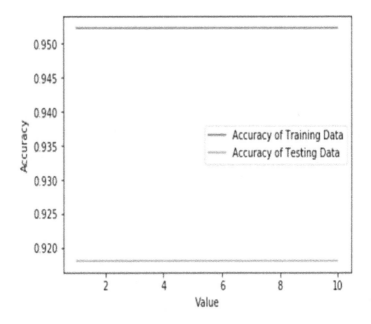

Accuracies of training and testing on Breast cancer dataset
using KNN with 3 neighbors without split command

By change in value of n_neighbors (representing the number of neighbors) from 2 to 3 in the below-mentioned command, you can observe the increase in accuracy of the KNN algorithm. As with the increase in the value of the nearest neighbors, the accuracy of the KNN algorithm increases. But by increasing too many nearest neighbors, the complexity, and simulation time will be increased as well.

knn = KNN(n_neighbors = 2)

You need to change parameters of algorithms to check their performances. You can change number of neighbors. Can you

237

change it to 10? Why not try it out yourself? What do you suppose the output will be? Will it change the accuracy?

Currently, this example is using 70% of data for training and 30% data for testing. Try and change the partition to 50% each and see what the results are. You can do that by altering the value in "trs = round(0.7 * ts)". Remember, the percentage you use here will automatically assign the remainder to the testing data. Check the results by changing these values for the testing data. You will notice how the changes take effect.

It is to be kept in mind that 70-30 partition is only applicable in this specific dataset. It is a good likelihood that this might not work in other cases. Therefore, we will now look at how to deal with such cases the split command.

Applying KNN on Breast cancer dataset with the split command

Input:

```
# Importing required libraries

from sklearn.datasets import load_breast_cancer as cancer

from sklearn.neighbors import KNeighborsClassifier as KNN

from sklearn.model_selection import train_test_split as tss

import matplotlib.pyplot as plt
```

```
# Loading input data

value = cancer()
```

```
# Splitting input data into training and testing data

Data_trn, Data_tst, Target_trn, Target_tst = tss(value.data,
value.target, random_state=10)
```

```
# Printing size of training and testing data

print(Data_trn.shape)

print(Data_tst.shape)
```

Output:

 (426, 30)

(143, 30)

Input:

```
accuracy_trn = []

accuracy_tst = []
```

```
limit = range(1, 11)
```

```
for i in limit:

    # Training the model

    knn = KNN(n_neighbors = 2)

    knn.fit(Data_trn, Target_trn)

    # Calculating accuracy of Training Data

    accuracy_trn.append(knn.score(Data_trn,
Target_trn))

    # Calculating accuracy of Testing Data

    accuracy_tst.append(knn.score(Data_tst, Target_tst))


# Plotting accuracy of training and testing data

plt.plot(limit, accuracy_trn, label = "Accuracy of Training
Data")

plt.plot(limit, accuracy_tst, label = "Accuracy of Testing Data")

plt.xlabel("Value")

plt.ylabel("Accuracy")

plt.legend()
```

Output:

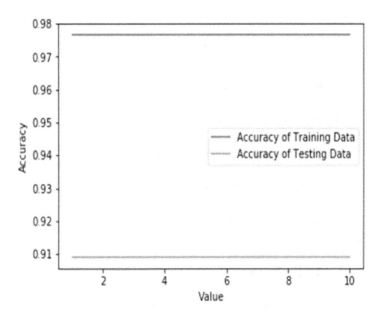

*Accuracies of training and testing on Breast cancer dataset
using KNN with 2 neighbors with split command*

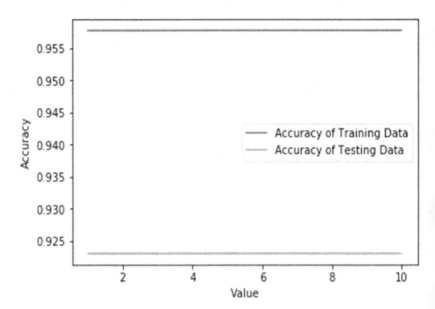

*Accuracies of training and testing on Breast cancer dataset
using KNN with 3 neighbors with split command*

Again, you can observe that by changing the value of
n_neighbors from 2 to 3 in the below-mentioned command,
accuracy of KNN algorithm will increase.

knn = KNN(n_neighbors = 2)

Play with this code again. Try to change the parameters of
algorithms to check their performances. Can you change
number of neighbors to 5? What output will you get now?
Will it change the accuracy? Remember, through trial and
error, we get to learn a lot. Do not be overwhelmed by any
error you might encounter as this is a part of the learning.

Decision Tree

The decision tree method is another example of machine
learning, which is used for both classification and regression
processes. They work on making trees based on decisions to
classify the datasets. This method contains if and else
statements. The tree starts with data points having maximum
probability among others. It makes multiple trees that are
connected with each other. We will apply Decision tree on
both Iris and Breast cancer datasets to perform classification
process and then we will check its performance in terms of
accuracy.

Applying Decision Tree on Breast cancer dataset

Input:

```
# Importing required libraries

from sklearn.datasets import load_breast_cancer as cancer

from sklearn.tree import DecisionTreeClassifier as DTC

from sklearn.model_selection import train_test_split as tss

import matplotlib.pyplot as plt


# Loading input data

value = cancer()


# Splitting input data into training and testing data

Data_trn, Data_tst, Target_trn, Target_tst = tss(value.data,
value.target, random_state=10)
```

```
accuracy_trn = []

accuracy_tst = []


limit = range(1, 11)

for i in limit:


        # Training the model

        dtc = DTC(criterion = 'entropy', min_samples_split = 50,
        max_features = 3, max_depth = 2)

        dtc.fit(Data_trn, Target_trn)

        # Calculating accuracy of Training Data

    accuracy_trn.append(dtc.score(Data_trn, Target_trn))

        # Calculating accuracy of Testing Data

    accuracy_tst.append(dtc.score(Data_tst, Target_tst))


# Plotting accuracy of training and testing data

plt.plot(limit, accuracy_trn, label = "Accuracy of Training
Data")

plt.plot(limit, accuracy_tst, label = "Accuracy of Testing Data")

plt.xlabel("Value")

plt.ylabel("Accuracy")
```

plt.legend()

Output:

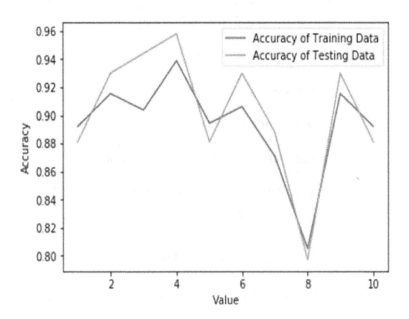

Accuracies accuracy of training and testing of Breast cancer dataset using DTC with 3 features

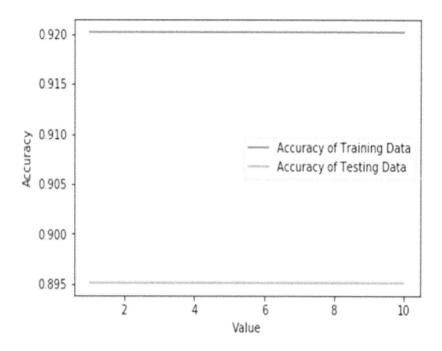

Accuracies of training and testing of Breast cancer dataset using DTC with 30 features

If you change the value of max_features (representing maximum features) from 3 to 30, the accuracy of DT algorithm will increase. Accuracy is increased with increase in number of features because the dataset contains 30 features. When the algorithm uses all features, the algorithm classifies effectively and hence accuracy is increased. While the accuracy of the DT algorithm increases with the increase in numbers and features, complexity and simulation time will increase as well.

```
dtc = DTC(criterion = 'entropy', min_samples_split = 50,
max_features = 3, max_depth = 2)
```

Change parameters of DTC to check the results. You can see the effects of changing maximum features. If you try to change the value of features to more than 30, what will be the result?

You will be encountered with an error. Do not be alarmed as it can easily be explained. We have just surpassed the maximum value of features, which is why the program is unable to compute and hence returns an error.

Applying Decision Tree on Iris dataset

Input:

Importing required libraries

from sklearn.datasets import load_iris as iris

from sklearn.tree import DecisionTreeClassifier as DTC

from sklearn.model_selection import train_test_split as tss

import matplotlib.pyplot as plt

Loading input data

value = iris()

Data = value.data

Target = value.target

```python
# Splitting input data into training and testing data

Data_trn, Data_tst, Target_trn, Target_tst = tss(value.data,
value.target, random_state=10)


# Printing size of training and testing data

print(Data_trn.shape)

print(Data_tst.shape)


accuracy_trn = []

accuracy_tst = []


limit = range(1, 11)

for i in limit:

        # Training the model

        dtc = DTC(criterion = 'entropy', min_samples_split = 50,
        max_features = 3, max_depth = 2)

        dtc.fit(Data_trn, Target_trn)

        # Calculating accuracy of Training Data

    accuracy_trn.append(dtc.score(Data_trn, Target_trn))

        # Calculating accuracy of Testing Data
```

```
accuracy_tst.append(dtc.score(Data_tst, Target_tst))


# Plotting accuracy of training and testing data

plt.plot(limit, accuracy_trn, label = "Accuracy of Training
Data")

plt.hold

plt.plot(limit, accuracy_tst, label = "Accuracy of Testing Data")

plt.xlabel("Value")

plt.ylabel("Accuracy")

plt.legend()


# Plotting prediction

plt.figure(2)

plt.plot(Data_trn[Target_trn == 0,0], Data_trn[Target_trn ==
0,1], 'rs', label = value.target_names[0])

plt.hold

plt.plot(Data_trn[Target_trn == 1,0], Data_trn[Target_trn ==
1,1], 'g.', label = value.target_names[1])

plt.legend()

plt.xlabel(value.feature_names[0])

plt.ylabel(value.feature_names[1])
```

Output:

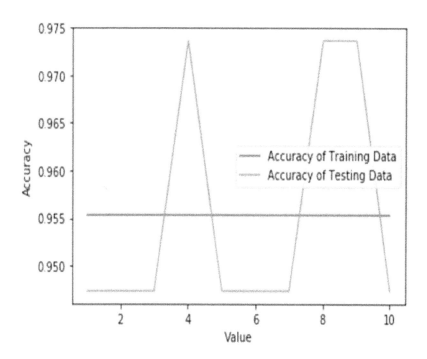

Accuracies of training and testing of iris dataset using DT with 3 features

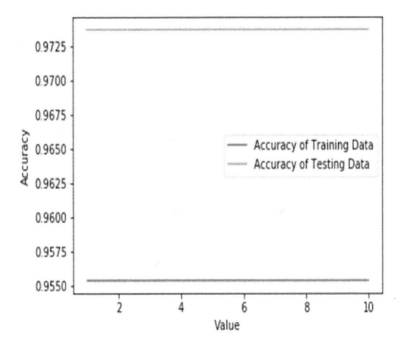

Accuracies of training and testing of iris dataset using DT with 4 features

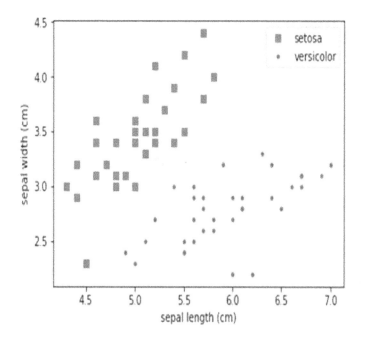

Predictions of iris dataset using DT with 3 features

By changing the value of max_features representing maximum features from three to four, you can observe that the accuracy of DT algorithm increases. As dataset contains four features and when algorithm uses all features, the algorithm classifies effectively and hence accuracy is increased and simulation time as well. Prediction achieved using four features instead of three is visually same, hence its plot is not shown.

dtc = DTC(criterion = 'entropy', min_samples_split = 50, max_features = 3, max_depth = 2)

Try changing the value to more than four. What results do you believe you will obtain? Again, do not worry should you encounter an error. This is to familiarize yourself with such situations and understanding the maximum values of such components. It is not necessary that these maximum values are predefined as we will look further in detail in future chapters.

Support Vector Machine

Support vector machines (SVM) are another example of machine learning, which is also used for both classification and regression processes. As it is used for supervised machine learning, labeled training data is given to a model. That model then assigns new values to these datasets. It works by creating categories separated by clear gap. The data belongs to a class, which is near to the line representing specific classes. This process proceeds until each dataset gets assigned.

Applying support vector classification on Breast cancer dataset

Input:

Importing required libraries

```python
from sklearn.svm import SVC

from sklearn.datasets import load_breast_cancer as cancer

from sklearn.model_selection import train_test_split as tss

import matplotlib.pyplot as plt


# Loading input data

value = cancer()


# Splitting input data into training and testing data

Data_trn, Data_tst, Target_trn, Target_tst = tss(value.data,
value.target, random_state=10)


accuracy_trn = []
accuracy_tst = []


limit = range(1, 11)
for i in limit:
        # Training the model
        svc = SVC(C = 1.0, gamma = 'auto', kernel = 'rbf')
    svc.fit(Data_trn,Target_trn)
```

```python
# Calculating accuracy of Training Data

accuracy_trn.append(svc.score(Data_trn, Target_trn))

# Calculating accuracy of Testing Data

accuracy_tst.append(svc.score(Data_tst, Target_tst))


# Plotting accuracy of training and testing data

plt.plot(limit, accuracy_trn, label="Accuracy of Training Data")

plt.plot(limit, accuracy_tst, label="Accuracy of Testing Data")

plt.xlabel("Neighbors")

plt.ylabel("Accuracy")

plt.legend()
```

Output:

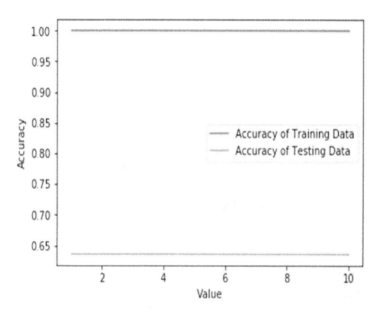

Accuracies of training and testing of Breast cancer dataset
using SVC with rbf kernel

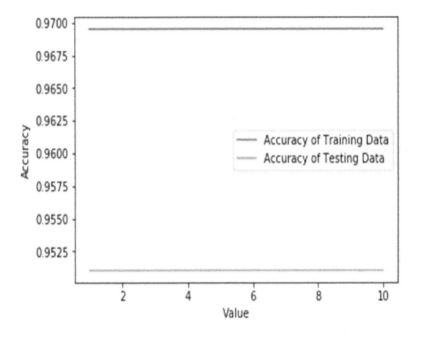

*Accuracies of training and testing of Breast cancer dataset
using SVC with linear kernel*

By changing the kernel from 'rbf' to linear, it leads to better accuracy. The accuracy is increased because the problem is linear. The rbf can also work fine but in cases where problem is nonlinear.

svc = SVC(C = 1.0, gamma = 'auto', kernel = 'rbf')

Applying support vector classification on Iris dataset

Input:

Importing required libraries

from sklearn.svm import SVC

```python
from sklearn.datasets import load_iris as iris

from sklearn.model_selection import train_test_split as tss

import matplotlib.pyplot as plt

# Loading input data

value = iris()


# Splitting input data into training and testing data

Data_trn, Data_tst, Target_trn, Target_tst = tss(value.data,
value.target, random_state=10)

accuracy_trn = []

accuracy_tst = []


limit = range(1, 11)

for i in limit:

        # Training the model

        svc = SVC(C = 1.0, gamma = 'auto', kernel = 'rbf')

        svc.fit(Data_trn, Target_trn)

        # Calculating accuracy of Training Data

    accuracy_trn.append(svc.score(Data_trn, Target_trn))

        # Calculating accuracy of Testing Data
```

```python
accuracy_tst.append(svc.score(Data_tst, Target_tst))


# Plotting accuracy of training and testing data

plt.plot(limit, accuracy_trn, label = "Accuracy of Training
Data")

plt.plot(limit, accuracy_tst, label = "Accuracy of Testing Data")

plt.xlabel("Value")

plt.ylabel("Accuracy")

plt.legend()


# Plotting prediction

plt.figure(2)

plt.plot(Data_trn[Target_trn == 0,0], Data_trn[Target_trn ==
0,1], 'rs', label = value.target_names[0])

plt.hold

plt.plot(Data_trn[Target_trn == 1,0], Data_trn[Target_trn ==
1,1], 'g.', label = value.target_names[1])

plt.legend()

plt.xlabel(value.feature_names[0])

plt.ylabel(value.feature_names[1])
```

Output:

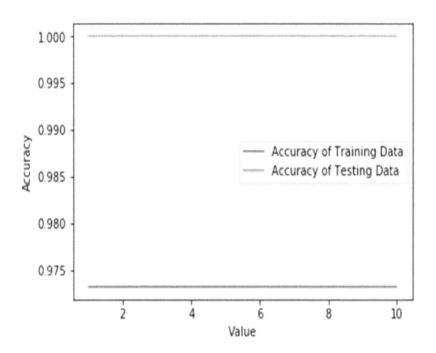

Accuracies of training and testing of iris dataset using SVC with rbf kernel

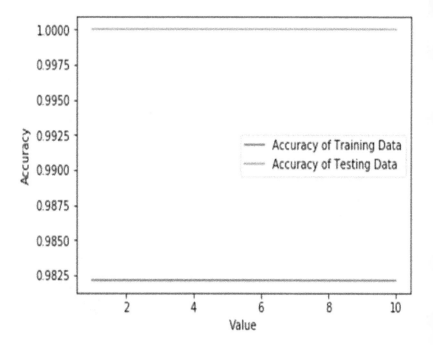

Accuracies of training and testing of iris dataset using SVC with linear kernel

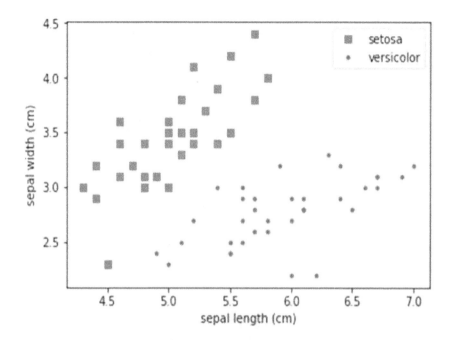

Predictions of iris dataset using SVC with rbf kernel

Again you can observe that by the change in the value of kernel from RBF to linear, the accuracy of the SVC algorithm increases. Accuracy is increased because problem is linear. The RBF can also work fine, but generally it is used in other cases where the problem is nonlinear. Predictions achieved using linear kernel instead of rbf kernel are visually the same and hold very minor details, not enough to be mapped or displayed, hence its plot is not shown.

svc = SVC(C = 1.0, gamma = 'auto', kernel = 'rbf')

Naive Bayes Classification

Naive Bayes classification method is another example of machine learning, which is used for classification process. This works by calculating probabilities of each dataset and assigns them new values depending on the value of their probabilities. This process continues until each dataset is assigned. Like previous methods, Naive Bayes will also be applied on both Iris and Breast cancer datasets for classification and then performances will be evaluated. Remember, you can use your preferred datasets instead of the ones shown in the book. The aim here is to provide you with a visual data representation of how accuracy varies and how we can use various methods on the same datasets to bring out unique results, based on the situation.

Applying naive Bayes classification on Breast cancer dataset

Input:

Importing required libraries

from sklearn.naive_bayes import GaussianNB as NB

from sklearn.datasets import load_breast_cancer as cancer

from sklearn.model_selection import train_test_split as tss

import matplotlib.pyplot as plt

Loading input data

```
value = cancer()


# Splitting input data into training and testing data

Data_trn, Data_tst, Target_trn, Target_tst = tss(value.data,
value.target, random_state=10)


accuracy_trn = []

accuracy_tst = []


limit = range(1, 11)

for i in limit:

    # Training the model

    nb = NB()

    nb.fit(Data_trn, Target_trn)

    # Calculating accuracy of Training Data

  accuracy_trn.append(nb.score(Data_trn, Target_trn))

    # Calculating accuracy of Testing Data

  accuracy_tst.append(nb.score(Data_tst, Target_tst))


# Plotting accuracy of training and testing data
```

```
plt.plot(limit, accuracy_trn, label = "Accuracy of Training
Data")

plt.plot(limit, accuracy_tst, label = "Accuracy of Testing Data")

plt.xlabel("Value")

plt.ylabel("Accuracy")

plt.legend()
```

Output:

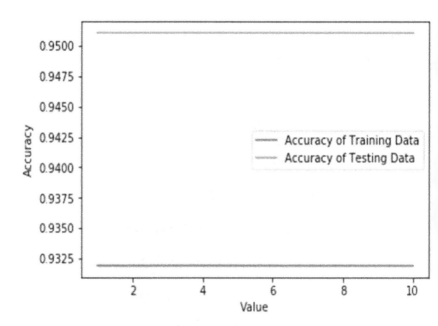

Accuracies of training and testing of Breast cancer dataset using NB

Naive Bayes method is applied with default settings of parameters. You can play with command below by passing various arguments:

```
nb = NB()
```

Applying naive Bayes classification on Iris dataset

Input:

```
# Importing required libraries

from sklearn.naive_bayes import GaussianNB as NB

from sklearn.datasets import load_iris as iris

from sklearn.model_selection import train_test_split as tss

import matplotlib.pyplot as plt


# Loading input data

value = iris()


# Splitting input data into training and testing data

Data_trn, Data_tst, Target_trn, Target_tst = tss(value.data,
value.target, random_state=10)


accuracy_trn = []
```

```python
accuracy_tst = []


limit = range(1, 11)
for i in limit:
        # Training the model
        nb = NB()
        nb.fit(Data_trn, Target_trn)
        # Calculating accuracy of Training Data
    accuracy_trn.append(nb.score(Data_trn, Target_trn))
        # Calculating accuracy of Testing Data
    accuracy_tst.append(nb.score(Data_tst, Target_tst))


# Plotting accuracy of training and testing data
plt.plot(limit, accuracy_trn, label = "Accuracy of Training
Data")
plt.plot(limit, accuracy_tst, label = "Accuracy of Testing Data")
plt.xlabel("Value")
plt.ylabel("Accuracy")
plt.legend()
```

```
# Plotting prediction

plt.figure(2)

plt.plot(Data_trn[Target_trn == 0,0], Data_trn[Target_trn ==
0,1], 'rs', label = value.target_names[0])

plt.hold

plt.plot(Data_trn[Target_trn == 1,0], Data_trn[Target_trn ==
1,1], 'g.', label = value.target_names[1])

plt.legend()

plt.xlabel(value.feature_names[0])

plt.ylabel(value.feature_names[1])
```

Output:

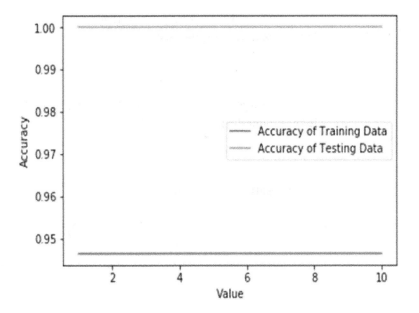

Accuracies of training and testing of Iris dataset using NB

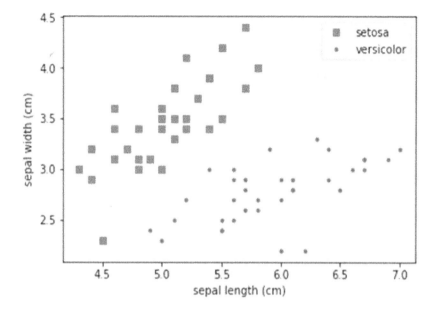

Predictions of iris dataset using NB

Logistic Regression

The logistic regression method is used for classification process as well for machine learning. Although its name suggests that this method may work better for the regression process, but it actually works just for classification process.

This method belongs to the linear classification. It can also be known as binary classification as it assigns zeros and ones to dataset in order to perform the process of classification. This method also works by calculating probabilities of each dataset and then assigns them new values depending on the value of their probabilities. Logistic Regression method will also be applied on both Iris and Breast cancer datasets for classification and then performances will be analyzed.

Applying logistic regression on Breast cancer dataset

Input:

```
# Importing required libraries

from sklearn.linear_model import LogisticRegression as LR

from sklearn.datasets import load_breast_cancer as cancer

from sklearn.model_selection import train_test_split as tss

import matplotlib.pyplot as plt


# Loading input data

value = cancer()


# Splitting input data into training and testing data

Data_trn, Data_tst, Target_trn, Target_tst = tss(value.data,
value.target, random_state=10)



accuracy_trn = []

accuracy_tst = []
```

```python
limit = range(1, 11)

for i in limit:


    # Training the model

    lr = LR(tol = 0.01, C = 1.0, max_iter = 100, n_jobs = 1)

    lr.fit(Data_trn, Target_trn)

    # Calculating accuracy of Training Data

    accuracy_trn.append(lr.score(Data_trn, Target_trn))

    # Calculating accuracy of Testing Data

  accuracy_tst.append(lr.score(Data_tst, Target_tst))


# Plotting accuracy of training and testing data

plt.plot(limit, accuracy_trn, label = "Accuracy of Training Data")

plt.plot(limit, accuracy_tst, label = "Accuracy of Testing Data")

plt.xlabel("Value")

plt.ylabel("Accuracy")

plt.legend()
```

Output:

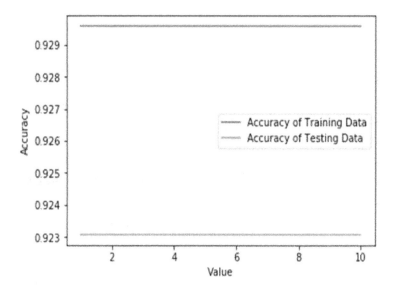

Accuracies of training and testing of Breast cancer dataset
using LR with tolerance of 0.01

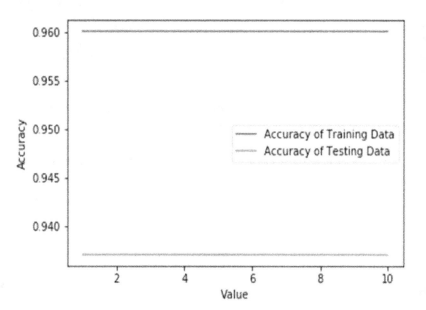

*Accuracies of training and testing of Breast cancer dataset
using LR with tolerance of 0.0001*

By changing the value of tolerance from 0.01 to 0.0001 through the command shown below, the accuracy of LR algorithm is increased. Accuracy is increased as less tolerance is accepted. With decreasing tolerance, quality output is achieved.

lr = LR(tol = 0.01, C = 1.0, max_iter = 100, n_jobs = 1)

Experiment with the parameters and check how the results vary. You can try and change the value of max_iter as well. However, can the accuracy increase if we reduce the tolerance? That's something for you to check by manipulating the values.

Remember, experiments have lead to great discoveries, we are just trying to gain a bit of an understanding here. Through trial and error, we will soon be able to understand how most of these methods work and how the data output would be like when we change certain values.

Applying logistic regression on Iris dataset

Input:

Importing required libraries

from sklearn.linear_model import LogisticRegression as LR

from sklearn.datasets import load_iris as iris

```python
from sklearn.model_selection import train_test_split as tss

import matplotlib.pyplot as plt


# Loading input data

value = iris()


# Splitting input data into training and testing data

Data_trn, Data_tst, Target_trn, Target_tst = tss(value.data,
value.target, random_state=10)


accuracy_trn = []

accuracy_tst = []

limit = range(1, 11)

for i in limit:

        # Training the model

        lr = LR(tol = 0.01, C = 10.0, max_iter = 100, n_jobs = 1)

    lr.fit(Data_trn, Target_trn)

        # Calculating accuracy of Training Data

    accuracy_trn.append(lr.score(Data_trn, Target_trn))

        # Calculating accuracy of Testing Data
```

```
accuracy_tst.append(lr.score(Data_tst, Target_tst))
```

```
# Plotting accuracy of training and testing data
```

```
plt.plot(limit, accuracy_trn, label = "Accuracy of Training
Data")
```

```
plt.plot(limit, accuracy_tst, label = "Accuracy of Testing Data")
```

```
plt.xlabel("Value")
```

```
plt.ylabel("Accuracy")
```

```
plt.legend()
```

```
# Plotting prediction
```

```
plt.figure(2)
```

```
plt.plot(Data_trn[Target_trn == 0,0], Data_trn[Target_trn ==
0,1], 'rs', label = value.target_names[0])
```

```
plt.hold
```

```
plt.plot(Data_trn[Target_trn == 1,0], Data_trn[Target_trn ==
1,1], 'g.', label = value.target_names[1])
```

```
plt.legend()
```

```
plt.xlabel(value.feature_names[0])
```

```
plt.ylabel(value.feature_names[1])
```

Output:

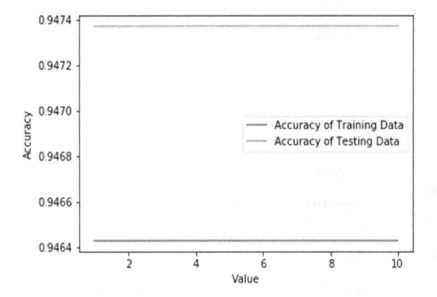

Accuracies of training and testing of Iris dataset using LR with C of 1

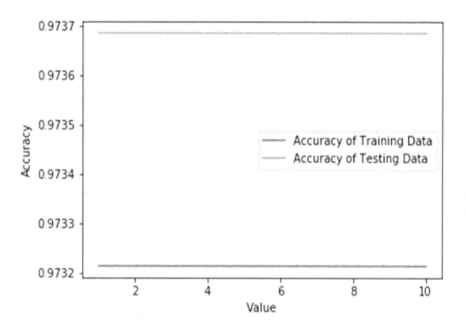

Accuracies of training and testing of Iris dataset using LR with
C of 10

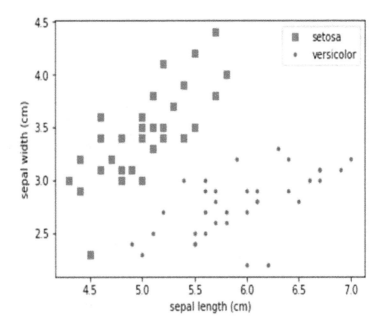

Predictions of iris dataset using LR using LR with C of 1

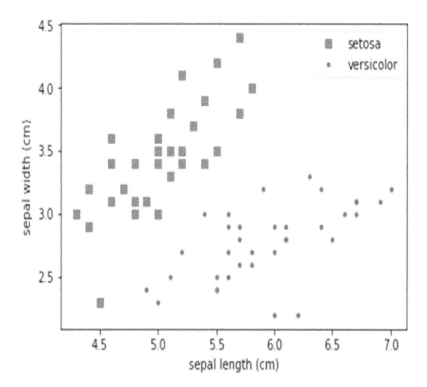

Predictions of iris dataset using LR with value of C of 10

You can observe in this example that by a change in the value of tolerance from 0.01 to 0.0001, no change appeared. We then changed value of C from 1 to 10 which increased the accuracy. Different parameters work differently for different problems. Just like we saw when we looked into Support vector, one example favored linear kernel while other favored rbf kernel. Similarly, change in value of tolerance did not affect the accuracy but C affected the accuracy.

lr = LR(tol = 0.01, C = 1.0, max_iter = 100, n_jobs = 1)

Neural Network

Neural network (NN) is another method of machine learning. It has been used often as a preferred method in machine learning problems. It uses multiple methods, which are modeled much similar to human brain to check patterns for predictions. We will apply NN for classification processes in this chapter. We will apply NN classification to Breast cancer and Iris datasets to validate its working capacity and accuracy.

Applying Neural network on Breast cancer dataset

Input:

```
# Importing required libraries

from keras.models import Sequential as NN

from keras.layers import Dense

from sklearn.datasets import load_breast_cancer as cancer

from sklearn.model_selection import train_test_split as tss

import matplotlib.pyplot as plt

import numpy as np


# Loading input data

value = cancer()
```

```python
# Splitting input data into training and testing data

Data_trn, Data_tst, Target_trn, Target_tst = tss(value.data,
value.target, random_state=10)

accuracy_trn = []

accuracy_tst = []


limit = range(1, 11)

for i in limit:


        # Training the model

        nn = NN()


        nn.add(Dense(1, activation = 'relu'))

        # compile the keras model

        nn.compile(loss = 'binary_crossentropy', optimizer =
'adam', metrics = ['accuracy'])

        # fit keras model on dataset

        nn.fit(Data_trn, Target_trn, epochs = 150, batch_size
= 10)

        # Calculating accuracy of Training Data
```

```
accuracy_trn.append(nn.evaluate(Data_trn, Target_trn))

    # Calculating accuracy of Testing Data

accuracy_tst.append(nn.evaluate(Data_tst, Target_tst))


A = np.array([accuracy_trn])

B = np.array([accuracy_tst])


AA = A[0, :, 1]

BB = B[0, :, 1]


# Plotting accuracy of training and testing data

plt.plot(limit, AA, label = "Accuracy of Training Data")

plt.plot(limit, BB, label = "Accuracy of Testing Data")

plt.xlabel("Value")

plt.ylabel("Accuracy")

plt.legend()
```

Output:

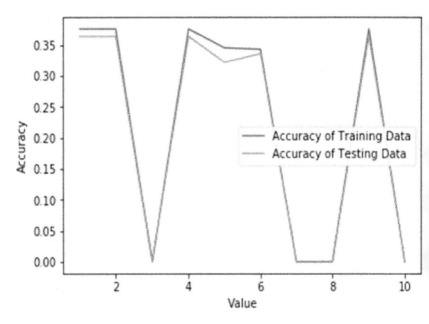

Accuracies of training and testing of Breast cancer dataset
using NN with relu activation

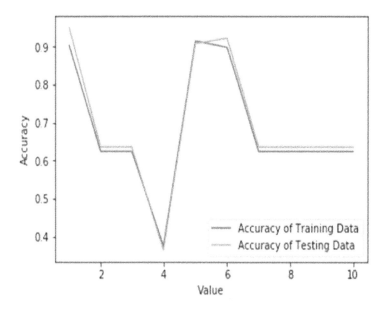

Accuracies of training and testing of Breast cancer dataset using NN with sigmoid activation

Change in the value of activation from 'relu' to 'sigmoid' in the command mentioned below, you can observe the increase in accuracy of NN algorithm.

nn.add(Dense(1, activation = 'relu'))

You can shuffle the activation to check the performance of the NN algorithm as well.

Applying Neural network on Iris dataset

Input:

Importing required libraries

```python
from keras.models import Sequential as NN

from keras.layers import Dense

from sklearn.datasets import load_iris as iris

from sklearn.model_selection import train_test_split as tss

import matplotlib.pyplot as plt

import numpy as np


# Loading input data

value = iris()


# Splitting input data into training and testing data

Data_trn, Data_tst, Target_trn, Target_tst = tss(value.data,
value.target, random_state=10)


accuracy_trn = []

accuracy_tst = []


limit = range(1, 11)

for i in limit:

        # Training the model
```

```
nn = NN()

nn.add(Dense(1, activation = 'relu'))

# compile the keras model

nn.compile(loss = 'binary_crossentropy', optimizer =
'adam', metrics = ['accuracy'])

# fit keras model on dataset

nn.fit(Data_trn, Target_trn, epochs = 150, batch_size
= 10)

# Calculating accuracy of Training Data

accuracy_trn.append(nn.evaluate(Data_trn, Target_trn))

# Calculating accuracy of Testing Data

accuracy_tst.append(nn.evaluate(Data_tst, Target_tst))


A = np.array([accuracy_trn])

B = np.array([accuracy_tst])

AA = A[0, :, 1]

BB = B[0, :, 1]


# Plotting accuracy of training and testing data

plt.plot(limit, AA, label = "Accuracy of Training Data")

plt.plot(limit, BB, label = "Accuracy of Testing Data")
```

```
plt.xlabel("Value")

plt.ylabel("Accuracy")

plt.legend()


# Plotting prediction

plt.figure(2)

plt.plot(Data_trn[Target_trn == 0,0], Data_trn[Target_trn ==
0,1], 'rs', label = value.target_names[0])

plt.hold

plt.plot(Data_trn[Target_trn == 1,0], Data_trn[Target_trn ==
1,1], 'g.', label = value.target_names[1])

plt.legend()

plt.xlabel(value.feature_names[0])

plt.ylabel(value.feature_names[1])
```

Output:

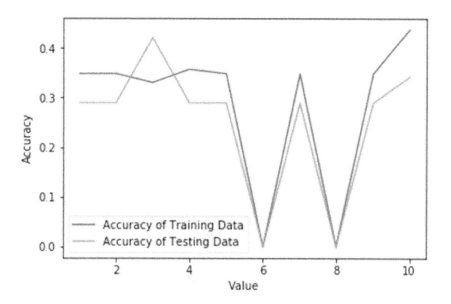

Accuracies of training and testing of Iris dataset using NN with relu activation

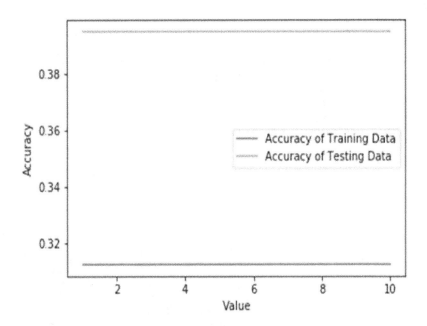

Accuracies of training and testing of Iris dataset using NN with sigmoid activation

By changing the value further, you can observe the increase in accuracy of NN algorithm.

nn.add(Dense(1, activation = 'relu'))

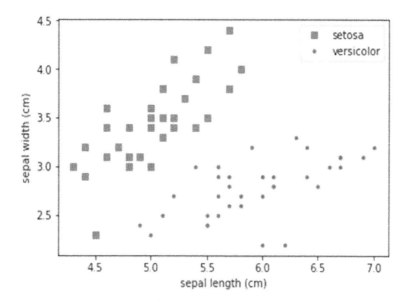

Predictions of iris dataset using NN with relu activation

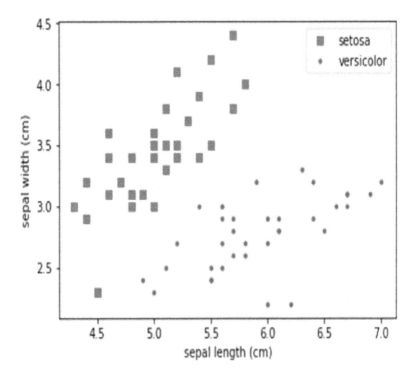

Predictions of iris dataset using NN with sigmoid activation

By changing the value further, you can observe the increase in accuracy of NN algorithm. The prediction achieved through sigmoid activation instead of relu activation is exactly the same, which is why we will not be looking at the plotting of the same.

```
nn.add(Dense(1, activation = 'relu'))
```

Things to remember:

We learned how we apply various classifications using numerous methods and functions. Each one of them has its unique use and application. Their accuracy in mapping and plotting varies, which is why it is ideal to get yourself familiarized with these through practice.

There are hundreds of thousands of datasets available for practice purposes. You can simply browse the internet and download these datasets from various websites. It is recommended that you continue practicing and learning numerous methods to gain the competitive advantage you are looking for. Since this book is targeting advanced learning, we will not continue with practices and move toward our next aspect of learning.

Chapter 3: Supervised Machine Learning for Continuous Class Label

Understanding the Concept of Regression

We already have discussed in the previous chapter that the term Supervised learning originated from the term supervision. Supervised learning takes data as inputs, and it also knows its corresponding outputs as well, and when different inputs are provided to that system, it can predict its output using that trained model.

We also discussed in the previous chapter that supervised machine learning comprises of two types: classification and regression. We discussed classification earlier in detail, which is used to predict discrete label, which means that it provides discrete output of specific input for training.

In this chapter, we will discuss the regression method that is used to predict continuous label which means that provides continuous output of specific input for training.

You can distinguish between two categories of supervised machine learning, classification and regression, by checking whether your output, given by prediction, contains any continuity or not. If the data contains continuity, then it is an example of regression and if it contains discrete output then it can safely be deduced as an example of classification. If you may recall, we already have discussed an example an individual's annual income when we initially touched upon regression.

We can have multiple applications of regression. We can have both sets of data either discrete or continuous. We need to understand both the schemes of machine learning in order to apply these methods in practical problems.

Regression Models

We have discussed the classification versions of KNN, Decision tree, SVM, Naive Bayes, logistic regression and Neural Network in the previous chapter. We applied those classification methods on Iris and Breast cancer datasets. Some of them contained features of regression as well.

There are many regression models that will be used in this chapter to predict continuous labels. We will discuss regression using KNN, Decision tree, SVM, Random forest, linear regression and Neural Network. We will apply these regression methods on Boston and Diabetes datasets; these are pre-defined datasets, available within the Scikit-Learn.

While performing the process of regression, we need to keep the factors of overfitting and underfitting in consideration. We need to know if our training datasets or models will work just on the training, test data and/or with new test data. We also should keep an eye out to know if we need to completely change the model to work for other test data.

K-Nearest Neighbors Regression

As we discussed in the previous chapter, KNN is the simplest machine learning algorithm that is used for both classification and regression processes. We used this method for classification process in the previous chapter, and this time, we will use it for the application of regression process.

The working procedure will remain the same for KNN for regression. This means, as before, it will take k nearest neighbors to calculate a new data point for any given data. If we keep value of k as one, it will be simplest version of KNN regression, which will take only one nearest neighbor as reference to calculate new data point for an input data. It will work exactly the same for calculating new data points for all the given data. We will apply the KNN-based regression to Boston and Diabetes datasets to analyze the accuracy. The value of K can also be varied to observe changes in the prediction.

Applying KNN regression on Boston dataset

Input:

Importing required libraries

from sklearn.neighbors import KNeighborsRegressor as KNN

from sklearn.datasets import load_boston as boston

from sklearn.model_selection import train_test_split as tss

import matplotlib.pyplot as plt

```python
import pandas as pd


# Loading input data

value = boston()

df = pd.DataFrame(value.data, columns =
value.feature_names)

df["MEDV"] = value.target

X = df.drop("MEDV",1)   # Feature Matrix

Y = df["MEDV"]          # Target Vector


# Splitting input data into training and testing data

Data_trn, Data_tst, Target_trn, Target_tst = tss(X, Y,
random_state = 10)


# Printing size of training and testing data

print(Data_trn.shape)

print(Data_tst.shape)
```

Output:

(379, 13)

(127, 13)

Input:

```
accuracy_trn = []

accuracy_tst = []


limit = range(1, 11)

for i in limit:

        # Training the model

        knn = KNN(n_neighbors = 1)

        knn.fit(Data_trn, Target_trn)

        # Calculating accuracy of Training Data

        accuracy_trn.append(knn.score(Data_trn,
Target_trn))

        # Calculating accuracy of Testing Data

        accuracy_tst.append(knn.score(Data_tst, Target_tst))


# Plotting accuracy of training and testing data

plt.plot(limit, accuracy_trn, label = "Accuracy of Training
Data")

plt.plot(limit, accuracy_tst, label = "Accuracy of Testing Data")

plt.xlabel("Value")
```

plt.ylabel("Accuracy")

plt.legend()

Output:

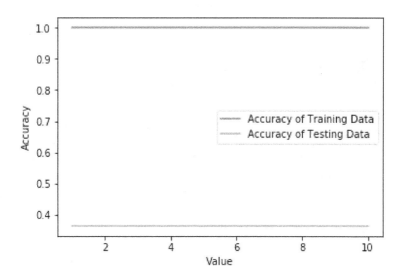

Accuracies of training and testing on Boston dataset using KNN with 2 neighbors

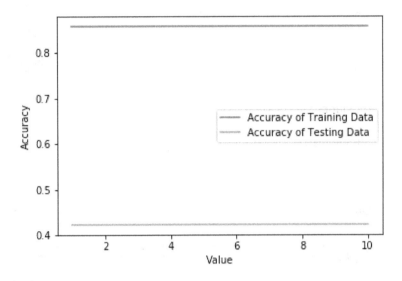

Accuracies of training and testing on Boston dataset using KNN with 3 neighbors

As before, if we change the value of n_neighbors while predicting its output from 1 to 2, we can observe the increase in accuracy of the KNN algorithm. Increasing the value of the nearest neighbors, the accuracy of KNN algorithm also increases. However, by increasing too many nearest neighbors, the complexity and simulation time increases as well.

Similarly, by using a much bigger value of number for neighbors, it can lead to lesser classes. You can further change value of k to check the change in accuracy of the prediction. Try to use different values for the code and analyze the performance of KNN algorithm. You can also apply this code to another dataset as well.

knn = KNN(n_neighbors = 2)

Applying KNN regression on

Diabetes dataset

Input:

```
# Importing required libraries

from sklearn.neighbors import KNeighborsRegressor as KNN

from sklearn.datasets import load_diabetes as diabetes

from sklearn.model_selection import train_test_split as tss

import matplotlib.pyplot as plt

import pandas as pd


# Loading input data

value = diabetes()

df = pd.DataFrame(value.data, columns =
value.feature_names)

df["MEDV"] = value.target

X = df.drop("MEDV",1)   # Feature Matrix

Y = df["MEDV"]          # Target Vector


# Splitting input data into training and testing data

Data_trn, Data_tst, Target_trn, Target_tst = tss(X, Y,
random_state = 10)
```

```
# Printing size of training and testing data

print(Data_trn.shape)

print(Data_tst.shape)
```

Output:

(331, 10)

(111, 10)

Input:

```
accuracy_trn = []

accuracy_tst = []


limit = range(1, 11)

for i in limit:

        # Training the model

        knn = KNN(n_neighbors = 2)

        knn.fit(Data_trn, Target_trn)

        # Calculating accuracy of Training Data

        accuracy_trn.append(knn.score(Data_trn,
```

Target_trn))

    # Calculating accuracy of Testing Data

  accuracy_tst.append(knn.score(Data_tst, Target_tst))

Plotting accuracy of training and testing data

plt.plot(limit, accuracy_trn, label = "Accuracy of Training Data")

plt.plot(limit, accuracy_tst, label = "Accuracy of Testing Data")

plt.xlabel("Value")

plt.ylabel("Accuracy")

plt.legend()

Output:

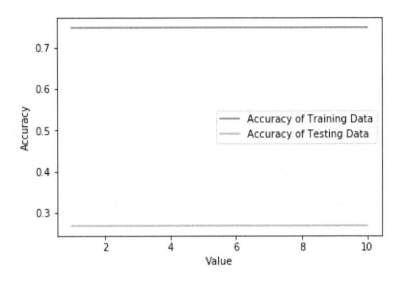

Accuracies of training and testing on Diabetes dataset using KNN with 2 neighbors

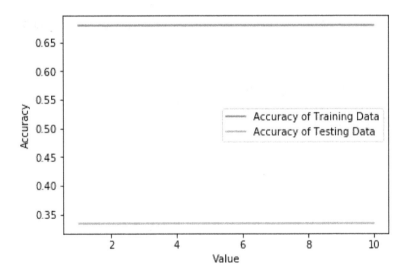

Accuracies of training and testing on Diabetes dataset using KNN with 3 neighbors

Decision Tree Regression

We have discussed in the previous chapter about usage of Decision Tree method for classification process. We discussed that it makes a tree-based decision in classifying the data sets. We used this method for classification process previously but in this chapter, we will apply regression process using Decision tree regression. We will apply Decision tree to Boston and Diabetes datasets to validate its accuracy.

Applying Decision Tree regression on Boston dataset

Input:

Importing required libraries

from sklearn.tree import DecisionTreeRegressor as DTR

from sklearn.datasets import load_boston as boston

from sklearn.model_selection import train_test_split as tss

import matplotlib.pyplot as plt

import pandas as pd

Loading input data

value = boston()

df = pd.DataFrame(value.data, columns = value.feature_names)

df["MEDV"] = value.target

```python
X = df.drop("MEDV",1)   # Feature Matrix

Y = df["MEDV"]          # Target Vector


# Splitting input data into training and testing data

Data_trn, Data_tst, Target_trn, Target_tst = tss(X, Y,
random_state = 10)


accuracy_trn = []

accuracy_tst = []

limit = range(1, 11)

for i in limit:

        # Training the model

        dtr = DTR(min_samples_split = 50, max_features = 3,
max_depth = 2)

        dtr.fit(Data_trn, Target_trn)

        # Calculating accuracy of Training Data

    accuracy_trn.append(dtr.score(Data_trn, Target_trn))

        # Calculating accuracy of Testing Data

    accuracy_tst.append(dtr.score(Data_tst, Target_tst))


# Plotting accuracy of training and testing data
```

```
plt.plot(limit, accuracy_trn, label = "Accuracy of Training
Data")

plt.plot(limit, accuracy_tst, label = "Accuracy of Testing Data")

plt.xlabel("Value")

plt.ylabel("Accuracy")

plt.legend()
```

Output:

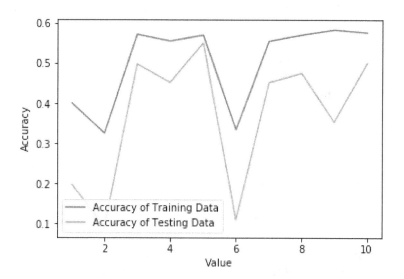

*Accuracies accuracy of training and testing of Boston dataset
using DTR with 3 features*

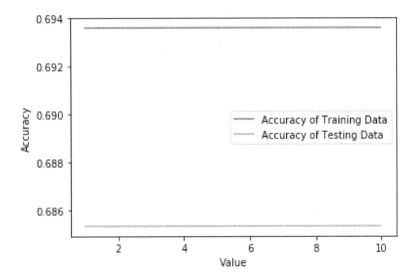

*Accuracies of training and testing of Boston cancer dataset
using DTR with 13 features*

If we change the value of max_features, which represents the
maximum features of the algorithm, from 3 to 13 in the
below-mentioned command, we can observe that the
accuracy of DT algorithm is greatly increased. Accuracy is
increased with increase in the number of features because
the dataset actually contains all 13 features and when
algorithm uses all features, the algorithm is classified
effectively and hence the accuracy is spot on.

As with the increase in the value of features, accuracy of DT
algorithm increases, along with the complexity and the
simulation time. Owing to the nature of this output, we need
to strike a healthy balance between accuracy and simulation
time.

dtr = DTR(min_samples_split = 50, max_features = 3,
max_depth = 2)

You can again change value of max_features to check the

change in accuracy of the prediction. Go ahead and change the values to analyze the performance of DTR algorithm. You should apply this code to other dataset as well to see how it performs with them.

Applying Decision Tree regression on Diabetes dataset

Input:

Importing required libraries

from sklearn.tree import DecisionTreeRegressor as DTR

from sklearn.datasets import load_diabetes as diabetes

from sklearn.model_selection import train_test_split as tss

import matplotlib.pyplot as plt

import pandas as pd

Loading input data

value = diabetes()

df = pd.DataFrame(value.data, columns = value.feature_names)

df["MEDV"] = value.target

X = df.drop("MEDV",1)   # Feature Matrix

Y = df["MEDV"]   # Target Vector

```python
# Splitting input data into training and testing data

Data_trn, Data_tst, Target_trn, Target_tst = tss(X, Y,
random_state = 10)


accuracy_trn = []

accuracy_tst = []


limit = range(1, 11)

for i in limit:

        # Training the model

        dtr = DTR(min_samples_split = 50, max_features = 3,
max_depth = 2)

        dtr.fit(Data_trn, Target_trn)

        # Calculating accuracy of Training Data

    accuracy_trn.append(dtr.score(Data_trn, Target_trn))

        # Calculating accuracy of Testing Data

    accuracy_tst.append(dtr.score(Data_tst, Target_tst))


# Plotting accuracy of training and testing data

plt.plot(limit, accuracy_trn, label = "Accuracy of Training
Data")
```

plt.plot(limit, accuracy_tst, label = "Accuracy of Testing Data")

plt.xlabel("Value")

plt.ylabel("Accuracy")

plt.legend()

Output:

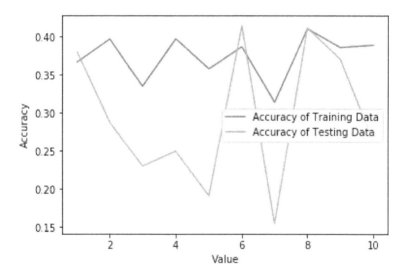

Accuracies of training and testing of iris dataset using DTR
with 3 features

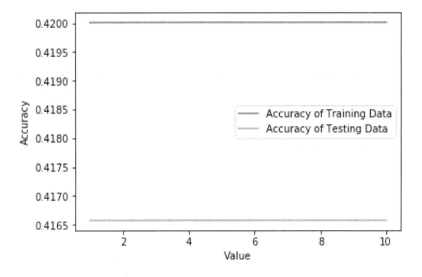

Accuracies of training and testing of iris dataset using DTR
with 10 features

Support Vector Regression

We have discussed Support vector machines in a previous chapter. We have discussed its classification method in that chapter, and we will apply SVM for regression process in this chapter. We will apply SVM to Boston and Diabetes datasets to validate its accuracy. As it belongs to supervised machine learning, labeled training data are given to that model, and that model assigns new values to these datasets. It creates categories separated by clear gap. The data belongs to class which is near to that line representing specific class. This process proceeds until each data set gets assigned.

Applying support vector regression on Boston dataset

Input:

Importing required libraries

from sklearn.svm import SVR

from sklearn.datasets import load_boston as boston

from sklearn.model_selection import train_test_split as tss

import matplotlib.pyplot as plt

import pandas as pd

Loading input data

value = boston()

df = pd.DataFrame(value.data, columns = value.feature_names)

df["MEDV"] = value.target

X = df.drop("MEDV",1)   # Feature Matrix

Y = df["MEDV"]   # Target Vector

Splitting input data into training and testing data

Data_trn, Data_tst, Target_trn, Target_tst = tss(X, Y, random_state = 10)

accuracy_trn = []

```python
accuracy_tst = []


limit = range(1, 11)
for i in limit:
        # Training the model
        svr = SVR(C = 1.0, gamma = 'auto', kernel = 'rbf')
        svr.fit(Data_trn, Target_trn)
        # Calculating accuracy of Training Data
        accuracy_trn.append(svr.score(Data_trn, Target_trn))
        # Calculating accuracy of Testing Data
    accuracy_tst.append(svr.score(Data_tst, Target_tst))


# Plotting accuracy of training and testing data
plt.plot(limit, accuracy_trn, label = "Accuracy of Training
Data")
plt.plot(limit, accuracy_tst, label = "Accuracy of Testing Data")
plt.xlabel("Value")
plt.ylabel("Accuracy")
plt.legend()
```

Output:

315

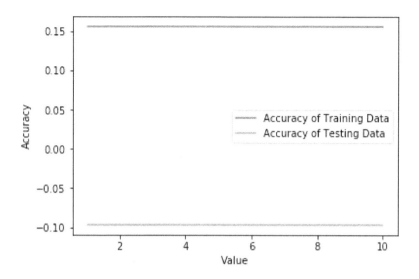

Accuracies of training and testing of Boston dataset using SVR with rbf kernel

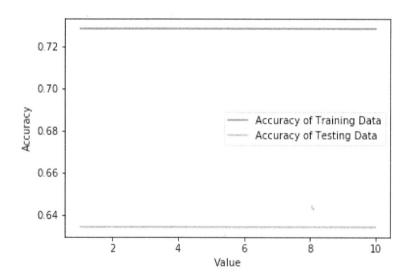

Accuracies of training and testing of Boston dataset using SVR with linear kernel

```
svr = SVR(C = 1.0, gamma = 'auto', kernel = 'rbf')
```

You can change the kernel value above to linear, as the above case is linear in nature, to improve the accuracy. Remember, had this been a nonlinear version, we would have preferred the 'RBF' instead.

Changing values of kernel is a great way to check the change in accuracy of the prediction. You can change the value of C as well. In many cases, C plays a vital role; however, will it play its role in this algorithm? Try it out yourself and see what happens when you change the value of C to anything else than 1.0.

While you practice using these methods and codes, try to change the value of gamma as well. Sometimes, you may need to fine tune your adjustments and values in order to bring out the best results and accuracy possible. If you are presented with an error, you would immediately know that the program is unable to compute using the given values and hence you can find out about their minimum and maximum values as well.

Applying support vector regression on Diabetes dataset

Input:

Importing required libraries

from sklearn.svm import SVR

```python
from sklearn.datasets import load_diabetes as diabetes

from sklearn.model_selection import train_test_split as tss

import matplotlib.pyplot as plt

import pandas as pd


# Loading input data

value = diabetes()

df = pd.DataFrame(value.data, columns =
value.feature_names)

df["MEDV"] = value.target

X = df.drop("MEDV",1)   # Feature Matrix

Y = df["MEDV"]          # Target Vector


# Splitting input data into training and testing data

Data_trn, Data_tst, Target_trn, Target_tst = tss(X, Y,
random_state = 10)


accuracy_trn = []

accuracy_tst = []


limit = range(1, 11)
```

```python
for i in limit:

    # Training the model

    svr = SVR(C = 1000.0, gamma = 'auto', kernel = 'rbf')

    svr.fit(Data_trn, Target_trn)

    # Calculating accuracy of Training Data

    accuracy_trn.append(svr.score(Data_trn, Target_trn))

    # Calculating accuracy of Testing Data

    accuracy_tst.append(svr.score(Data_tst, Target_tst))


# Plotting accuracy of training and testing data

plt.plot(limit, accuracy_trn, label = "Accuracy of Training
Data")

plt.plot(limit, accuracy_tst, label = "Accuracy of Testing Data")

plt.xlabel("Value")

plt.ylabel("Accuracy")

plt.legend()
```

319

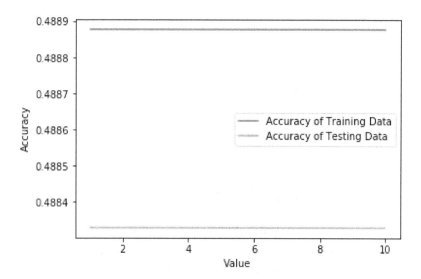

Accuracies of training and testing of Diabetes dataset using SVR with rbf kernel

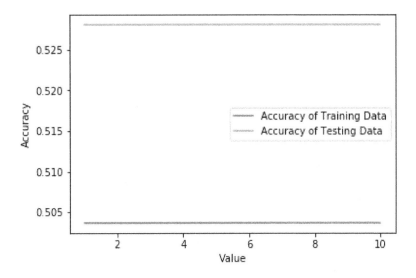

Accuracies of training and testing of Diabetes dataset using SVR with linear kernel

Random Forest Regression

Random forest method is another example of machine learning that is mainly used for regression process. This also work same as decision tree to some extent as it calculates probabilities of each data set and assign them new values depending on the value of their probabilities. It is used to take mode of classes or mean of trees in order to predict new value of data. This process proceeds until each data set get assigned. We will apply Random forest regression to Boston and Diabetes datasets to analyze its working and accuracy.

Applying Random Forest

Regression on Boston dataset

Input:

```
# Importing required libraries

from sklearn.ensemble import RandomForestRegressor as RFR

from sklearn.datasets import load_boston as boston

from sklearn.model_selection import train_test_split as tss

import matplotlib.pyplot as plt

import pandas as pd


# Loading input data

value = diabetes()

df = pd.DataFrame(value.data, columns = value.feature_names)

df["MEDV"] = value.target

X = df.drop("MEDV",1)   # Feature Matrix

Y = df["MEDV"]          # Target Vector


# Splitting input data into training and testing data

Data_trn, Data_tst, Target_trn, Target_tst = tss(X, Y, random_state = 10)
```

```
accuracy_trn = []

accuracy_tst = []


limit = range(1, 11)

for i in limit:

        # Training the model

        rfr = RFR(n_estimators = 10, random_state = 0)

        rfr.fit(Data_trn, Target_trn)

        # Calculating accuracy of Training Data

        accuracy_trn.append(rfr.score(Data_trn, Target_trn))

        # Calculating accuracy of Testing Data

    accuracy_tst.append(rfr.score(Data_tst, Target_tst))

# Plotting accuracy of training and testing data

plt.plot(limit, accuracy_trn, label = "Accuracy of Training
Data")

plt.plot(limit, accuracy_tst, label = "Accuracy of Testing Data")

plt.xlabel("Value")

plt.ylabel("Accuracy")

plt.legend()
```

Output:

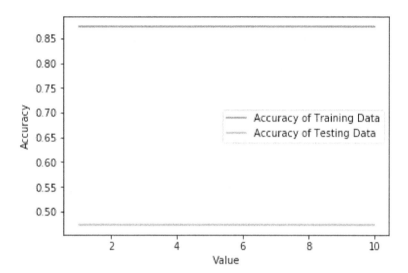

Accuracies of training and testing of Boston dataset using RFR with n_estimators of 10

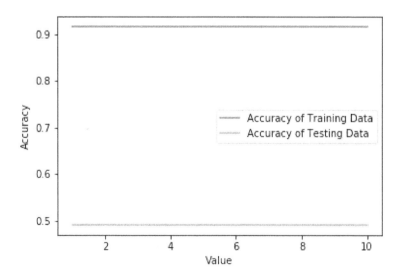

Accuracies of training and testing of Boston dataset using RFR
with n_estimators of 100

Applying Random Forest Regression on Diabetes dataset

Input:

Importing required libraries

from sklearn.ensemble import RandomForestRegressor as RFR

from sklearn.datasets import load_diabetes as diabetes

from sklearn.model_selection import train_test_split as tss

import matplotlib.pyplot as plt

import pandas as pd

Loading input data

value = diabetes()

df = pd.DataFrame(value.data, columns = value.feature_names)

df["MEDV"] = value.target

X = df.drop("MEDV",1)   # Feature Matrix

Y = df["MEDV"]   # Target Vector

```
# Splitting input data into training and testing data

Data_trn, Data_tst, Target_trn, Target_tst = tss(X, Y,
random_state = 10)


accuracy_trn = []

accuracy_tst = []


limit = range(1, 11)

for i in limit:

        # Training the model

        rfr = RFR(n_estimators = 10, random_state = 0)

        rfr.fit(Data_trn, Target_trn)

        # Calculating accuracy of Training Data

    accuracy_trn.append(rfr.score(Data_trn, Target_trn))

        # Calculating accuracy of Testing Data

        accuracy_tst.append(rfr.score(Data_tst, Target_tst))


# Plotting accuracy of training and testing data

plt.plot(limit, accuracy_trn, label = "Accuracy of Training
Data")

plt.plot(limit, accuracy_tst, label = "Accuracy of Testing Data")
```

```python
plt.xlabel("Value")

plt.ylabel("Accuracy")

plt.legend()
```

Output:

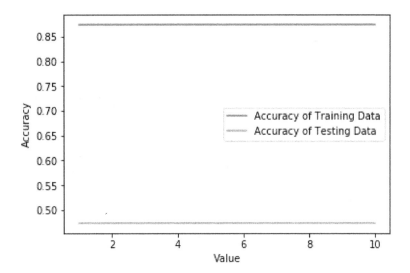

Accuracies of training and testing of Diabetes dataset using
RFR with n_estimators of 10

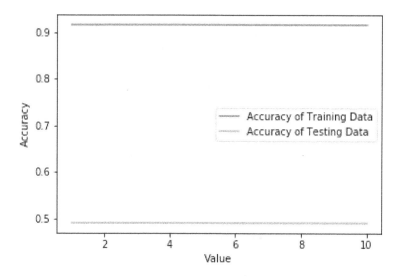

Accuracies of training and testing of Diabetes dataset using RFR with n_estimators of 100

In both the examples here and above, one parameter is playing a vital part. Changing that will alter the rate of accuracy. This is represented as:

rfr = RFR(n_estimators = 10, random_state = 0)

You can try to modify the value of n_estimators, which denotes the number of estimators. You can vary the numeric value from 10 to 100 and see how the accuracy is affected. Alternatively, you can also try to change the value of the random_state variable to anything other than zero.

Linear Regression

Linear regression method is another basic method of machine learning that is just used for regression process. This method belongs to linear classification. As its name suggests, once the model is trained, it uses linear functions to predict the output value of given data. These models are also known as linear models. This method is being used much as compare to other predictive methods. The reason behind its success is that the models that rely linearly on unknown parameters can fit better than those models who rely nonlinearly on unknown parameters. This process proceeds until each data set get assigned. We will apply linear regression to Boston and Diabetes datasets to validate its working and accuracy.

Applying linear regression on Boston dataset

Input:

```
# Importing required libraries

from sklearn.linear_model import LinearRegression as LR

from sklearn.datasets import load_boston as boston

from sklearn.model_selection import train_test_split as tss

import matplotlib.pyplot as plt

import pandas as pd


# Loading input data

value = boston()

df = pd.DataFrame(value.data, columns = value.feature_names)

df["MEDV"] = value.target
```

```python
X = df.drop("MEDV",1)   # Feature Matrix

Y = df["MEDV"]          # Target Vector


# Splitting input data into training and testing data

Data_trn, Data_tst, Target_trn, Target_tst = tss(X, Y,
random_state = 10)


accuracy_trn = []

accuracy_tst = []


limit = range(1, 11)

for i in limit:

        # Training the model

        rf = LR(n_jobs = 1)

        rf.fit(Data_trn, Target_trn)

        # Calculating accuracy of Training Data

        accuracy_trn.append(rf.score(Data_trn, Target_trn))

        # Calculating accuracy of Testing Data

    accuracy_tst.append(rf.score(Data_tst, Target_tst))
```

Plotting accuracy of training and testing data

```
plt.plot(limit, accuracy_trn, label = "Accuracy of Training
Data")

plt.plot(limit, accuracy_tst, label = "Accuracy of Testing Data")

plt.xlabel("Value")

plt.ylabel("Accuracy")

plt.legend()
```

Output:

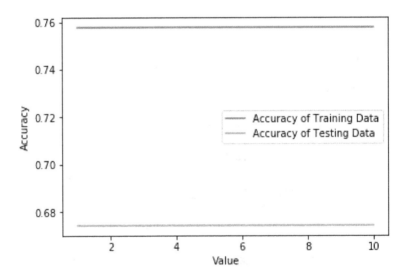

Accuracies of training and testing of Boston dataset using LR

Have a look at the command highlighted below. We can see that once again a single parameter plays a vital role to run this method.

```
rf = LR(n_jobs = 1)
```

Change value of n_jobs and check the result. Try to find out how large can you set its value.

Applying linear regression on Diabetes dataset

Input:

```
# Importing required libraries

from sklearn.linear_model import LinearRegression as LR

from sklearn.datasets import load_diabetes as diabetes

from sklearn.model_selection import train_test_split as tss

import matplotlib.pyplot as plt

import pandas as pd


# Loading input data

value = diabetes()

df = pd.DataFrame(value.data, columns = value.feature_names)

df["MEDV"] = value.target

X = df.drop("MEDV",1)   # Feature Matrix

Y = df["MEDV"]          # Target Vector
```

```
# Splitting input data into training and testing data

Data_trn, Data_tst, Target_trn, Target_tst = tss(X, Y,
random_state = 10)


accuracy_trn = []

accuracy_tst = []


limit = range(1, 11)

for i in limit:

        # Training the model

        rf = LR(n_jobs = 1)

        rf.fit(Data_trn, Target_trn)

        # Calculating accuracy of Training Data

    accuracy_trn.append(rf.score(Data_trn, Target_trn))

        # Calculating accuracy of Testing Data

    accuracy_tst.append(rf.score(Data_tst, Target_tst))


# Plotting accuracy of training and testing data

plt.plot(limit, accuracy_trn, label = "Accuracy of Training
Data")

plt.plot(limit, accuracy_tst, label = "Accuracy of Testing Data")
```

```
plt.xlabel("Value")

plt.ylabel("Accuracy")

plt.legend()
```

Output:

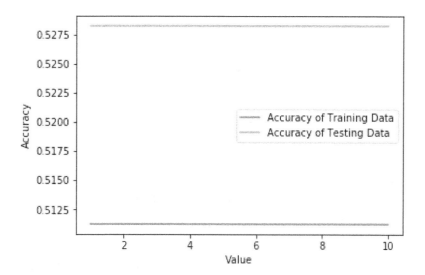

Accuracies of training and testing of Diabetes dataset using LR

By applying various methods to the same datasets, we can see how the variations occur and how much accuracy we can obtain. While the charts may seemingly appear the same, the finer details are being changed to either provide a greater accuracy or otherwise.

Neural Network Regression

We have discussed the application of NN in terms of classification in a previous chapter. Now, we shall apply the NN for regression process. We will apply NN regression to Boston and Diabetes datasets to validate its working and accuracy.

Applying neural network regression on Boston dataset

Input:

```
# Importing required libraries

from sklearn.neural_network import MLPRegressor as MLPR

from sklearn.datasets import load_boston as boston

from sklearn.model_selection import train_test_split as tss

import matplotlib.pyplot as plt

import pandas as pd


# Loading input data

value = boston()

df = pd.DataFrame(value.data, columns =
```

```
value.feature_names)

df["MEDV"] = value.target

X = df.drop("MEDV",1)   # Feature Matrix

Y = df["MEDV"]       # Target Vector


# Splitting input data into training and testing data

Data_trn, Data_tst, Target_trn, Target_tst = tss(X, Y,
random_state = 10)


accuracy_trn = []

accuracy_tst = []


limit = range(1, 11)

for i in limit:

        # Training the model

        mlpr = MLPR(activation = 'tanh',max_iter = 1000,
random_state = 0)

        mlpr.fit(Data_trn, Target_trn)

        # Calculating accuracy of Training Data

    accuracy_trn.append(mlpr.score(Data_trn, Target_trn))

        # Calculating accuracy of Testing Data
```

```
        accuracy_tst.append(mlpr.score(Data_tst,
Target_tst))
```

```
# Plotting accuracy of training and testing data

plt.plot(limit, accuracy_trn, label = "Accuracy of Training
Data")

plt.plot(limit, accuracy_tst, label = "Accuracy of Testing Data")

plt.xlabel("Value")

plt.ylabel("Accuracy")

plt.legend()
```

Output:

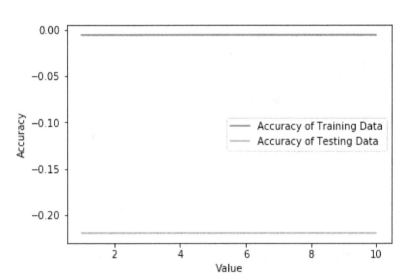

337

Accuracies of training and testing of Boston dataset using NN with max_iters of 100

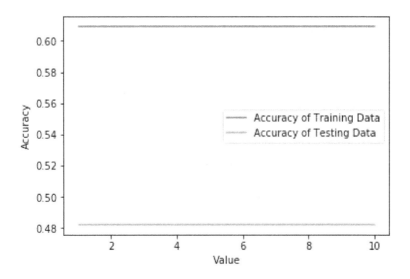

Accuracies of training and testing of Boston dataset using NN with max_iters of 1000

We can observe that NN algorithm is using 'tanh' as activation. If we change the value of max_iter, which represents the maximum iterations from 100 to 1000, we can observe the increase in accuracy of the NN algorithm. It is obvious that accuracy of any algorithm increases with the increase in number of iterations. It takes quite a bit of processing to perform any task. It might consume more time, but it will come up with a better accuracy.

mlpr = MLPR(activation = 'tanh',max_iter = 1000, random_state = 0)

Applying neural network

regression on Diabetes dataset

Input:

```python
# Importing required libraries

from sklearn.neural_network import MLPRegressor as MLPR

from sklearn.datasets import load_diabetes as diabetes

from sklearn.model_selection import train_test_split as tss

import matplotlib.pyplot as plt

import pandas as pd


# Loading input data

value = diabetes()

df = pd.DataFrame(value.data, columns = value.feature_names)

df["MEDV"] = value.target

X = df.drop("MEDV",1)   # Feature Matrix

Y = df["MEDV"]          # Target Vector

# Splitting input data into training and testing data

Data_trn, Data_tst, Target_trn, Target_tst = tss(X, Y, random_state = 10)


accuracy_trn = []
```

```
accuracy_tst = []


limit = range(1, 11)

for i in limit:

    # Training the model

    mlpr = MLPR(activation = 'tanh',max_iter = 1000,
random_state = 0)

    mlpr.fit(Data_trn, Target_trn)

    # Calculating accuracy of Training Data

  accuracy_trn.append(mlpr.score(Data_trn, Target_trn))

    # Calculating accuracy of Testing Data

  accuracy_tst.append(mlpr.score(Data_tst, Target_tst))


# Plotting accuracy of training and testing data

plt.plot(limit, accuracy_trn, label = "Accuracy of Training
Data")

plt.plot(limit, accuracy_tst, label = "Accuracy of Testing Data")

plt.xlabel("Value")

plt.ylabel("Accuracy")

plt.legend()
```

Output:

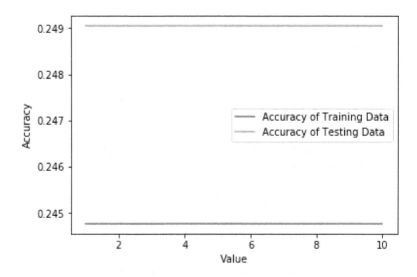

Accuracies of training and testing of Diabetes dataset using NN with max_iters of 1000

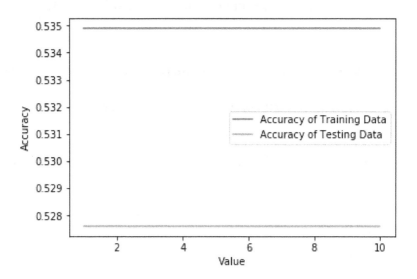

Accuracies of training and testing of Diabetes dataset using

NN with max_iters of 10000

Once again, the NN algorithm is using tanh as activation. If we change the value of max_iter from 1000 to 10000, it will increase the accuracy of the NN algorithm. It is therefore understandable that accuracy of any algorithm increases with the increase in number of iterations.

In the previous chapter, we learned about discrete class labels and classification methods; however, this chapter introduced us to continuous class label classification methods. We went through a few examples and used Boston and Diabetes datasets to draw outputs from.

In the next chapter, we will be diving into the world of unsupervised learning to see just why it is slightly difficult to get a grasp on things. We will look into the concept of clustering and map out a few examples and codes to see how we can use unsupervised learning to bring out results that we require.

It is of the utmost importance that you continue practicing the codes to develop a firm understanding of the matter. Learning "Machine Learning" within a matter of days is not possible without ample practice, clarification of concepts and the usage of the right tools, libraries and understanding of Python as a programming language.

Chapter 4: Unsupervised Machine Learning

Earlier, at the start of the first chapter, we discussed how unsupervised learning is a method of machine learning that is used to gather information from the datasets. However, unlike supervised learning, it does not know the outputs to specific inputs, and when other inputs are given to it, it can just categorize outputs on the basis of some parameters such as Euclidean distance, etc. In short, unsupervised learning does not create datasets to be used for training the model for prediction of outputs.

Understanding the Concept of Clustering

Clustering can easily be defined as a method that partitions or divides the given data into sets of groups. These groups are called clusters. Each cluster contains data that is specific and contains items, components or data that matches. Think of two clusters named 'even' and 'odd,' One of these will contain numbers that are even, while the other would contain numbers that are odd.

There are two main types of unsupervised learning: transformation and clustering. The transformation method can relate with dimension reduction. It takes a high dimensional data, containing many samples of each features or many features, and converts it into low dimensional data. It removes less impactful samples or features.

In many cases, dimension reduction methods reduce to two dimensions. It is very important to apply dimension reduction methods as it can save processing time and avoid confusion, which is usually created when seeing high dimensional data. The dimension reduction methods provide a much-needed motivation to the programmer to dive deep into the data and visualize it better.

The other method of unsupervised learning is clustering. It is used to divide the data on the basis of similarities. If you want to deal with big data, you need it to be divided into multiple groups so that you can carry out efficient and effective analysis. For example, if you want to upload multiple photos to any social media site, you would like to add those photos in groups so that you can keep track of those pictures easily, if and when required. One way would be to add pictures of a similar person in one group. Although the sites don't know about you personally and don't know which picture represents whom, but the site still wants us to divide those pictures into groups as it is a sensible way of managing data.

Challenges in Unsupervised Learning

Unsupervised learning does not contain any information of label, which means we do not know the right output for the corresponding input. The model cannot come to a conclusion whether it went well or not. In such a case, algorithms will divide data on the basis of similarity of some of their features, and while doing so, it does not ensure the output of our choices.

For example, the model can group pictures in a way that one group will contain picture with various people in it, which does not necessarily fulfill the requirement of one who wants to have a group on the basis of individuals (each group containing pictures of a specific person).

Unsupervised learning can be used in cases where a programmer just wishes to understand the data instead of using it for any automation solution. Similarly, unsupervised learning can be used as a *preprocessing* step for supervised learning. In some cases, it might help to get better accuracy from supervised learning, and it can get less memory data and might be able to save time as well.

Preprocessing and Scaling

Many classification and regression methods have been discussed in previous chapters. We have observed that some of these methods require some work as their accuracies are not up to the mark. Some unsupervised-based preprocessing steps and scaling is performed before applying supervised methods.

Types of Preprocessing

There are different types of preprocessing. StandardScalar is one of the libraries used for preprocessing. It makes sure that each feature of dataset has a mean of zero and variance of one. It is used to keep all features to the same level. Although it does not have any specific minimum or maximum values for features, but it still works fine as it contains features of maintaining required mean and variance.

RobustScaler is another library that is used for preprocessing. It is also used to keep all features to the same level. It uses median and quartiles instead of mean and variance. Due to using different parameters, it ignores the data points which are far away from others. These data points are often known as outliers, which create complications for other scaling methods. Hence, RobustScaler is better in use than StandardScalar.

Then we have the MinMaxScaler library, which is used for preprocessing. It is used to keep the data between 0 and 1 by shifting the data. That means that if the data is plotted, then the scale of the x-axis and y-axis will be between 0 and 1. It can also produce acceptable results.

Normalizer is the last library to be discussed for preprocessing. It scales data points in a way that keeps the distance between the feature vectors of unity. Every data point is scaled at a different value. It is normally used when direction does matter.

Effects of Preprocessing on Supervised Learning

Preprocessing plays a very important role, especially for methods that are sensitive to these scalers. As mentioned earlier, many preprocessing scales can be used. Below is an example of preprocessing using MinMaxScaler.

Input:

Importing required libraries

from sklearn.svm import SVC

from sklearn.datasets import load_breast_cancer as cancer

from sklearn.model_selection import train_test_split as tss

import matplotlib.pyplot as plt

from sklearn.preprocessing import MinMaxScaler as MMS

```python
# Loading input data

value = cancer()


# Splitting input data into training and testing data

Data_trn, Data_tst, Target_trn, Target_tst = tss(value.data,
value.target,

                                        random_stat
                                        e = 10)

accuracy_trn = []

accuracy_tst = []

Data_trn_scld = []

Data_tst_scld = []


mms = MMS()

mms.fit(Data_trn)


Data_trn_scld = mms.transform(Data_trn)

Data_tst_scld = mms.transform(Data_tst)


limit = range(1, 11)

for i in limit:
```

```
# Training the model

svc = SVC(C = 1.0, gamma = 'auto', kernel = 'rbf')

svc.fit(Data_trn_scld, Target_trn)

# Calculating accuracy of Training Data

accuracy_trn.append(svc.score(Data_trn_scld, Target_trn))

# Calculating accuracy of Testing Data

accuracy_tst.append(svc.score(Data_tst_scld, Target_tst))


# Plotting accuracy of training and testing data

plt.plot(limit, accuracy_trn, label = "Accuracy of Training Data")

plt.plot(limit, accuracy_tst, label = "Accuracy of Testing Data")

plt.xlabel("Value")

plt.ylabel("Accuracy")

plt.legend()
```

Output:

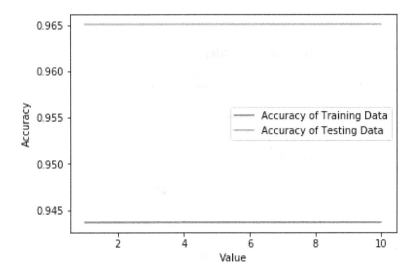

*Accuracies of training and testing of Breast cancer dataset
using SVC with MinMaxScaler*

Let us look at an example of preprocessing using the
StandardScaler.

Input:

Importing required libraries

from sklearn.svm import SVC

from sklearn.datasets import load_breast_cancer as cancer

from sklearn.model_selection import train_test_split as tss

import matplotlib.pyplot as plt

from sklearn.preprocessing import StandardScaler as SS

```python
# Loading input data

value = cancer()


# Splitting input data into training and testing data

Data_trn, Data_tst, Target_trn, Target_tst = tss(value.data,
value.target,

                                          random_stat
                                          e = 10)

accuracy_trn = []

accuracy_tst = []

Data_trn_scld = []

Data_tst_scld = []


ss = SS()

ss.fit(Data_trn)


Data_trn_scld = ss.transform(Data_trn)

Data_tst_scld = ss.transform(Data_tst)


limit = range(1, 11)

for i in limit:
```

```
# Training the model

svc = SVC(C = 1.0, gamma = 'auto', kernel = 'rbf')

svc.fit(Data_trn_scld, Target_trn)

# Calculating accuracy of Training Data

accuracy_trn.append(svc.score(Data_trn_scld, Target_trn))

# Calculating accuracy of Testing Data

accuracy_tst.append(svc.score(Data_tst_scld, Target_tst))


# Plotting accuracy of training and testing data

plt.plot(limit, accuracy_trn, label = "Accuracy of Training
Data")

plt.plot(limit, accuracy_tst, label = "Accuracy of Testing Data")

plt.xlabel("Value")

plt.ylabel("Accuracy")

plt.legend()
```

Output:

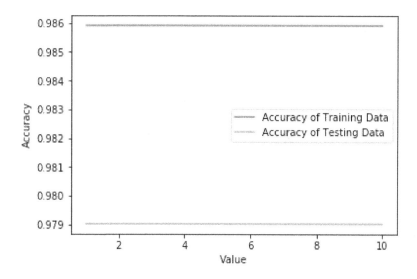

Accuracies of training and testing of Breast cancer dataset using SVC with StandardScaler

You can observe that SVM based classification provided an accuracy of around 0.64, but when we applied the MinMaxScaler based scaling and then applied classification using SVM, an accuracy of around 0.97 is achieved. Similarly, when we applied the StandardScaler based scaling and then applied classification using SVM, an accuracy of around 0.98 was achieved. Results can show that preprocessing is required, and MinMaxScaler and StandardScaler based preprocessing perform well.

Dimension Reduction

Many datasets contain high dimensions, which take long processing times. Along with processing problems, these datasets become difficult to visualize. Dimension reduction is required to reduce the dimensions of high dimensional datasets. It is also very important to retain maximum information even after reducing dimensions of the datasets. There are many methods that are used for dimension reduction.

Principal Component Analysis is famous for dimension reduction. It provides the principal components of the datasets. It removes the least impactful features and retains the highest impactful ones. This way, the datasets will not lose much information and will still be able to represent all the data.

Principal Component Analysis

Principal Component Analysis is a statistical method that works on orthogonal transformation to measure the correlation between variables. It finds out the principal components of datasets. An example of Dimension reduction using PCA is given below.

Applying Principal Component Analysis on Breast cancer dataset

Input [1]:

Importing required libraries

from sklearn.decomposition import PCA

from sklearn.datasets import load_breast_cancer as cancer

from sklearn.model_selection import train_test_split as tss

```python
import matplotlib.pyplot as plt

from sklearn.preprocessing import StandardScaler as SS

# Loading input data

value = cancer()


# Splitting input data into training and testing data

Data_trn, Data_tst, Target_trn, Target_tst = tss(value.data,
value.target, random_state = 10)

Data_trn_scld = []

Data_tst_scld = []


ss = SS()

ss.fit(Data_trn)


Data_trn_scld = ss.transform(Data_trn)

Data_tst_scld = ss.transform(Data_tst)


# Training the model with Principal components of 2

pca = PCA(n_components = 2)

pca.fit(Data_trn_scld)
```

```
X_pca = pca.transform(Data_trn_scld)
```

```
print("Original Dimension:
{}".format(str(Data_trn_scld.shape)))
```

```
print("Reduced Dimension: {}".format(str(X_pca.shape)))
```

Output [1]:

Original Dimension: (426, 30)

Reduced Dimension: (426, 2)

Input [2]:

```
# plotting First versus second principal component
```

```
plt.plot(X_pca[Target_trn == 0,0], X_pca[Target_trn == 0,1],
'rs', label = value.target_names[0])
```

```
plt.hold
```

```
plt.plot(X_pca[Target_trn == 1,0], X_pca[Target_trn == 1,1],
'g.', label = value.target_names[1])
```

```
plt.legend()
```

```
plt.xlabel("First principal component")
```

```
plt.ylabel("Second principal component")
```

Output [2]:

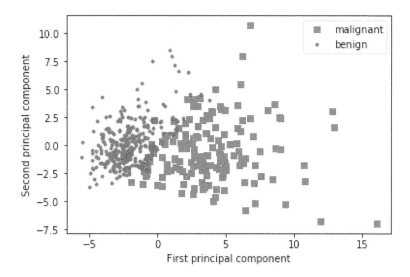

First Principal component versus Second Principal component of Breast cancer dataset using PCA and StandardScaler

Input [2]:

```
print("Dimension of PCA components:
{}".format(pca.components_.shape))
```

Output [2]:

Dimension of PCA components: (2, 30)

Input [3]:

```
print("Components of PCA:\n{}".format(pca.components_))
```

Output [3]:

Components of PCA:

[[0.22497118 0.10209091 0.23305712 0.22669916
0.13095741 0.23777761

  0.26054451 0.26113228 0.11857964 0.04990416
0.20451814 0.01547142

  0.21189041 0.2032527   0.00835308 0.17314863
0.18095912 0.18353095

  0.03353539 0.10045326 0.23188534 0.09793079
0.24072506 0.22923198

  0.11457974 0.20876477 0.22872514 0.2501444
0.10389674 0.12133481]

 [-0.22383928 -0.06901511 -0.20453941 -0.22094646
0.20201801 0.16857578

  0.04865932 -0.02438319 0.19604069 0.37928075 -
0.09722973 0.0862208

 -0.07797413 -0.13996098 0.20813873 0.237834
0.17790854 0.12701146

  0.18413975 0.28625985 -0.21230329 -0.06003402 -
0.1898874 -0.21147895

  0.18822065 0.14823507 0.08302158 -0.00246167
0.13405653 0.28669719]]

Applying Principal Component Analysis on Digits dataset

Input [1]:

```
# Importing required libraries

from sklearn.decomposition import PCA

from sklearn.datasets import load_digits as Value

import matplotlib.pyplot as plt


# Plotting Digits Dataset

value = Value()

fig, axes = plt.subplots(2, 5, figsize=(10, 5),

subplot_kw={'xticks':(), 'yticks': ()})

for ax, img in zip(axes.ravel(), value.images):

        ax.imshow(img)


# Training the model with Principal components of 2

pca = PCA(n_components = 2)

pca.fit(value.data)


# PCA Transform
```

```
value_pca = pca.transform(value.data)

colors = ["#A83683", "#4E655E", "#853541", "#3A3120",
"#535D8E",

"#476A2A", "#7851B8", "#BD3430", "#4A2D4E", "#875525"]
```

Output [1]:

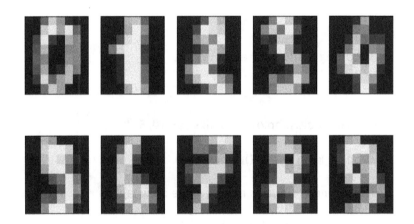

Digits dataset

Input [2]:

```
# Plotting Principal components

plt.figure(figsize = (10, 10))

plt.xlim(value_pca[:, 0].min(), value_pca[:, 0].max())

plt.ylim(value_pca[:, 1].min(), value_pca[:, 1].max())
```

```
for i in range(len(value.data)):

    plt.text(value_pca[i, 0], value_pca[i, 1], str(value.target[i]),
color =

        colors[value.target[i]], fontdict = {'weight': 'bold',
        'size': 9})

plt.xlabel("First principal component")

plt.ylabel("Second principal component")
```

Output [2]:

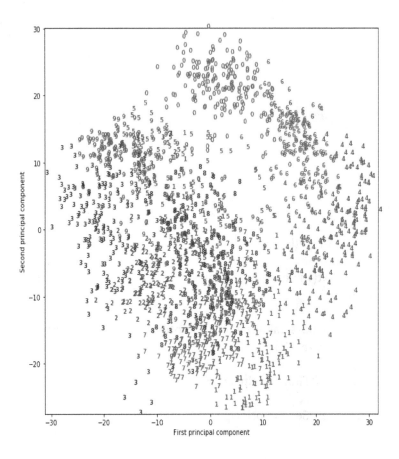

First Principal component versus Second Principal component of Digits dataset using PCA

Manifold Learning with t-SNE

We have discussed PCA for dimension reduction and data visualization. t-SNE is another method that is used to visualize data. It provides a better visualization of data as compared to PCA. An example of visualization of data using t-SNE method is given below.

Applying t-SNE on Digits dataset

Input:

Importing required libraries

```
from sklearn.manifold import TSNE

from sklearn.datasets import load_digits as Value

import matplotlib.pyplot as plt


value = Value()

tsne = TSNE(random_state = 42)


# TSNE Transform

value_tsne = tsne.fit_transform(value.data)

colors = ["#A83683", "#4E655E", "#853541", "#3A3120",
"#535D8E",

"#476A2A", "#7851B8", "#BD3430", "#4A2D4E", "#875525"]


# Plotting Feature components

plt.figure(figsize = (10, 10))

plt.xlim(value_tsne[:, 0].min(), value_tsne[:, 0].max() + 1)
```

```
plt.ylim(value_tsne[:, 1].min(), value_tsne[:, 1].max() + 1)

for i in range(len(value.data)):

    plt.text(value_tsne[i, 0], value_tsne[i, 1],
str(value.target[i]),color = colors[value.target[i]],fontdict =
{'weight': 'bold', 'size': 9})

plt.xlabel("First Feature of t-SNE")

plt.xlabel("Second Feature of t-SNE")
```

Output :

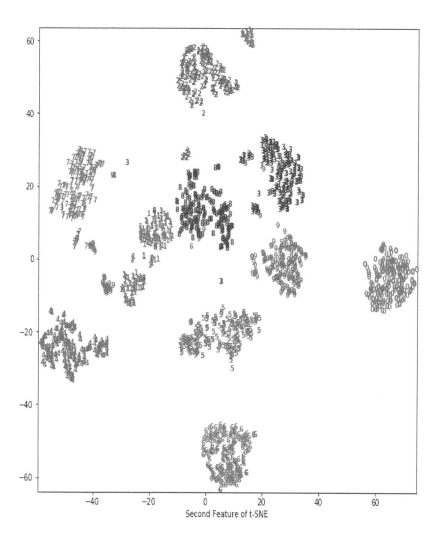

First Feature component versus Second Feature component of Digits dataset using t-SNE

You can observe through the result that t-SNE method is far better than PCA in terms of visualization of data. It divided classes better than PCA method. There are other methods as well for visualization of data.

Clustering Models

We already know that clustering is used to divide the dataset into groups known as clusters. As it belongs to unsupervised machine learning, it deals without the knowledge of labels. There are many methods for clustering process. We will discuss K-Means clustering, Agglomerative clustering, and DBSCAN methods.

K-Means Clustering

K-means clustering is a commonly used method due to it being the simplest method of clustering. It finds the center of clusters that belong to certain regions of dataset. The user gives an input to the method by providing the required number of clusters, and by using that information, it starts with random centers of those number of clusters, takes the mean of these cluster centers with each data point, and then finds the updated cluster center. It keeps on doing this process in multiple iterations until no further change is detected. The result can be contradictory as method does not have the knowledge of labels, so it just makes the clusters by using specific techniques.

Applying K-Means Clustering on Blobs dataset

Input [1]:

```
# Importing required libraries

from sklearn.datasets import make_blobs as blobs

from sklearn.cluster import KMeans

import matplotlib.pyplot as plt
```

```
# Reading input data

Data, Target = blobs(random_state = 1)

# Making clustering model

kmeans = KMeans(n_clusters = 3)

kmeans.fit(Data)

print("Clusters:\n{}".format(kmeans.labels_))
```

Output [1]:

Clusters:

[0 2 2 2 1 1 1 2 0 0 2 2 1 0 1 1 1 0 2 2 1 2 1 0 2 1 1 0 0 1 0 0 1 0
2 1 2

2 2 1 1 2 0 2 2 1 0 0 0 0 2 1 1 1 0 1 2 2 0 0 2 1 1 2 2 1 0 1 0 2 2
2 1 0

0 2 1 1 0 2 0 2 2 1 0 0 0 0 2 0 1 0 0 2 2 1 1 0 1 0]

Input [2]:

```
print("Predictions:\n{}".format(kmeans.predict(Data)))
```

Output [2]:

Predictions:

[0 2 2 2 1 1 1 2 0 0 2 2 1 0 1 1 1 0 2 2 1 2 1 0 2 1 1 0 0 1 0 0 1 0
2 1 2

2 2 1 1 2 0 2 2 1 0 0 0 0 2 1 1 1 0 1 2 2 0 0 2 1 1 2 2 1 0 1 0 2 2
2 1 0

0 2 1 1 0 2 0 2 2 1 0 0 0 0 2 0 1 0 0 2 2 1 1 0 1 0]

Input [3]:

plt.scatter(X[: , 0], X[: , 1], c = kmeans.labels_)

plt.legend()

plt.xlabel(kmeans.labels_[0])

plt.ylabel(kmeans.labels_[1])

plt.hold

plt.show

Output [3]:

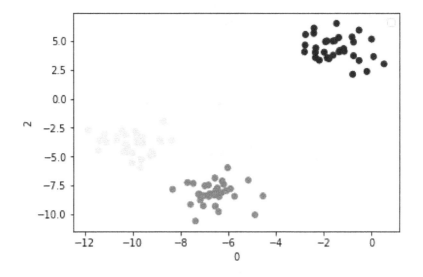

Prediction of Blobs Dataset using K-Means

Applying K-Means Clustering on Dense Blobs dataset

Input [1]:

```
# Importing required libraries

from sklearn.datasets import make_blobs as blobs

from sklearn.cluster import KMeans

import matplotlib.pyplot as plt

# Reading input data

Data, Target = blobs(n_samples = 200,cluster_std = [1.0, 2.5,
0.5],random_state = 170)

# Making clustering model
```

```
kmeans = KMeans(n_clusters = 3, random_state = 0)

kmeans.fit(Data)

print("Clusters:\n{}".format(kmeans.labels_))
```

Output [1]:

Clusters:

```
[1 2 2 0 0 1 2 0 1 0 2 1 1 0 1 2 0 0 1 0 1 0 0 1 0 0 0 0 2 1 2 0 1 1
0 1 2

 2 1 1 2 0 1 0 2 0 2 2 0 2 2 1 1 2 1 0 2 2 0 2 2 0 1 1 2 1 2 0 1 1 2
2 1 1

 2 2 0 2 1 2 2 0 1 1 0 0 0 1 0 2 0 0 0 0 2 0 0 0 2 2 1 1 2 0 1 1 2 1
1 2 2

 1 0 1 1 2 2 0 0 0 0 1 1 2 1 0 1 1 1 1 2 0 1 0 0 1 0 0 1 1 1 2 1 0 0
2 0 1

 1 0 2 1 0 1 1 1 2 1 2 2 0 1 1 0 0 0 1 0 1 1 1 0 0 0 2 0 0 0 0 0 0 2
0 2 2

 1 0 2 0 1 0 1 2 1 2 0 0 0 0 2]
```

Input [2]:

```
print("Predictions:\n{}".format(kmeans.predict(Data)))
```

Output [2]:

Predictions:

[1 2 2 0 0 1 2 0 1 0 2 1 1 0 1 2 0 0 1 0 1 0 0 1 0 0 0 0 2 1 2 0 1 1 0 1 2

2 1 1 2 0 1 0 2 0 2 2 0 2 2 1 1 2 1 0 2 2 0 2 2 0 1 1 2 1 2 0 1 1 2 2 1 1

2 2 0 2 1 2 2 0 1 1 0 0 0 1 0 2 0 0 0 0 2 0 0 0 2 2 1 1 2 0 1 1 2 1 1 2 2

1 0 1 1 2 2 0 0 0 0 1 1 2 1 0 1 1 1 1 2 0 1 0 0 1 0 0 1 1 1 2 1 0 0 2 0 1

1 0 2 1 0 1 1 1 2 1 2 2 0 1 1 0 0 0 1 0 1 1 1 0 0 0 2 0 0 0 0 0 0 2 0 2 2

1 0 2 0 1 0 1 2 1 2 0 0 0 0 2]

Input [3]:

plt.scatter(Data[: , 0], Data[: , 1], c = kmeans.labels_)

plt.xlabel(kmeans.labels_[0])

plt.ylabel(kmeans.labels_[1])

plt.hold

plt.show

Output [3]:

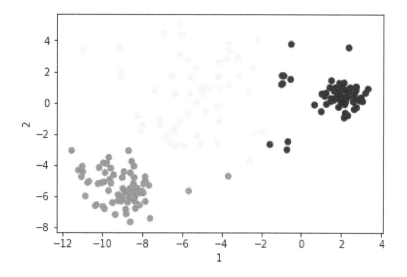

Prediction of Dense Blobs Dataset using K-Means

Applying K-Means Clustering on Stretched Blobs dataset

Input [1]:

```
# Importing required libraries

from sklearn.datasets import make_blobs as blobs

from sklearn.cluster import KMeans

import matplotlib.pyplot as plt

import numpy as np


# Reading input data
```

```python
Data, Target = blobs(random_state = 170, n_samples = 600)

rnd = np.random.RandomState(74)


# Data stretching through transformation

transformation = rnd.normal(size = (2, 2))

Data = np.dot(Data, transformation)


# Making clustering model

kmeans = KMeans(n_clusters = 3)

kmeans.fit(Data)


plt.scatter(Data[: , 0], Data[: , 1], c = kmeans.labels_)

plt.xlabel(kmeans.labels_[0])

plt.ylabel(kmeans.labels_[1])

plt.hold

plt.show
```

Output:

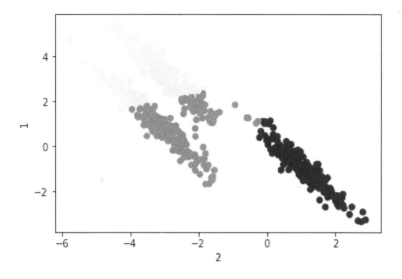

Prediction of Stretched Blobs Dataset using K-Means

You can observe that as long as we are making complex data, the performance of k-means method is decreasing. We are trying more complex data to further validate its performance.

Applying K-Means Clustering on Moons dataset

Input [1]:

Importing required libraries

from sklearn.datasets import make_moons as moons

from sklearn.cluster import KMeans

import matplotlib.pyplot as plt

```
# Reading input data

Data, Target = moons(n_samples = 200, noise = 0.05,
random_state = 0)


# Making clustering model

kmeans = KMeans(n_clusters = 2)

kmeans.fit(Data)

plt.scatter(Data[: , 0], Data[: , 1], c = kmeans.labels_)

plt.xlabel(kmeans.labels_[0])

plt.ylabel(kmeans.labels_[1])

plt.hold

plt.show
```

Output:

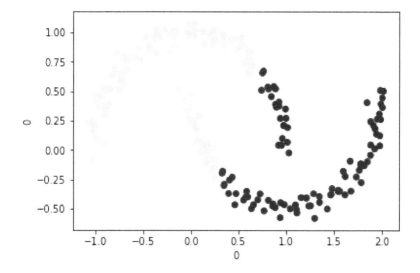

Prediction of Moons Dataset using K-Means

Here, we can evidently see that K-means was performing well on simple data, but when we moved to the Moons dataset, which is comparatively complex than Blobs dataset, K-means failed to make proper clusters. Both predicted classes contain members of other classes. We can analyze that k-Means does not work on complex datasets. For these problems, we need to look for other clustering methods.

Agglomerative Clustering

Agglomerative clustering is another method of clustering, which is somehow similar to the K-means clustering method as it also starts with random cluster. It then merges those clusters into similar clusters until no change occurs. We will apply Agglomerative clustering on blobs dataset to compare its performance with k-means.

Applying Agglomerative Clustering on Blobs dataset

Input:

```
# Importing required libraries

from sklearn.datasets import make_blobs as blobs

from sklearn.cluster import AgglomerativeClustering as Agg

import matplotlib.pyplot as plt


# Reading input data

Data, Target = blobs(random_state = 1)

# Making clustering model

agg = Agg(n_clusters = 3)

agg.fit_predict(Data)


plt.scatter(Data[: , 0], Data[: , 1], c = agg.labels_)

plt.legend()

plt.xlabel(agg.labels_[0])

plt.ylabel(agg.labels_[1])

plt.hold

plt.show
```

Output:

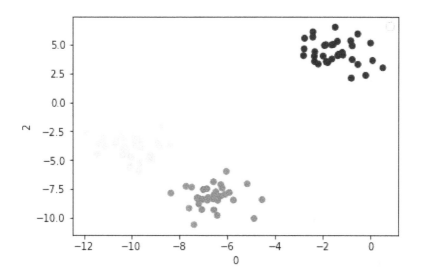

Prediction of Blobs Dataset using Agglomerative Clustering

You can observe that the performance of the Agglomerative clustering is much better than that of K-means clustering as it made clusters effectively. It has made clear clusters as compared to the ones K-means clustering came up with.

Applying Agglomerative Clustering on Moons dataset

Input:

```
# Importing required libraries

from sklearn.datasets import make_moons as moons
```

```python
from sklearn.cluster import AgglomerativeClustering as Agg

import matplotlib.pyplot as plt


# Reading input data

Data, Target = moons(random_state = 1)


# Making clustering model

agg = Agg(n_clusters = 3)

agg.fit_predict(Data)


plt.scatter(Data[:,0], Data[:,1], c = agg.labels_)

plt.legend()

plt.xlabel(agg.labels_[0])

plt.ylabel(agg.labels_[1])

plt.hold

plt.show
```

Output:

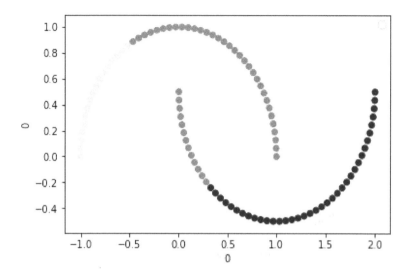

Prediction of Moons Dataset using Agglomerative Clustering

You can again observe that although the Agglomerative clustering method could not perform perfectly in prediction of the Moons dataset, its performance is still much better than K-means clustering.

DBSCAN

DBSCAN is yet another clustering method that is different from previous clustering methods we have looked upon so far. It works on points that are situated in the crowd region. Those crowd regions are also known as dense regions. It performs slower than Agglomerative clustering but gives better results than K-means clustering and Agglomerative clustering. Let us look at how this fares by applying the DBSCAN on moons dataset.

Applying DBSCAN Clustering on Blobs dataset

Input:

```
# Importing required libraries

from sklearn.datasets import make_blobs as blobs

from sklearn.cluster import DBSCAN as DB

import matplotlib.pyplot as plt


# Reading input data

Data, Target = blobs(random_state = 0, n_samples = 12)


# Making clustering model

db = DB()

dd = db.fit_predict(Data)


print("Cluster:\n{}".format(dd))
```

Output:

Cluster:

[-1 -1 -1 -1 -1 -1 -1 -1 -1 -1 -1 -1]

Applying DBSCAN Clustering on Moons dataset

Input [1]:

```
# Importing required libraries

from sklearn.datasets import make_moons as moons

from sklearn.preprocessing import StandardScaler as SS

from sklearn.cluster import DBSCAN as DB

import matplotlib.pyplot as plt


# Reading input data

Data, Target = moons(n_samples = 200, noise = 0.05,
random_state = 0)

ss = SS()

ss.fit(Data)

Data_scaled = ss.transform(Data)


# Making clustering model

db = DB()

dd = db.fit_predict(Data_scaled)


print("Cluster:\n{}".format(dd))
```

Output [1]:

Cluster:

[0 1 1 0 1 1 0 1 0 1 0 1 1 1 0 0 0 1 0 0 1 1 0 1 0 1 1 1 1 0 0 0 1 1
0 1 1

0 0 1 1 0 0 1 1 0 0 0 1 1 0 1 1 0 1 0 0 1 0 0 1 0 1 0 1 0 0 1 0 0 1
0 1 1

1 0 1 0 0 1 1 0 1 1 1 0 0 0 1 1 0 0 1 0 1 1 1 1 0 1 1 1 0 0 0 1 0 0
1 0 0

0 0 0 0 1 0 1 1 0 0 0 1 0 1 0 0 1 1 1 0 0 0 1 1 1 1 0 1 0 1 1 0 0 0
0 1 1

0 1 1 1 0 0 1 0 1 1 0 0 1 1 0 1 1 1 0 1 1 1 0 0 0 0 1 1 1 0 0 0 1 0
1 1 1

0 0 1 0 0 0 0 0 0 1 0 1 1 0 1]

Input [2]:

plt.scatter(Data[:,0], Data[:,1], c = db.labels_)

plt.xlabel(db.labels_[0])

plt.ylabel(db.labels_[1])

plt.hold

plt.show

Output [2]:

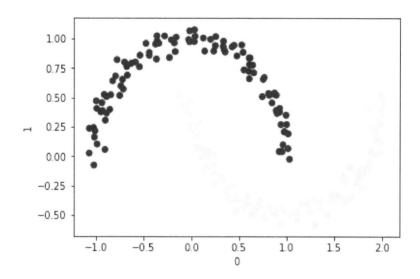

Prediction of Moons Dataset using DBSCAN

Sure enough, the performance of the DBSCAN clustering is best among all clustering algorithms. It has made many clear clusters as compared to K-means clustering and Agglomerative clustering. Although it has used StandardScaler, it has still performed well in dividing the classes.

Rounding off clustering:

We have seen various methods of clustering and how these can help us achieve significant results. Some of these have are quicker while others are more accurate. We have gone through a few visual representations to see exactly how each of these work and how they produce results accordingly.

In the next chapter, we will be looking at how we can work with data that contains text. We will go through sentiment analysis with appropriate examples, we will look at what

'stopwords' are and how we can use methods to analyze the
text to fetch desired results.

Chapter 5: Working with Text Data

We have discussed two types of features to represent our dataset. One type comprises a continuous feature that describes the quantity, and the other one is a categorical feature that represents items from fixed list. There is another type of data, which is text. Text data has many applications all over the world.

We have discussed one example of the email message in the 2nd chapter, in which we discussed that email messages could be an example of classification in which one has to classify the email as genuine or spam. The classification will be performed using the provided data. In fact, that email message might contain textual data, which is represented as strings. Similarly, if someone wants to learn about the opinion of any politician on any specific topic, we can take help from his/her speeches or tweets related to that topic to come to a conclusion. That speech or tweets will also contain some textual data that can further help us acquire a better understanding.

In a similar way, in case of customer services, a company needs to check whether the customer has lodged a complaint or an inquiry. This can be done by the representative of the company after checking the subject line of the email that has been sent by the customer. The subject line alone should provide a clue as to what nature of email the customer has sent. One can easily classify it as a complaint or inquiry. That email or document will also contain some textual data.

There are many scenarios in which we deal with textual data, and therefore we need to understand how to deal with textual data. We can perform some machine learning methods to perform classification, clustering or regression depending on these specific problems.

Types of Data Represented as Strings

Text in any dataset consists of strings, but it does not mean that all string features will be assumed as text data. A feature containing strings can represent categorical features as well, which is why we first need to check the data to analyze the constituents of datasets. The string can be comprised of four types, such as text data, categorical data, structured string data and free strings that can be semantically mapped to categories.

Categorical data comes from a fixed list. For example, you have a list of colors such as 'red,' 'green,' 'pink,' 'purple,' 'orange,' 'brown,' 'yellow' and 'black' and you ask someone to select his favorite color from specific list. The person will then select his/her favorite color present within the specific list. Each color will be represented by a categorical variable. As there are eight colors, there should be eight categorical variables. If he/she sees more than eight variables, it will no longer be an example of Categorical data.

This can happen as any color like black was misspelled as blak or blac, and that will lead to the creation of two or more variables for a specific color. As these different variables are representing the same color, these variables can be mapped to the same category.

If the person's favorite color is not present in that specific list, it is either because the person is looking for an unusual color, or that person is confused between 'gray' or 'grey,' or the person can come up with names like 'midnight blue,' which are difficult to be mapped into any color. Depending on the response you get, if the said response does not belong to the primary list, it is considered to be a part of a secondary list. It will then be referred as free strings that can be semantically mapped to categories.

The other type is structured string data. It does not come from fixed categories. It contains structures such as names and addresses of people, telephone numbers, and dates. These types of data demand more effort to deal with.

Text data is the last type of string data that consists of phrases or sentences. This type contains examples of tweets, chats, and reviews. For text analysis, natural language processing (NLP) plays a vital role here.

Sentiment Analysis of Movie Reviews

Sentiment analysis has become a very popular field these days. We will apply sentiment analysis to movie reviews. Reviews comprise of either positive or negative feedback from the audience. The dataset is collected from the Internet Movie Database website. It contains text-based movie reviews.

You will need to download this dataset and then load it in Python. This dataset contains two folders, one is for training data, and the other one is the test data. Both of these folders are further divided into subfolders where one is 'pos' and the other one is 'neg'. The 'pos' folder contains positive reviews while the 'neg' folder contains negative reviews. The dataset is available at
http://ai.stanford.edu/~amaas/data/sentiment/.

Input [1]:

```
# Importing required libraries

from sklearn.datasets import load_files

import matplotlib.pyplot as plt

import numpy as np


# Reading input Training data

reviews_trn = load_files("acllmdb/train/")


# Extracting data and target values from Training data

Data_trn = reviews_trn.data

Target_trn = reviews_trn.target


print("Type of Data_trn: {}".format(type(Data_trn)))
```

Output [1]:

```
Type of Data_trn: <class 'list'>
```

Input [3]:

```
print("Length of Data_trn: {}".format(len(Data_trn)))
```

Output [2]:

Length of Data_trn: 75000

Input [3]:

print("Data_trn [1]:\n{}".format(Data_trn[1]))

Output [3]:

Data_trn [1]:

b"Amount of disappointment I am getting these days seeing movies like Partner, Jhoom Barabar and now, Heyy Babyy is gonna end my habit of seeing first day shows.

The movie is an utter disappointment because it had the potential to become a laugh riot only if the d\xc3\xa9butant director, Sajid Khan hadn't tried too many things. Only saving grace in the movie were the last thirty minutes, which were seriously funny elsewhere the movie fails miserably. First half was desperately been tried to look funny but wasn't. Next 45 minutes were emotional and looked totally artificial and illogical.

OK, when you are out for a movie like this you don't expect much logic but all the flaws tend to appear when you don't enjoy the movie and thats the case with Heyy Babyy. Acting is good but thats not enough to keep one interested.

For the positives, you can take hot actresses, last 30 minutes, some comic scenes, good acting by

the lead cast and the baby. Only problem is that these things
do not come together properly to make a good movie.

Anyways, I read somewhere that It isn't a copy of
Three men and a baby but I think it would have been better if
it was."

Input [4]:

```
Data_trn = [doc.replace(b"<br />", b" ") for doc in Data_trn]
print("Samples per class: {}".format(np.bincount(Target_trn)))
```

Output [4]:

```
Samples per class: [12500 12500 50000]
```

Input [5]:

```
# Reading input Test data
reviews_tst = load_files("data/acllmdb/test/")
# Extracting data and target values from Test data
Data_tst = reviews_tst.data
Target_tst = reviews_tst.target
```

```
print("Number of documents in test data:
{}".format(len(Data_tst)))
```

Output [5]:

Number of documents in test data: 25000

Input [6]:

```
Data_tst = [doc.replace(b"<br />", b" ") for doc in Data_tst]

print("Samples per class (test):
{}".format(np.bincount(Target_tst)))
```

Output [6]:

Samples per class (test): [12500 12500]

Representing Text Data as Bags of Words

We already have discussed the importance of text data. The usage of bags of words for machine learning methods has become very popular. While dealing with this representation, we usually remove some of the structures, such as words, sentences, paragraphs, chapters, and formatting. It only counts words that appear in each text. By removing structure and counting just word, it provides a representation of text in the form of a 'bag.'

While carrying out a representation of bags of words, the steps required are as follows;

·   Splitting each document into words that are known as tokens and the process, that is known as tokenization.

·   The collection of vocabulary of all words appearing in each document and numbering them is known as vocabulary building.

·   Counting words in vocabulary is known as encoding.

Applying Bag of Words on a Toy dataset

Bag of words is applied in CountVectorizor, which is used to perform transformation. We are applying bag of words to the toy dataset.

Input [1]:

Initializing words

words = ["Every one is not wise,","Every one can not be wise,"]

Importing required libraries

from sklearn.feature_extraction.text import CountVectorizer

Cvect = CountVectorizer()

Cvect.fit(words)

Output [1]:

CountVectorizer(analyzer='word', binary=False, decode_error='strict',

    dtype=<class 'numpy.int64'>, encoding='utf-8', input='content',

    lowercase=True, max_df=1.0, max_features=None, min_df=1,

    ngram_range=(1, 1), preprocessor=None, stop_words=None,

    strip_accents=None, token_pattern='(?u)\\b\\w\\w+\\b',

    tokenizer=None, vocabulary=None)

Input [2]:

print("Size of Vocabulary: {}".format(len(Cvect.vocabulary_)))

Output [2]:

Size of Vocabulary: 7

Input [3]:

print("Content of Vocabulary:\n

{}".format(Cvect.vocabulary_))

Output [3]:

Content of Vocabulary:

{'every': 2, 'one': 5, 'is': 3, 'not': 4, 'wise': 6, 'can': 1, 'be': 0}

You can observe the size of vocabulary and counts of each word in the list of words. It is showing the number of occurrences for each word.

If you want to get the bag of words representation of training data, you can use 'transform'.

Input [1]:

bag_of_words = Cvect.transform(words)

print("bag_of_words: {}".format(repr(bag_of_words)))

Output [1]:

bag_of_words: <2x7 sparse matrix of type '<class 'numpy.int64'>'

   with 11 stored elements in Compressed Sparse Row format>

You can observe the bag of words representation of training data. Bag of words representation is stored in SciPy sparse matrix which only stores non-zero entries. If you want to mapping of words you can perform below steps.

Input [2]:

```
print("Dense Representation of bag of
words:\n{}".format(bag_of_words.toarray()))
```

Output [2]:

Dense Representation of bag of words:

[[0 0 1 1 1 1 1]

 [1 1 1 0 1 1 1]]

You can see that words have been mapped to either 0 or 1.

Applying Bag of Words on Movie Reviews

Input [1]:

```
# Importing required libraries

from sklearn.datasets import load_files

from sklearn.feature_extraction.text import CountVectorizer

import matplotlib.pyplot as plt

import numpy as np
```

```
# Reading input data

reviews_trn = load_files("acllmdb/train/")

reviews_tst = load_files("acllmdb/test/")


# Extracting data and target values from Training data

Data_trn = reviews_trn.data

Target_trn = reviews_trn.target


# Extracting data and target values from Test data

Data_tst = reviews_tst.data

Target_tst = reviews_tst.target


Cvect = CountVectorizer()

Cvect.fit(Data_trn)


Data_trn = Cvect.transform(Data_trn)

print("Data_trn:\n{}".format(repr(Data_trn)))
```

Output [1]:

Data_trn:

<75000x124255 sparse matrix of type '<class 'numpy.int64'>'

 with 10359806 stored elements in Compressed
Sparse Row format>

You can check that the shape of Data_trn after bag of words representation is 75000 x 124255 with a vocabulary of 124,255. Once again, the Bag of words representation is stored in SciPy sparse matrix which only stores non-zero entries. If you want to get details of vocabulary, you can perform the following steps:

Input [1]:

names_feature = Cvect.get_feature_names()

print("Number of features: {}".format(len(names_feature)))

Output [1]:

Number of features: 124255

Input [2]:

print("First 20 features:\n{}".format(names_feature[:20]))

Output [2]:

First 20 features:

```
['00', '000', '0000',
'0000000000000000000000000000000001',
'0000000000001', '000000001', '000000003', '00000001',
'000001745', '00001', '0001', '00015', '0002', '0007', '00083',
'000ft', '000s', '000th', '001', '002']
```

Input [3]:

```
print("Features from 50010 to
50030:\n{}".format(names_feature[50010:50030]))
```

Output [3]:

Features from 50010 to 50030:

```
['heatman', 'heatmiser', 'heaton', 'heats', 'heatseeker',
'heatwave', 'heave', 'heaved', 'heaven', 'heavenlier',
'heavenliness', 'heavenly', 'heavens', 'heavenward', 'heaves',
'heavier', 'heavies', 'heaviest', 'heavily', 'heaviness']
```

Input [4]:

```
print("Every 5000th
feature:\n{}".format(names_feature[::5000]))
```

Output [4]:

Every 5000th feature:

```
['00', 'aluin', 'banquière', 'brandie', 'chcialbym', 'corruptible',
'devagan', 'eisenburg', 'fetiches', 'ghar', 'heathen', 'indy',
'kerchner', 'locasso', 'meistersinger', 'narrators',
```

'overwhelmingly', 'portugese', 'recreating', 'samharris', 'silveira', 'stolen', 'themself', 'undeveloped', 'weidler']

We can observe that data is very big, and maybe some of it is useless, which is why we should apply a better feature extraction. We first need to apply classification so that we can compare its performance with one after removing some features.

Applying Logistic Regression on Movie Reviews

Input:

```
# Importing required libraries

from sklearn.datasets import load_files

from sklearn.feature_extraction.text import CountVectorizer

from sklearn.model_selection import cross_val_score

from sklearn.linear_model import LogisticRegression

import matplotlib.pyplot as plt

import numpy as np


# Reading input data

reviews_trn = load_files("acllmdb/train/")

reviews_tst = load_files("acllmdb/test/")
```

```
# Extracting data and target values from Training data

Data_trn = reviews_trn.data

Target_trn = reviews_trn.target


# Extracting data and target values from Test data

Data_tst = reviews_tst.data

Target_tst = reviews_tst.target


Cvect = CountVectorizer()

Cvect.fit(Data_trn)


Data_trn = Cvect.transform(Data_trn)


scores = cross_val_score(LogisticRegression(), Data_trn,
Target_trn, cv = 5)

print("Accuracy: {:.2f}".format(np.mean(scores)))
```

Output:

Accuracy: 0.71

Applying Logistic Regression with Gridsearch on Movie Reviews

Input:

Importing required libraries

from sklearn.datasets import load_files

from sklearn.model_selection import cross_val_score

from sklearn.linear_model import LogisticRegression

from sklearn.feature_extraction.text import CountVectorizer

from sklearn.model_selection import GridSearchCV

import matplotlib.pyplot as plt

import numpy as np

Reading input data

reviews_trn = load_files("aclImdb/train/")

reviews_tst = load_files("aclImdb/test/")

Extracting data and target values from Training data

Data_trn = reviews_trn.data

Target_trn = reviews_trn.target

```python
# Extracting data and target values from Test data

Data_tst = reviews_tst.data

Target_tst = reviews_tst.target


Cvect = CountVectorizer()

Cvect.fit(Data_trn)


Data_trn = Cvect.transform(Data_trn)


prm_grd = {'C': [0.001, 0.01, 0.1, 1, 10]}

grd = GridSearchCV(LogisticRegression(), prm_grd, cv = 5)

grd.fit(Data_trn, Target_trn)

print("Cross validation score: {:.2f}".format(grd.best_score_))

print("Parameter with best performance: ",
grd.best_params_)
```

Output:

Cross validation score: 0.72

Parameter with best performance: {'C' : 0.1}

You can observe that cross validation score using value of C = is achieved. We should check performance on test data as well which will further describe the performance of algorithm.

Input:

Data_tst = Cvect.transform(Target_tst)

print("{:.2f}".format(grd.score(Data_tst, Target_tst)))

Output:

0.70

We have checked the accuracies of logistic regression with and without GridSearch. We need to apply a better feature extraction here, as well. We should look to remove useless or less impactful features. It can be observed that we have used CountVectorizer, which converts all words to lowercase characters, which means 'Some', 'some'' and sOme will correspond to the same token.

It is a good thing to have as some words can be mistakenly written in uppercase and can be differentiated with the same word in lowercase, but despite this feature of CountVectorizer, we have observed that there are still some useless features or words which need to be removed.

Stopwords

We can remove the useless words by using stopwords. It removes words that are repeated over and over again.

Input [1]:

```
# Importing required libraries

from sklearn.datasets import load_files

from sklearn.model_selection import cross_val_score

from sklearn.linear_model import LogisticRegression

from sklearn.feature_extraction.text import CountVectorizer

from sklearn.model_selection import GridSearchCV

import matplotlib.pyplot as plt

import numpy as np


# Reading input data

reviews_trn = load_files("acllmdb/train/")

reviews_tst = load_files("acllmdb/test/")


# Extracting data and target values from Training data

Data_trn = reviews_trn.data

Target_trn = reviews_trn.target
```

```
# Extracting data and target values from Test data

Data_tst = reviews_tst.data

Target_tst = reviews_tst.target

Cvect = CountVectorizer(min_df = 5).fit(Data_trn)

X_train = Cvect.transform(Data_trn)

print("X_train with min_df: {}".format(repr(X_train)))
```

Output [1]:

X_train with min_df: <75000x124055 sparse matrix of type '<class 'numpy.int64'>'

with 10359846 stored elements in Compressed Sparse Row format>

We can observe that with demanding at least five occurrences, we have reduced features from 124255 to 124055, which means reduction of 200 features. Now we need to check the accuracy of logistic regression algorithm after reducing useless words.

Input [2]:

```
grd = GridSearchCV(LogisticRegression(), prm_grd, cv = 5)

grd.fit(Data_trn, Target_trn)
```

```
print("Cross validation score: {:.2f}".format(grd.best_score_))
```

Output [2]:

Cross validation score: 0.72

We can observe that even after reducing useless words, accuracy of logistic regression algorithm is unchanged. Although the accuracy has not improved, we have reduced the number of features by getting the same performance, which means we have done good by reducing words that are meaningless.

Applying Logistic Regression with Gridsearch and Stopwords on Movie Reviews

Input [1]:

```
# Importing required libraries

from sklearn.datasets import load_files

from sklearn.model_selection import cross_val_score

from sklearn.linear_model import LogisticRegression

from sklearn.feature_extraction.text import CountVectorizer

from sklearn.model_selection import GridSearchCV

import matplotlib.pyplot as plt
```

```python
import numpy as np


# Reading input data

reviews_trn = load_files("acllmdb/train/")

reviews_tst = load_files("acllmdb/test/")


# Extracting data and target values from Training data

Data_trn = reviews_trn.data

Target_trn = reviews_trn.target


# Extracting data and target values from Test data

Data_tst = reviews_tst.data

Target_tst = reviews_tst.target


Cvect = CountVectorizer(min_df = 5, stop_words = "english").fit(Data_trn)

X_train = Cvect.transform(Data_trn)

print("X_train with stop words:\n{}".format(repr(X_train)))
```

Output [1]:

X_train with stop words:

<75000x123865 sparse matrix of type '<class 'numpy.int64'>'

with 10359836 stored elements in Compressed Sparse Row format>

We can again observe that with applying stopwords, we have reduced features from 124,055 to 123,865, which means a reduction of 190 features. Now, we need to check the accuracy of the logistic regression algorithm after the reduction.

Input [2]:

```
grd = GridSearchCV(LogisticRegression(), param_grid, cv = 5)

grd.fit(Data_trn, Target_trn)

print("Cross validation score: {:.2f}".format(grid.best_score_))
```

Output [2]:

Cross validation score: 0. 73

Applying Logistic Regression with tf-id Vectorizer and Stopwords on Movie Reviews

Input [1]:

```python
# Importing required libraries

from sklearn.datasets import load_files

from sklearn.model_selection import cross_val_score

from sklearn.linear_model import LogisticRegression

from sklearn.model_selection import GridSearchCV

from sklearn.feature_extraction.text import TfidfVectorizer

from sklearn.pipeline import make_pipeline

import matplotlib.pyplot as plt

import numpy as np


# Reading input data

reviews_trn = load_files("acllmdb/train/")

reviews_tst = load_files("acllmdb/test/")


# Extracting data and target values from Training data

Data_trn = reviews_trn.data

Target_trn = reviews_trn.target


# Extracting data and target values from Test data

Data_tst = reviews_tst.data
```

```
Target_tst = reviews_tst.target

ppe = make_pipeline(TfidfVectorizer(min_df = 5, norm =
None), LogisticRegression())

prm_grd = {'logisticregression__C': [0.001, 0.01, 0.1, 1, 10]}

grd = GridSearchCV(ppe, prm_grd, cv = 5)

grd.fit(Data_trn, Target_trn)

print("Cross validation score: {:.2f}".format(grd.best_score_))
```

Output [1]:

Cross validation score: 0.73

Applying Natural language toolkit on Email

We will be processing some emails now. We will first look at the original email and the one after some processing to get a better understanding. You can use any email and carry out the process on it.

Input [1]:

```
# Importing required libraries

from nltk.stem import SnowballStemmer

import string
```

The first part is to give an appropriate path of the file and read the file.

d6=[]

d=open("2","r")

d1 = d.read()

Output [1]:

Message-ID: <26985403.1075859469480.JavaMail.evans@thyme>

Date: Wed, 26 Dec 2001 09:41:22 -0800 (PST)

From: susan.bailey@enron.com

To: stephanie.panus@enron.com

Subject: FW: People on Termination List

Cc: stewart.rosman@enron.com

Mime-Version: 1.0

Content-Type: text/plain; charset=us-ascii

Content-Transfer-Encoding: 7bit

Bcc: stewart.rosman@enron.com

X-From: Bailey, Susan
</O=ENRON/OU=NA/CN=RECIPIENTS/CN=SBAILE2>

X-To: Panus, Stephanie

</O=ENRON/OU=NA/CN=RECIPIENTS/CN=Spanus>

X-cc: Rosman, Stewart
</O=ENRON/OU=NA/CN=RECIPIENTS/CN=Srosman>

X-bcc:

X-Folder: \Susan_Bailey_Jan2002\Bailey, Susan\Deleted Items

X-Origin: Bailey-S

X-FileName: sbaile2 (Non-Privileged).pst

Stephanie,

Please add the following individuals set forth below to list of recipients to receive the Master Termination Log.

Also, please add Steve Hall to that list.

Thanks,

Susan

-----Original Message-----

From: Rosman, Stewart

Sent: Wednesday, December 26, 2001 11:37 AM

To: Bailey, Susan

Subject: People on Termination List

Sean Crandall

Diana Scholtes

Jeff Richter

Chris Mallory

Mark Fischer

Tom Alonso

Input [2]:

Once the contents are available in Python, the next step is to remove the metadata from the email.

the string 'X-FileName'. This string is present in every email and can be 'split'.

d2=d1.split('X-FileName')

Output [2]:

% First part of d2

Message-ID:
<26985403.1075859469480.JavaMail.evans@thyme>

Date: Wed, 26 Dec 2001 09:41:22 -0800 (PST)

From: susan.bailey@enron.com

To: stephanie.panus@enron.com

Subject: FW: People on Termination List

Cc: stewart.rosman@enron.com

Mime-Version: 1.0

Content-Type: text/plain; charset=us-ascii

Content-Transfer-Encoding: 7bit

Bcc: stewart.rosman@enron.com

X-From: Bailey, Susan
</O=ENRON/OU=NA/CN=RECIPIENTS/CN=SBAILE2>

X-To: Panus, Stephanie
</O=ENRON/OU=NA/CN=RECIPIENTS/CN=Spanus>

X-cc: Rosman, Stewart
</O=ENRON/OU=NA/CN=RECIPIENTS/CN=Srosman>

X-bcc:

X-Folder: \Susan_Bailey_Jan2002\Bailey, Susan\Deleted
Items

X-Origin: Bailey-S

% First part of d2

: sbaile2 (Non-Privileged).pst

Stephanie,

Please add the following individuals set forth below to list of recipients to receive the Master Termination Log.

Also, please add Steve Hall to that list.

Thanks,

Susan

-----Original Message-----

From: Rosman, Stewart

Sent: Wednesday, December 26, 2001 11:37 AM

To: Bailey, Susan

Subject: People on Termination List

Sean Crandall

Diana Scholtes

Jeff Richter

Chris Mallory

Mark Fischer

Tom Alonso

Input [3]:

```
# Once the email body is retrieved, the next step is to remove punctuation, and split the text into individual words.

for c in string.punctuation:

        d3= d2[1].replace(c,"")

d4=d3.split(' ')
```

Output [3]:

```
% d3
```

: sbaile2 (Non-Privileged).pst

Stephanie,

Please add the following individuals set forth below to list of recipients to receive the Master Termination Log.

Also, please add Steve Hall to that list.

Thanks,

Susan

-----Original Message-----

From: Rosman, Stewart

Sent: Wednesday, December 26, 2001 11:37 AM

To: Bailey, Susan

Subject: People on Termination List

Sean Crandall

Diana Scholtes

Jeff Richter

Chris Mallory

Mark Fischer

Tom Alonso

% d4

:

sbaile2

(Non-Privileged).pst

Stephanie,

Please

add

the

following

individuals

set

forth

below

to

list

of

recipients

to

receive

the

Input [4]:

```
# Now apply SnowballStemmer on each word. [hint: use
.append() method to make a continual list of words]

stemmer = SnowballStemmer("english")

for i in range(len(d4)):

    d5=stemmer.stem(d4[i])

        d6.append (d5)


# The resulting list of words is then 'joined' again into a single
string.

d6 = " ".join(d6)
```

Output [4]:

% d5

alonso

% d6

: sbaile2 (non-privileged).pst

stephanie,

pleas add the follow individu set forth below to list of recipi to receiv the master termin log.

also, pleas add steve hall to that list.

thanks,

susan

-----origin message-----

from: rosman, stewart

sent: wednesday, decemb 26, 2001 11:37 am

to: bailey, susan

subject: peopl on termin list

sean crandall

diana scholtes

jeff richter

chri mallory

mark fischer

tom alonso

In the above example, we have successfully processed an email. We began with an email that contained far too much information, most of which we were neither interested in nor looking forward to.

We then processed the same email and removed meta descriptions and other unnecessary words to bring out only the information we were interested in. The end result is an information extracted from the email that is relevant and needed.

While this process is lengthy, it does beg the question, why would you do all that when you can copy and paste the email body yourself? Remember, we are undergoing Machine learning and naturally, we are expecting to deal with a bulk of data. There is every likelihood that you will not be dealing with data that is only comprising of a single email. By training the model to filter out unnecessary information for hundreds of thousands of email in the shortest span of time, you are saving yourself quite a lot of process. The machine will now be able to carry out the same for you instead, at a rate far quicker than an individual can deliver.

To conclude this chapter, we have learned how to handle data that comprises of text. Unlike previous chapters, where we were manipulating numeric values and methods to plot graphs and visualize the data, this chapter dealt with 'strings' of text as you would normally find in emails and movie reviews.

Major organizations use sentiment analysis to tailor recommendations using this information for the members of the general audience. Through using such methods and algorithms, we can train the model of the machine to learn and store words as 'vocabulary' and then ensure that the machine can use these to gain valuable data and analyze the same. Through effective analysis, we can have quite a lot of work carried out in the least timeframe possible.

In the final chapter, we will be looking at the real world applications of Machine learning. While there are quite a lot of these in existence, we will only be focusing on a select few to provide data scientists and machine learners a better understanding of the applications in the real world.

Chapter 6: Machine Learning Real World Applications

Machine learning is an all-important field throughout the world. Its application can be seen in many apps, software, and research-based projects of various magnitudes. Machine learning has been around for quite some time now; however, recently it has garnered a massive attention from the worldwide audience and computer experts.

It can be used in medical fields for diagnosing various diseases using classification or regression methods, within social networks to locate your friends, get suggestions and a feed that is tailor-made for your liking, and in forecasting weather conditions by providing the model with a number of features that can further train and classify, predict or forecast weather when required. It is capable of processing extensively large data for large organizations or small-sized data for smaller organizations as well.

Where can you use machine learning?

We can use machine learning in many applications when it comes to the real world. Before we go ahead, let us quickly stroll through the previous examples discussed to remind ourselves of some practical examples. Then, we shall look at four more large-scale uses of machine learning. For this book, we will not be covering small scale usage of machine learning. After all, we are trying to learn to be a part of a bigger picture.

In the beginning, we discussed how the spam filter used a list of blacklisted words which helped the filter to identify spam words or emails. This filter can be used as one of the examples of intelligent applications. This problem can be solved by a human as well, but in that case, a person requires thorough understanding of processes in order to come up with such a model. Manual or hand-coded rules can be useful but not in every case.

Similarly, in another example we learned that the hand-coded method fails in a specific aspect, and that is the detection of a face in an image. Although every smartphone these days can detect and identify faces in the pictures, this was far from possible in the past. The reason behind failure in detection and identification of faces in an image in the recent past is due to the difference in perception of pixels between a human and a computer.

Apart from these, The application of machine learning can be seen across various sectors of our daily lives. These include and are not limited to the following:

1.   Financial institutions – Financial institutions like banks have greatly benefited from machine learning and have used machine learning to create complex algorithms to learn and identify suspicious or fraudulent transactions. There were times when a transaction could not be identified at such a rapid pace and most of the people who carried out these illegal activities got away with it. Now, things are different. With large processing power and memory available for the systems of today, financial institutions can run transactions through a trained model and immediately identify if any transaction, regardless of how genuine it looks, is flagged as suspicious or fraudulent. These transaction checks have greatly improved the leakages in reserves and allowed the world to host better banking systems where the money and financial records remain safe and secure, away from prying

eyes.

2. Sentiment Analysis – Major streaming platforms across the globe, such as Netflix and Amazon Prime, are using sentiment analysis to analyze the behavior of the user and learn of what the user might like or dislike. This saves quite a lot of time and guess work as the entire profile is categorized by labels such as likes, dislikes, and only then recommendations are proposed for the users. This creates a high chance that the user might end up clicking on the said recommendation. This isn't just limited to streaming services, many other websites use the same approach, such as Facebook, twitter and many more. This is why you normally end up getting feeds that are more likely to engage you.

3. Healthcare – We have looked at a few variations of machine learning methods using Iris and Breast Cancer datasets. However, the reason we used those is because machine learning plays a vital role in the health sector. With top-notch machineries, equipment and analysis tools, machine learning provides ground-breaking results in the least amount of time imaginable. What was once done in days can now be done within minutes. No longer do you need to consult various doctors regarding a scan just to find out the condition of your ailment. Now, the clever machines and models continue to evolve and learn to decode the films and scans to predict the answers with amazing accuracy. The bright side is, this field will continue to use machine learning for generations to come.

4. E-Commerce – Sure enough, businesses that operate online, such as Amazon, eBay, Alibaba, use machine learning

to understand the buying patterns, wishlisted items and items the users might browse through to come up with recommendations. For any business person, it is imperative to propose or recommend items which have a high likelihood of being sold to a specific type of customer. Through machine learning, that is being done every single minute of every day. The more you browse such e-commerce websites, the more data they compile to refine their accuracy in recommending products. Eventually, you will be spoiled for choice as these recommendations, almost all of them, will be too tempting to resist. The fact of the matter is that these existed within the website before as well, the only difference is, you may have skipped past these. Now, since the machine has learned of your shopping behavior and the kind of items you are interested in, the model will propose the ones which are most likely to be sold to you.

The world continues to evolve and with it the data that is being collected. Every day we spend hours on our cell phones and computers, scrolling through websites, products and even social media pages. This data is growing larger and larger for every single one of us. Imagine the amount of data that exists on the internet now. Processing that will require hundreds of years, if not thousands, if done by human beings.

Machine learning has drastically changed everything for us and taken over the arduous task of carrying out such large operations in unbelievably short span of time. Not only does that save us time, it saves us quite a lot of effort and possibly money as well. Now, we can create our own models and use the data we have gathered to tailor the kind of recommendations we would like the customers to see, effectively increasing our chances for great sales.

Before we end the chapter, below are some working data

using a few more datasets. Have a look through and try to find out what is being done here. You can try and alter the variables, the methods and see how that would affect the overall output of the same.

Applying Machine Learning methods on Wine Data

Input [1]:

```
# Importing required libraries

import pandas as pd

from sklearn.cluster import KMeans

from sklearn.preprocessing import StandardScaler

from sklearn.pipeline import make_pipeline


df = pd.read_csv('wine_data.csv')


samples = df.iloc[:, 2: 10].values

model = KMeans(n_clusters = 3)

labels = model.fit_predict(samples)


ct = pd.crosstab(labels,df['class_name'])

print("Crosstab with simple Kmeans:\n",ct)
```

Output [1]:

Crosstab with simple Kmeans:

```
class_name Barbera Barolo Grignolino

row_0

0          5     15      6

1         19      9     46

2         24     35     19
```

```
       class_label      alcohol   ...              od280
       proline

count  178.000000 178.000000  ...   178.000000
178.000000

mean     1.938202 13.000618 ...     2.611685  746.893258

std     0.775035        0.811827      ...    0.709990
314.907474

min     1.000000  11.030000   ...    1.270000  278.000000

25%     1.000000  12.362500   ...    1.937500  500.500000

50%     2.000000  13.050000   ...    2.780000  673.500000

75%     3.000000  13.677500   ...    3.170000  985.000000

max     3.000000  14.830000   ...    4.000000
1680.000000
```

Input [2]:

```
print(df.describe())


scaler = StandardScaler()

scaler.fit(samples)

scaled_samples = scaler.transform(samples)

# Applying KMeans and pd.crosstab on the scaled_samples

Model = KMeans(n_clusters = 3)

labels = model.fit_predict(scaled_samples)

ct = pd.crosstab(labels,df['class_name'])

print("Crosstab with StandardScaler and Kmeans:\n",ct)
```

Output [2]:

[8 rows x 14 columns]

Crosstab with StandardScaler and Kmeans:

class_name	Barbera	Barolo	Grignolino
row_0			
0	0	55	4
1	46	0	13
2	2	4	54

Input [3]:

```
#%% Pipeline
Scaler = StandardScaler()
Kmeans = KMeans(n_clusters = 3)
pipeline = make_pipeline(scaler,kmeans)


pipeline.fit(samples)
labels = pipeline.predict(samples)
ct = pd.crosstab(labels,df['class_name'])
print("Crosstab with pipeline:\n",ct)
```

Output [3]:

```
Crosstab with pipeline:
 class_name  Barbera  Barolo  Grignolino
row_0
0                1       5          44
1               47       0          22
2                0      54           5
```

Applying Machine Learning methods on Banknote Authentication Data

Input [1]:

```python
# Importing required libraries

from sklearn.model_selection import train_test_split

import pandas as pd

from sklearn.tree import DecisionTreeClassifier

from matplotlib import pyplot as plt

file = pd.read_csv('bank_note.txt')

data = file.values

x = data[: , 0:4]

y = data[: , 4]


#Data Splitting

x_train, x_test, y_train, y_test = train_test_split(x, y, test_size
= 0.3,
```

```
                                        rand
                                        om_s
                                        tate
                                        = 15)


clf = DecisionTreeClassifier(criterion = 'gini',
min_samples_split = 65,

                                max_features = 3,
                                max_depth = 150)

clf.fit(x_train,y_train)

out = clf.predict(x_test)

acc = (sum(out == y_test))/len(out)

print('Accuracy of the classifier is {:.4f}'.format(acc*100))



#Data Plotting

plt.plot(x_train[y_train == 0,0],x_train[y_train == 0,1],'rs',label
= 'Original')

plt.hold

plt.plot(x_train[y_train == 1,0],x_train[y_train ==
1,1],'g.',label='Fake')

plt.legend()

plt.xlabel('variance of Wavelet Transformed image')

plt.ylabel('skewness of Wavelet Transformed image')
```

```
plt.figure(2)

plt.plot(x_train[y_train == 0,2],x_train[y_train == 0,3],'rs',label
= 'Original')

plt.hold

plt.plot(x_train[y_train == 1,2],x_train[y_train == 1,3],'g.',label
= 'Fake')

plt.legend()

plt.xlabel('curtosis of Wavelet Transformed image ')

plt.ylabel('entropy of image')
```

Output [1]:

Accuracy of the classifier is 93.4466

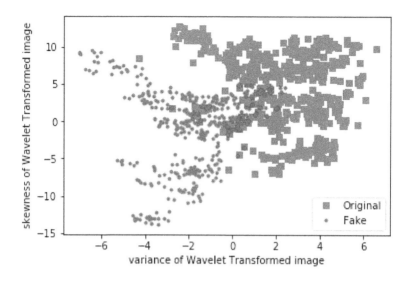

Prediction of first two features of Banknote Dataset using Decision Tree Classifier

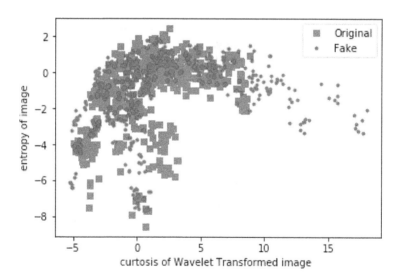

Prediction of last two features of Banknote Dataset using Decision Tree Classifier

Both of these datasets are collected from https://archive.ics.uci.edu/ml/datasets.php. You can use this repository to download and use any dataset you might like. It is recommended that you continue practicing your codes and machine learning by downloading various machine learning datasets. These will help you grasp the concepts far better than just repeating everything the book has to offer.

Conclusion

Admittedly, the book comprises of quite a few codes, all of which may seem daunting and rather overwhelming at first. If you have a good understanding of the Python programming language, you should easily be able to relate to the code and understanding what is being done at a certain given point. While our main objective was to ensure we visit some of the more technically advanced approaches and test out various models, check their accuracy and put them to work, we cannot deny that at the heart of the entire Machine Learning lies Python; a beautiful and intriguing language that continues to amaze the world.

In the start of this book, we looked upon various components, went through some details and established that this book caters to people with a good knowledge of Python and other important libraries. The purpose of this book was to allow you to seek out further datasets, libraries and components which would allow you to enhance your Machine Learning skills by using practical, real world examples.

We then discussed many machine learning methods and their applications as well. We also learned that machine learning can be divided into two types, supervised machine learning and unsupervised machine learning. Supervised machine learning contains the information of output label. Supervised machine learning is further split into two types, classification, and regression. Classification is used to predict discrete labels while regression is used to predict continuous numbers or floating-point numbers.

Classification is further divided into two categories, binary classification and multi-classification. Binary classification divides two classes while multi-classification separates multiple classes. In other words, we can say that binary classification provides either a yes or no as an answer. We discussed the example of classification of emails as an example of binary classification.

We also visited examples of regression such as prediction of an individual's annual income from his/her education, age and other related 'features' where predicted output will be an amount of any value. The predicted output can be any number, varying on the kind of data provided.

Unsupervised machine learning does not contain the information of the output label. It applies multiple methods including Euclidean distance. It contains k-means, agglomerative and DBSCAN methods which divide the datasets without knowing the information of output label.

Multiple methods of each category have been applied. We observed that linear kernel worked better than other kernels in classification. Some methods worked well by increasing the value of C while others performed well by reducing the value of tolerance.

We also observed that we should limit the number of features while training and predicting output otherwise we can lead to lack of accuracy.

We observed that K-means clustering performed well but in simple problems. For problems which were complex in nature, it failed.

Agglomerative and DBSCAN methods performed better than K-means clustering, especially in difficult cases. We also observed that many scales can be used to increase the efficiency of algorithms. It was also shown that many scales can be used as preprocessing especially before applying classification as some methods are sensitive to scales and perform well with application of scales such as SVM and NN.

Finally, we analyzed some text data and were successfully able to remove unnecessary data from the said email while retaining the one that we require the most.

While the book has left out hundreds of other applications of machine learning, and thousands of datasets which could have been used, it is done deliberately to allow the aspiring learners to carry out experimentations and come up with better solutions through effective approach and model training. Where possible, the links were shared so that you can gain access to such training model datasets.

Machine learning has gained quite a pace and promises to be a worthy field of interest for those willing to pursue a career in it. We have barely uncovered the tip of the iceberg, there is quite a lot remaining that we might not know yet. Machine learning will soon revolutionize ad impact quite a lot of things, which makes this the perfect time to get into some practice and start making your way to the top.

While you can continue to read various books and scroll through a gazillion videos available all over the internet, the best way to master machine learning is to implement the codes and try writing new ones. Come up with genuine ideas by visualizing a scenario and then focusing on the task. Learn and then teach the same to the model by supplying the appropriate data. The end results will always bring out something unique each time.

Great programmers and inventors have gone through extensive trial and error methods to come up with contributions which have helped the society, if not the world. However, you hold a distinct advantage over such success stories; they relied on man hours while you now have a machine to carry out the same extensive work but in a fraction of the time you may have taken otherwise. Use the knowledge and use it well!

Remember, there is no such thing as being "too late to learn." All it needs is commitment and a will to learn. Great inventors used the same age-old principles to come up with brilliant, ground-breaking inventions. Do not let the thought of being late to begin learning something new get to you. Your creativity is yours, and you are unique in your own way. With the knowledge you have gathered, let your creativity flow and practice. Who knows, you might very well be the next great mind to rise.

Let Machine Learning help you achieve great new success. This field holds significant potential and the future is only looking to grow bigger. Despite all the competition, despite the sheer number of aspiring students and masters, there is much to be done in this world to help others and create a more safe, secure and efficient environment. All it takes is one brilliant idea to change everything.

Whether you wish to bring a revolutionary new model to analyze blood samples, or detect fraudulent online transactions, you have all the time in the world to come up with something truly unique.

The beauty about the entire Machine Learning process is that you can explore far greater and more promising opportunities for yourself. The field is quite vast and you can get into various projects and institutions. Here are a few of the top ones which use or need Machine Learning:

1. Virtual Assistants - We are referring to technologies like Siri for iPhones. The world of voice recognition and virtual assistants is rapidly evolving. Now, even the television remote controls come with voice assistance. Machine learning plays an important part to make these applications successful. By gathering the data of your selection, your voice samples, and your day-to-day commands, you start getting more personalized recommendations and outputs. This is just the start; there is a long way to go as the world has just started getting used to such virtual assistants.

2. Face tracking - Whether you use facial recognition apps for surveillance purposes or for cinematography, face tracking requires complex algorithms to train the model in order to learn what face it needs to track and how to keep its focus on the subject of choice. We are still in early days which is why there is quite a lot to be done in this field as well. The applications will further diversify the use of machine learning in CCTVs, surveillance, video making, aerial/drone imaging and much more.

3. Search engine queries - We have already seen how search engines tend to immediately understand what we are trying to search. Now, you know how! They use algorithms to try and understand the behavior of the user and identify what the user is trying to search for. Using features like their geographical location, age, and browsing habits, the search engines present results tailor-made for them.

4. Customer support - This might be a bit of a surprise, but the fact of the matter is that not always do you get to speak to a live customer service representative. There are quite a few occurrences where you will end up speaking to a 'bot' that is collecting the data and understanding what you are trying to find out. Using the abundant resources from the page, the bot will present the information to you accordingly while trying to gauge the exact nature of the query. This is far from perfect which is why if you can come up with an accurate model, you might be just moments away from becoming the next success story.

5. Traffic updates - Have you ever accessed the maps on your smartphone and come across warnings that the road you are travelling on is experiencing delays and severe traffic jams? Have you ever wondered how come your cell phone knows that? Using GPS satellites, the number of phones or GPS modules installed within cars, the speed at which they travel, the machines immediately compute if the road is facing blocks or letting the traffic flow easily. The problem is that not many GPS modules are active or installed, which does kind of create discrepancies and there is a certain lag within the actual situation and the data that it represents on the screen. While there is Machine Learning already at play, it does need upgrading. There is quite a lot of room for improvement and even new models to come and replace the old ones.

Finally, Machine Learning is still in its genesis. While the concept has lurked around for quite some time, it is only recently that things have truly started to manifest and bring forth successful stories and results. The applications go far beyond health care and financial institutions. The world awaits new ideas, there is always someone out there looking for a person of your caliber, understanding and knowledge. Train yourself by practicing and be the next success story; or better yet, train your machine to be one for you!

Bibliography

1.	Muller, A, C. & Guido, S. (2017). Introduction to Machine Learning with Python. Sebastopol, CA: O'Reilly Media Inc.

2.	Raschka, S. (2015). Python Machine Learning. Birmingham, UK: Packt Publishing Ltd.

3. Heyy Babyy, Retrieved 10/2019, from, https://www.imdb.com/title/tt0806088/reviews

4. Large Movie Review Dataset, Retrieved, 10/2019 from. http://ai.stanford.edu/~amaas/data/sentiment/

python data analytics

Introduction

Data is an essential part of the Information Technology ecosystem and is utilized to perform multiple operations in Machine Learning and Data Science. In order to analyze data for different types of predictions and business operations, it is mandatory to focus on mathematical models, graphs, data insights, databases, and statistics for developing deep learning models. Python programming language is considered as the best source for developing data science and deep learning models. Being a general-purpose programming language, Python is widely being used to gain insights from data and also serves as a powerful language to store, access and manipulate data in lists.

Python programming language is easy to understand, implement and interpret because it is an exceedingly powerful and effective general-purpose language. Over time, there have been several tools and integrated development environments created for data science and data analytics which support Python. Learning Python data science is also considered as the process of gaining knowledge and insights from diverse and huge datasets by analyzing, processing and organizing data. Programming of data science is flexible but involves the application of highly complex mathematical processes for which beginners are required to learn the basics of Python programming language.

Data science is based on complex algorithms and models for which a powerful programming language is required to handle mathematical processing.

Chapter 1: Python Data Science and Machine Learning

Artificial Intelligence, Machine Learning, and Data Science are the most commonly used technologies that are capable of performing complex operations and also bring long term benefits to businesses and industries. Over the past few years, researchers and developers have been working on creating machine learning models and algorithms that have the power to make accurate predictions and get trained by utilizing input data. Machine Learning is a data-driven system development algorithm that is based on data analysis, feedback, and data models which also help in refining algorithms for improving model accuracy and performance. Mainly, the machine learning systems analyze data to detect patterns and make accurate predictions by applying the predefined rules.

Data science is associated with data representation and scientific methodologies to transform algorithms for developing new solutions. By utilizing structured and raw data, data scientists make use of algorithms, mathematical models, and statistics to derive a specific solution. Generally, data science is based on the processes of data extraction, data cleansing, visualization, analysis and actionable insights generation. Furthermore, the approach also helps in predicting and understanding user behavior or recommendations. Machine learning is a major part of data science because it inherits aspects from algorithms and statistics to process the generated data and information extracted from multiple resources.

When it comes to dealing with enormous amounts of data,

machine learning and data science algorithms are implemented together for processing information and gaining actionable data insights. It is mandatory to obtain knowledge about probability, statistics and technical skills to create data science models with complete functionality. Machine learning is also a part of artificial intelligence and is capable of performing major tasks such as data extraction, processing, and loading.

In order to develop state of the art and high performing data science models, developers are required to upgrade themselves with new skills and programming techniques. This includes in depth understanding and implementation of supervised and unsupervised techniques. In particular, data science covers major topics like data integration, distributed architecture, data visualization, and deployment in production model.

Why Learn Python for Data Analysis?

Python is an essential language for data analysis because it is flexible and easy to learn. Developers who want to create machine learning and deep learning models can use Python scripts and libraries which are easy to implement. Furthermore, the language is simple to learn which makes it ideal for beginners. Without spending much time and effort on coding, developers can utilize the functionality of Python to accomplish tasks without any hassle.

Due to its increased performance and functionality, Python has a large following and is vastly used in industrial and academic processes. There is a wide range of useful analytics libraries available for Python and users can approach to various community platforms to discuss their problems with other Python developers. Libraries such as Pandas, Numpy, and Matplotlib allow data analysts to carry out different functions smoothly.

Basics of Python for Data Analysis

Python is a general-purpose programming language that includes dedicated libraries for predictive modeling and data analysis. These built-in library packages can be used to import data from Excel spreadsheets and for processing sets for time series analysis as well. Pandas is a helpful Python Data Analysis Library that supports advanced manipulation through its powerful data frames and advanced numerical analysis features. Moreover, Pandas is built through NumPy which is one of the best libraries for data science development. Other major libraries such as SciPy, Scikit-Learn, and PyBrain are popular machine learning libraries that bring modules for developing data preprocessing and neural network models.

Better understanding and implementation of NumPy will make it convenient to work on tools like Pandas for which learning basics of Python programming language is necessary. Basics of NumPy include indexing of arrays, development with N-dimensional arrays, universal functions, statistical methods, and transposing an array to create data science models and algorithms.

NumPy

NumPy stands for "Numerical Python" and is a library that is comprised of a collection of multidimensional arrays. This library can be implemented to perform both logical and mathematical operations on arrays related to linear algebra and random number generation process. Data manipulation in Python is also performed through NumPy array and the latest Python programming tools such as Pandas are all based on this library. NumPy operations include access of data and subarrays to reshape, split and join the arrays.

In NumPy library, Ndarray is an N-dimensional array type that describes items of the same type which can also be accessed through a zero based index. Syntax to create ndarray using an array function in NumPy is defined as follows:

Numpy.array(object, dtype = None, copy = True, order = None, subok = False, ndmin =0)

For example:

Import numpy as np

A = np.array([4,5,6])

Print x

Output: [4,5,6]

2-D and 3-D arrays

2 dimensional and 3 dimensional arrays in NumPy can be defined by using the following basic syntax:

For 2 dimensional arrays:

C= np.array([3,4,5),(6,7,8)])

Print(c.shape)

(2,3)

For 3 dimensional arrays:

C= np.array([

[[3,4,5], [6,7,8]],

[[7,5,4], [34,5,22]]

])

Print (d.shape)

(2,2,3)

Now, we can also create random arrays for which random function is used. Here is an example to specify the maximum value and size of an array in NumPy:

Random_array = np.random.randint(15, size =5)

Print(random_array)

Output: [1 3 56 98 45]

Boolean array

Array12_b = np.array([2,5,10], dtype='bool')

Arr2d_b

Array([True, False, True, dtype = bool)

Size and Shape

shape

print('Shape: ', arr2.shape)

dtype

```
print('Datatype: ', arr2.dtype)

# size

 print('Size: ', arr2.size)

# ndim

print('Num Dimensions: ', arr2.ndim) #>
```

Shape: (3, 4)

#> Datatype: float64

#> Size: 12

#> Num Dimensions: 2

Min, Max and Mean Operations on ndarray

```
# mean, max and min

print("Mean value is: ", arr2.mean())

print("Max value is: ", arr2.max())

print("Min value is: ", arr2.min())
```

#> Mean value is:

#> Max value is:

#> Min value is:

Adding Two Arrays

print(two_dim_array + two_dim_array)

Output:

[[4 2 6 15]

 [20 12 55 34]]

Function to convert an input to an array:

Numpy.asarray(data, dtype=None, order=None)[source]

Linspace and logspace functions:

Numpy.linespace(start, stop, num, endpoint)

Numoy.logspace(start, stop, num, endpoint)

SciPy

SciPy Python library is a built-in package which provides different resources to work on NumPy arrays. The library is mostly used in scientific computing, technical computing, mathematics and Engineering. It can operate on an array of NumPy library and also contains different types of sub packages which can be used to solve complex problems in scientific computation.

Packages:

Name	Description

Scipy.io	File input and output
Scipy.linalg	Linear Algebra
Scipy.special	Special Function
Scipy.interpolate	Interpolation
Scipy.stats	Statistics operations
Scipy.optimize	Optimization and fit.
Scipy.signal	Signal processing
Scipy.ndimage	Multidimensional image processing
Scipy.spatial	Spatial data structures and algorithms
Scipy.sparse	Sparse
Scipy.fftpack	Fast Fourier Transforms

Basic Functions

These are the basic functions that can be performed with SciPy library in Python:

Defining Data Types

import numpy as np

arr= np.arange(3, 5, dtype = np.float)

print arr

print " This is an Array data type :".arr.dtype

Output:[3. 4. 5.]

NumPy Vector

import numpy as np

list = [6,4,2,7]

arr = np.array(list)

print arr

Output: [6,4,2,7]

Installing the SciPy library:

Pip install scipy

Importing ScipPy library:

Import scipy

Single and Double Integrals

SciPy also supports general purpose integration which has only one variable present between two points. For example:

import scipy.integrate

f= lambda x: 12*x

i = scipy.integrate.quad(f, 0, 1)

print (i)

Output:

(6.0, 6.661338147750939e-14)

Source:
https://docs.scipy.org/doc/scipy/reference/tutorial/integrate.html

For double integral, dblquad function is used which is comprised of two variables with y being the first argument and x being the second argument.

import scipy.integrate

f = lambda x, y : 12*x

g = lambda x : 0

h = lambda y : 1

i = scipy.integrate.dblquad(f, 0, 0.5, g, h)

print(i)

Output:

(3.0, 6.661338147750939e-14)

Input and Output

To load and save a .mat file, we can use loadmat, savemat, and whosmat functions for a MATLAB file. For example:

import scipy.io as sio

import numpy as np

vect = np.arange(10)

sio.savemat('array.mat', {'vect':vect})

mat_file_content = sio.loadmat('array.mat')

Print mat_file_content

Source:
https://docs.scipy.org/doc/scipy/reference/tutorial/io.html

Linear Algebra

Mathematics is the basic concept of Python. To perform calculations, SciPy offers fast linear algebra operations because it is created through BLAS and ATLAS LAPACK libraries. Method for solving a linear algebra system is defined as follows:

Problem: 1x + 2y =5

3x + 4y =6

Solution:

Import required modules/ libraries

import numpy as np

from scipy import linalg

Create input array

A= np.array([[1,2],[3,4]])

Solution Array

B= np.array([[5],[6]])

Solve the linear algebra

X= linalg.solve(A,B)

Print results

print(X)

Checking Results

print("\n Checking results, following vector should be all zeros")

```
print(A.dot(X)-B)
```

SciPy library also supports gradient optimization, integration, and special functions that are a part of numerical computation. Being an open source project, SciPy can also be used as a system prototyping and data processing environment like R-lab or MATLAB. Furthermore, high level classes and commands for data visualization and data manipulation increase the functionality and performance of SciPy Python library.

Pandas

Pandas Python library is designed with powerful data structures to support data analysis and data manipulation in data science. The library is mainly used for performing web analytics, statistics, finance and economics operations through Python programming. For processing and analysis of data, developers can consider Pandas library because it has the capability to load, organize, analyze, manipulate, and model the data for all kinds of datasets and inputs. Pandas is an efficient and fast DataFrame object which can work on both customized and default indexing.

Furthermore, developers can perform label-based slicing, sub setting, and indexing of large datasets through Pandas library. Other features include data alignment, integrated handling of missing data, reshaping of data sets and tools for loading data into memory objects. Generally, Pandas only supports Series and DataFrame data structures that are built through Numpy array.

Operations

Creating a data frame by using a dictionary of existing NumPy 2D arrays:

d_dic ={'first_col_name':c1,'second_col_names':c2 } df = pd.DataFrame(data = d_dic

Getting column names in a list:

Df.columns.tolist()

Reading data from a text file or CSV file:

df = pd.read_csv(file_path, sep=',', header = 0, index_col=False,names=None)

Reset an index to another list, array or an existing column:

new_df = df.reset_index(drop=True,inplace=False)

Remove a column:

Df.drop(columns = list of cols to drop)

Slice a dataframe for a given condition:

mask = df['age'] == age_value

or

mask = df['age'].isin(list_of_age_values)

result = df[mask]

Sorting values by column:

df.sort_values(by = list_of_cols,ascending=True)

Applying a function to all elements in a data frame:

New_df = df.applymap (f)

Generally, Pandas is based on two major components that are Series and DataFrame. Series is referred to as a column, whereas a DataFrame is a multidimensional table comprised of a collection of Series for Pandas.

Creating DataFrames

DataFrames in Pandas can be created in multiple ways. Here is a sample code for generating DataFrames through dictionary:

dict = {"country": ["Brazil", "Russia", "India", "China", "South Africa"],

    "capital": ["Brasilia", "Moscow", "New Dehli", "Beijing", "Pretoria"],

    "area": [8.516, 17.10, 3.286, 9.597, 1.221],

    "population": [200.4, 143.5, 1252, 1357, 52.98] }

import pandas as pd

brics = pd.DataFrame(dict)

print(brics)

Source: https://www.learnpython.org/en/Pandas_Basics

Creating DataFrame through CSV:

Import pandas as pd

```python
import pandas as pd


# Import the cars.csv data: cars

cars = pd.read_csv('cars.csv')


# Print out cars

print(cars)
```

Indexing DataFrames

To index a Pandas DataFrame, we can use the simple technique of square bracket notation as follows:

```python
import pandas as pd

cars = pd.read_csv('cars.csv', index_col = 0)


# Print out country column as Pandas Series

print(cars['cars_per_cap'])


# Print out country column as Pandas DataFrame

print(cars[['cars_per_cap']])


# Print out DataFrame with country and drives_right columns
```

```
print(cars[['cars_per_cap', 'country']])
```

Importing Excel File

Importing an Excel file is possible through Python, for which we can use Pandas built-in library. We can use the read_excel function to import and manipulate data from a predefined Excel file. The syntax to import an Excel file in Python is defined as follows:

import pandas as pd

df = pd.read_excel('path')

print (df)

Capturing Data

To import an Excel file into Python Pandas, we have to first capture the file path where the Excel file is located on your computer. For example:

C:\Users\Admin\Desktop\Sample.xlsx

Applying Python code:

import pandas as pd

df = pd.read_excel (r "C:\Users\Admin\Desktop\Sample.xlsx")

print (df)

Syntax to run the code:

pip install xlrd

import pandas as pd

```
df = pd.read_excel (r "C:\Users\Admin\Desktop\Sample.xlsx")

df = pd.DataFrame(data, columns= ['Price']

print (df)
```

Matplotlib

Matplotlib Python library is used to design and create 2D graphs and plots. The process is done with the help of Python scripts and it is based on a named pyplot. This pyplot provides extra features such as styles, font properties, and formatting. The package can be imported into Python script by using the statement as mentioned below:

```
from matplotlib import pyplot as plt
```

Developers can use Python Matplotlib library features to design plots, histograms, error charts, power spectra, scatter plots, and bar charts. The library provides complete functionality for all kinds of font properties, axes properties, and line styles as well.

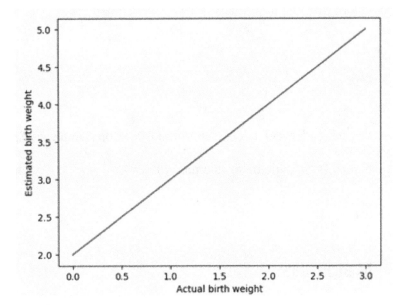

Source: https://data-flair.training/blogs/python-matplotlib-tutorial/

In the above graph, the methods xlabel() and ylabel() are used for setting labels for the x and y-axes. The values are taken from the list of parameters for y-axis whereas the values for x-axis are the four points 0.0, 1.0, 2.0 and 3.0.

Method to create pyplot interface:

Import matplotlib.pyplot as plt

Plt.plot ([2,3,4,5])

Data scientist can visualize the data to perform different types of data analysis operations. Here is an approach to plot a simple graph from matplotlib:

from matplotlib import pyplot as plt

plt.plot([1,2,3],[4,5,1])

plt.show()

Resulting graph:

Scatter Plot

For creating a scatter plot in Matplotlib, the following code based on the scatter method is used:

Fig, ax = plt.subplots()

ax. Scatter(iris['sepal_length'], iris['sepal_width])

ax.set_title('Iris Dataset')

ax.set_xlabel('sepal_length')

ax.set_ylabel('sepal_width)

Line Chart

Line chart can be created by calling the plot method in Matplotlib as follows:

Columns = iris.columns.drop(['class'])

X_data = range(0, isis.shape[0])

Fig, ax = plt.subplots()

For column in columns:

    Ax.plot(x_data, isis[column])

ax.set_title('Iris Dataset')

ax.legend()

Chapter 2: Basics of Python

Python IDE's

An Integrated Development Environment is a tool which provides facilities like build automation, testing, code lining and debugging for different programming languages. Python IDEs are best suited for developing machine learning and deep analytics models. Here are some of the best IDEs for Python programming:

Sublime Text

Sublime Text is an amazing code editor that provides high customizability and is best for beginners. Along with other popular programming languages, Sublime Text also supports Python execution and comes with a predefined support for the language. The editor can be downloaded free of cost and is considered as a full-fledged Python development environment. Sublime Text packages are written in Python programming language which provide a wide range of extensions and packages to support complex programming.

Atom

Atom is an open source integrated development environment designed and developed by Github. Users can download and install the IDE along with predefined development packages such as linter-flake8 and python-debugger. Being highly customizable, users can install packages and set up the environment to meet their development requirements.

Eclipse

Eclipse is an all-rounder integrated development environment that is available for Windows, Linux, and OS X. The tool has a rich marketplace of add-ons and extensions which makes it suitable for machine learning and Python development. Furthermore, PyDev extension allows the developers to perform Python debugging and utilize code completion facility as well.

Getting Starting with Python

Basic Syntax

For writing your first Python program, you are required to be well aware of the basic syntax and requirements of Python programming language. A Python program can be written and executed in two basic modes which are known as Interactive mode and Script mode. In Interactive mode, developers are supposed to write a program and execute it, whereas in the Script mode, files and code can be saved and accessed through Python program (.py file).

Identifiers

Identifiers are used to identify a module, class, function, or a variable in a program. In Python programming language, an identifier can be a letter from A to Z or from a to z followed by zero or more digits, underscores, or letters. Furthermore, Python language does not allow characters such as %, $ or @ within identifiers. Being a case sensitive language, programmers need to carefully place identifiers to execute the program without any error.

Python syntax can be executed by writing the following line in the command line:

>> print("Hello world!")

Hello world

Variables and Data Types

Similar to other major programming languages such as Java, C and C++, Python has predefined data types and rules for using variables. For Python programming, you must remember that a variable can have both short and descriptive variables like x, y, age or year. A variable name should always start with a letter and cannot start with a number. Moreover, variable names are case sensitive in Python and developers need to be careful when declaring variables in the program.

Data Types

Python has built-in or default data types which include text, numeric, sequence, mapping, Set and Boolean and Binary type. To get the data type in Python programming language, "type()" function can be used in the program.

Here are some examples to set data types in Python:

Sample	Data Type
x = " Python"	Str

x = 5	Int
x = 5.0	float
x = range (5)	range
x = ("Red", "Blue")	Tuple
x = ["Red", "Blue"]	list
x = True/False	Boolean
x = b "Python"	bytes

Decision Making and Basic Operators

Decision making is an essential part of any programming language because it specifies the program to take actions according to the given conditions.

If statement

Syntax:

if expression:

        statement

Sample program:

```
#!/use/bin/python

Var1 = 50

if var1:

        print"1- Expression value"

        print var1

var2 = 0

if var2:

        print "2- Expression value"

        print var 2

print "Value:"
```

If-else statement

Syntax:

if expression:

        statement

else:

        statement

Nested If statements

In a nested if statement, we can have an if, elif and else present within another if, elif and else statement. The syntax for implementing this statement is defined as follows:

If expression1:

Statement(s)

if expression2:

statement(s)

elif expression3:

statement(s)

else:

statement(s)

Functions and Modules

Python has built-in functions which can be used to create complex machine learning and deep learning models. Built in functions are also known as user defined functions. For defining a function in Python programming language, we can use the syntax as described below:

Def function name(parameters) :

"function docstring"

function suite

return [expression]

For example:

```
Def printme (str ):

    "Sample string passed into a function"

    print str

    return
```

Modules in Python programming allow developers to organize their code and develop code modules that can be used further in the program. A module is also referred to as a file made up of Python code which includes arbitrarily named attributes, classes, variables and functions. For example:

```
def print func( parameter ):

    print "Sample: ", parameter

    return
```

Furthermore, we can also import an existing module into the Python source code by using the import module support. Here are some of the import statement modules for Python programming language:

- import statement
- from.. import statement: from modname import*

Object Oriented Programming

Python is based on object-oriented programming modules which enables developers to perform different tasks through classes and objects. In OOP, a class is a user defined prototype which is defined for an object and contains a set of attributes, data members, class variables and instance variables. A class variable is shared with each instance of the class and is usually defined outside the class method. Furthermore, class variables cannot be used more often as compared to instance variables.

Instance variable is defined inside a method and only belongs to the current instance of a class. In object-oriented programming, function overloading approach is referred to as the implementation of more than one behavior to a specific function. To implement classes in a program, we are required to make use of objects and methods in the class definition. Here is the syntax to create a class in Python:

Class ClassName:

"class documentation string"

Class_suite

Sample student class in Python:

```python
class Student:

 'Base class for all Students"

 empCount = 0


 def __init__(self, name, Grade):

        self.name = name

        self.grade = grade

        Student.stuCount += 1


 def displayCount(self):
```

```
print "Total Students%d" % Student.stuCount
```

```
def displayStudent(self):
```

```
print "Name : ", self.name, ", Marks: ", self.marks
```

To access class attributes, we can use the following syntax:

```
stu.1displayStudent()
```

```
stu.2displayStudent()
```

```
print "Student %d" % Student.stuCount
```

In a Python class, there are several built-in attributes that can be accessed by using the dot operator. For example, dict, doc, name, module and bases.

Class Inheritance

In object-oriented programming, a class can be created by deriving it from an existing class. The child class inherits the attributes from its parent class and they can also be used to override data members, functions, and methods from the parent class. Furthermore, the derived classes are the same in functionality as their parent class. For example:

```
class A:        // Class A definition
```

```
..
```

```
class B:        // Class B definition
```

```
..
```

```
class C(A, B):  //Subclass A and B
```

Python syntax:

class SubClassName (ParentClass1[, ParentClass2, ..]):

"class documentation string"

Class_suite

Source:
https://www.tutorialspoint.com/python/pdf/python_classes_objects.pdf

Regular Expressions

Regular expression or RegEx is referred to as the sequence of characters which is implemented to create a search pattern. For developing machine learning and data analytics models, regular expressions are widely used for pattern matching and training of models. Python comes with a built-in regular expression module which is also known as re module or RegEx module. To import the module, we can use the "import re" statement in the program.

The re module is comprised of different functions which can be used to search a string for match. For example, search, split, sub and findall are the major functions that are used for pattern matching and learning in machine learning models.

Implementation:

findall () function

import re

str = "Machine learning"

```
x = re.findall("in", str)

print(x)
```

Search() function

```
import re

str = "Machine learning"

x = re.search("\s", str)

print("Position of first white-space character:", x.start())
```

Split () function

```
import re

str = "Machine learning"

x = re.split("\s", str)

print(x)
```

Match and Search functions

Match function has the capability to match re pattern to the string. The syntax for match function is defined as follows:

```
re.match(pattern, string, flags=0)
```

In the search function, the first occurrence of re pattern is searched within optional flags and the string. The syntax for search function is defined as follows:

```
re.search(pattern, string, flags=0)
```

Furthermore, regular expression literals can also include an optional modifier. The optional modifier has the capability to control different aspects of matching and they are also considered as an optional flag.

Exception Handling

An exception occurs during program execution and can disrupt the smooth flow of program instructions. When an exception occurs in a Python program, it can be handled through 'try' and 'except' statements as explained below:

try:

    statements

except Exception 1:

    //if exception 1 occurred, execute this block

exception 2:

    //if exception 2 occurred, execute this block

else

No exception occurred

There are different exceptions and assertions which can occur in a Python program. For example: Exception, StopIteration, SystemExit, StandardError, OverflowError, ArithmeticError, ZeroDivisionError, AssertionError, ImportError, KeyboardInterrupt, LookupError, IndexError, KeyError and NameError. It must be noted that a single try statement can have various except statements and they are only used when the try block has statements that might throw any type of exception. Furthermore, the Python program might also execute a generic except clause and handle any type of exception.

File Handling

File handling is an essential part of every web or desktop application. The approach is used to create, read, update and delete files from the database of the program. In Python programming, file handling is generally performed with open() function and includes filename and mode parameters.

Opening a File

To open a file through a Python program, we can use four different modes defined as follows:

Read: Opens file for reading and initiates an error in case the file does not exist.

Write: Opens file for writing and automatically creates a file if it is not available.

Append: Opens file for appending and creates if not available.

Create: Creates the required file and initiates an error if the file already exists.

Basic syntax for file handling operations:

To open a file: f = open("samplefile.txt"0

To open a file on server:

f = open("samplefile.txt", "r")

print(f.read())

Closing a File

f = open("Filename.txt","r")

print(f.readline())

f.close

Writing into Existing Files

f = open("samplefile.txt", "a")

f.write("New content")

f.close()

f = open("samplefile.txt", "r")

print(f.read())

Create new file: f = open("Newfile.txt", "x")

Deleting Files

To remove or delete a file in Python, you are required to import OS module for which os.remove() function is recommended. The syntax for deleting or removing a file in Python programming language is defined as follows:

import os

os.remove("Samplefile.txt")

Deleting a Folder

To delete a specific folder, we can use the following syntax:

import os

os.rmdir("Folder")

Chapter 3: Data Handling

Importing and handling datasets are the key functionalities of machine learning and artificial intelligence models. In Python programming language, there are different approaches and techniques that could be implemented to create data science projects and perform data handling operations. Comma Separated Value (CSV) files are the best suitable file format for storing and transferring data. Python provides the ability to read, write, and manipulate data to and from CSV files through Pandas library and data frames which makes it easier for data scientists to design and build machine learning models.

Importing Data with CSV files

Before building machine learning models, data scientists have to find the best suitable ways to gather and utilize datasets so that the models could be trained properly. Comma Separated Value (CSV) files are the ultimate source to import and export data for machine learning models. In Python programming language, Pandas library is used to deal with operations for importing and loading CSV files. Before using the file system, it is mandatory that you know where the data is located and what is the current working directory. All the information and data in computers is stored in directories which are generally known as folders.

There are different factors which need to be focused when importing data from CSV files. A CSV file has a predefined header that helps in assigning names to each column of data and in case the header is not available, you will have to define the names and attributes manually. Furthermore, you can also explicitly specify whether or not your CSV file had a header when loading the data. Generally, CSV files have a "#" sign at the start of a line which is used to indicate comments in the file. Depending upon the method, we can use different comments and characters to give information regarding the CSV file.

Loading CSV Files

CSV files are an essential part of machine learning models for which Python API comes with a predefined CSV module and reader() function to lead CSV files. After the loading is complete, the CSV data can be converted into a NumPy array to be used for building machine learning models.

Function to load CSV data through NumPy:

#load CSV

import numpy

filename = "Samplefile.csv"

rawdata = open(filename, 'rt')

data = numpy.loadtxt(rawdata, delimiter=",")

print(data.shape)

Function to Load CSV Data Through Pandas

We can also import data or CSV files through Pandas read.csv() function which is best suitable for building machine learning models. The syntax to implement read.csv() function is defined as follows:

#load CSV from Pandas

```
import pandas

filename = 'Samplefile.csv'

data = pandas.readcsv(filename, names= names)

print(data.shape)
```

Loading CSV File Data through Python Standard Library

Python language comes with a predefined API which provides reader() function and CSV module to load CSV files into the program. Once the data has been loaded, the CSV file can be converted into a NumPy array for utilizing it in machine learning models. Basic syntax for loading CSV file data through Python standard library is described as follows:

```
#load CSV

import csv

import numpy

filename = "Samplefile.csv"

rawdata = open(filename, 'rt')

reader = csv.reader(rawdata, delimiter=',')

x = list(reader)

data = numpy.array(x).astype('float')

print(data.shape)
```

Source: https://machinelearningmastery.com/load-machine-learning-data-python/

File System

Importing CSV files and data is possible by using Pandas and Python standard library. Before starting with importing data, it is mandatory that the developer is aware of file system location of data and the current working directory. 'ls' command is used to list all content in the current working directory whereas the 'cd' command gives you the name of the sub directory in which you can change your working directory. Furthermore, 'pwd' command can be considered to print the path of your current working directory and '..' command to navigate back to the parent directory of your current working directory.

To execute Shell commands directly from IPython, we can use IPython console which includes various magic command lines capable of performing multiple operations with a single command. When importing external files, we are required to focus on some important aspects to avoid any problems in execution of the program. You must make sure that data type variable is in a consistent date format and consider special values as missing values. Furthermore, check whether the header row is present or not and make sure that no truncation of rows occurs while fetching external data.

Importing Data File from URL

Here is the simple Python syntax to import file from URL in read_csv() function:

sampledata = pd.read_csv(http://sampleurl/file.csv)

Importing R data file

To import R data file, we can use pyreadr package and load .Rds and .RData format files from the R data frame by using the following syntax:

import pyreadr

result = pyreadr.read_r('C/desktop/sample.RData')

print(result.keys()

df1 = result["df1"]

Import Data from SQL Server and Tables Stored in SQL

We can read information and data from SQL Server by building a connection for which database details including server and user ID are required. Python syntax for importing data from tables in a database is defined as follows:

import pandas as pd

import pyodbc

conn – pyodbc.connect("Driver={SQL Server};Server=servername;UID=username;PWD=password;database=RCO_DW;")

df = pd.readsqlquerry('select*from dbTable WHERE AGE > 20', conn)

df.head()

Summarizing Data

Python gives us the power of packages, libraries, and data frames to perform manipulation and aggregation on data sets. Pandas library has built in functions which allow programmers to split a specific data set into subsets on a known criterion. Furthermore, you can also apply a function or a set of functions in your code to combine different results together. The goal of Pandas library is to perform data analysis by giving appropriate functions and data structures.

Splitting Data

After the data has been loaded, we can divide it into groups for which the following Python syntax is recommended:

bytreatment = data.groupby("Treatment")

bytreatment["Relalative Fitness"].describe()

Application of Data Functions

Grouped data can be manipulated into different forms by using statistical techniques in machine learning and deep learning models. In this regard, the describe() method is used to produce statistics for grouped data such as mean(), median() and max(). Furthermore, other arbitrary functions can also be applied over groups of data by using aggregate agg() method . For example:

bygroup.treatment["Sample"].aggregate(np.sum)

Or

bygroup.treatment["Sample"].aggregate(np.sum, np.mean, sp.std, len])

Furthermore, JSON files can also be used to store and manipulate data as text in human readable format. Pandas library comes with built in JSON files for which read_json function can be used. JSON is also known as JavaScript Object Notation and is saved with .json extension.

To input data using JSON file, we can use the following Python syntax:

import pandas as pd

data = pd.read_json('file/input path.json')

print (data)

Source: https://www.shanelynn.ie/summarising-aggregation-and-grouping-data-in-python-pandas/

Similarly, JSON function can also be used to read specific columns and rows from a CSV file. Pandas library supports read_json function which is implemented to read specific columns and rows after the JSON file is loaded into the DataFrame. Moreover, we can also use the .loc() method to load JSON file which is also known as the multi-axes indexing method.

Groupby method returns a groupby object which originally describes how the rows of original data have been split. The output of aggregation and groupby operations are different for Pandas Dataframes and Pandas Series for which we have to select the operation column separately. Moreover, the groupby output will be based on an index or multi-index rows depending upon the selected grouping variables.

Python Aggregation

Aggregation is generally performed through NumPy and Pandas libraries in Python. In most of the cases, the file data is not of a similar type or format and we are required to combine or group data into sets for further processing. However, in most of the cases, an aggregation function includes different rows combined together by the implementation of statistical algorithms like count, maximum, average, mean, mode, or median. In Python, data is aggregated to ensure the privacy of datasets and make it easier to analyze.

The most important aspect of using data aggregation is to meet legal and privacy concerns for a machine learning model. It is required that the data should be called to the group by using groupby() function to map values. The values can then be indexed and rely on the transform() function to develop aggregated data through NumPy and Pandas algorithms in Python programming language. Sample program showing aggregation in Python:

```
import pandas as pd

import numpy as np


df = pd.DataFrame(np.random.randn(10, 4),

        index = pd.date_range('5/4/2010', class=5),

        columns = ['1', '2', '3', '4'])


print df
```

r = df.rolling(window=3,min_class=2)

print r

Source: https://www.w3resource.com/python-exercises/pandas/python-pandas-data-frame-exercise-4.php

Unstructured Data

Data that is formatted in columns and rows can be simply converted into different structures to be implemented in the development of machine learning models. XLS, CSV and TXT files are the best examples of structured data because they have a predefined limiter and fixed width. On the other hand, there is data which does not have a specific format and is also known as unstructured data. Python libraries and predefined functions can be used to process unstructured files and utilize the data for processing.

The following example illustrates the reading of unstructured data in Python:

filename = 'input_data.txt'

with open(filename) as fn:

Read each line

ln = fn.readline()

Keep count of lines

lncnt = 1

while ln:

```
print("Line {}: {}".format(lncnt, ln.strip()))

    ln = fn.readline()

    lncnt += 1
```

Output:

Line 1: Python is a high-level programming language.

Line 2: It has a design philosophy that general-purpose interpreted,emphasizes code readability, notably using significant whitespace, interactive, object-oriented, and high-level programming language.

Line 3: It has grown from humble beginnings into one of the most popular programming languages on the planet.

Source: http://python-ds.com/python-processing-unstructured-data

Data Preparation for Analysis and Evaluation

Machine Learning and Artificial Intelligence models learn from the datasets and information they are fed with. Depending upon the labels and attributes of data, the models get trained to perform various operations and tasks in the future without human intervention. Data preparation is the first step that is performed after the data has been collected from one or more sources so that it is cleaned and transformed. Moreover, it is often merged with different sources having various levels of data and structures of data quality.

In order to create meaningful data insights, machine learning engineers and data scientists have to prepare data for analysis and outline the best sources to combine vital information and data.

How to Prepare Data

To prepare data for machine learning and predictive analysis models, we are required to focus on some simple approaches which will help us in collecting high quality data. After the objectives of model for predictive analysis have been defined, we can begin with data preparation. At first, you must identify your data sources because structured and unstructured data is available in different formats and types. Furthermore, data is mostly owned by a third party for which you need to acquire permissions to utilize the data.

Secondly, select the variables to add into your analysis for which you can start with multiple variables and eliminate the ones which offer no predictive values for the model. In most of the cases, derived variables have a greater direct impact on the model as compared to the raw variables which can in return affect performance of the machine learning model. To evaluate the quality of data, we need to understand the limitations and state of data because accuracy of the model is directly dependent upon data quality.

Although selecting and cleaning data is time consuming and requires a lot of hard effort, there are several effective data preparation techniques which can be followed to yield best results. Accuracy of machine learning models is directly dependent on the quality and accuracy of the training data.

How to Determine the Quality of Data

To explore the quality of input data, we need to understand the limitations and statistics that are required to operate the machine learning model with high accuracy. Make sure that the data is complete and perform any filtration before feeding the training data into the machine learning model. Furthermore, you are required to fill in the missing values or eliminate them if not needed. To perform analyzation and quality assurance, we can implement regression algorithms. Classification algorithms have the capability to analyze discrete data whereas the association algorithms can be considered for data having correlated attributes.

Datasets which are used to train and test the model should contain relevant business information. This will help companies to support their customers in a better way and provide them with the most suitable services as well. Smaller data files which have a good native structure can be opened through spreadsheets or editors, whereas larger or complicated datasets need to be handled with extraction or transformation software. Statistical adjustments can be applied to data which requires scale and weighting transformations. This will also help in cleaning data reviews for consistencies because generally inconsistencies may be found because of extreme, out of range or faulty logic.

In Big Data systems, preparing large datasets is time consuming and requires effort. To begin with the procedure, following data preparation rules on the sample data will reduce latency of iterative exploration and will make it easier to figure out large datasets. Data cleaning approach is used to find and eliminate errors in data.

Creating and Formatting New Variables

After the training data has been collected and finalized, the next step is to set up the variables which will directly respond to research queries and questions. Generally, datasets do not include measured variables and you are required to set up each variable individually. These operations include creating change scores, combining multiple categories of nominal variables, centering predictions and creating indices from scales.

Newly created and original variables need to be formatted properly for major reasons. Firstly, if you do not format a missing value or a dummy variable it will directly affect data analysis and predictions of your machine learning model. Secondly, it will save a lot of time and effort if a faulty variable is removed at first because setting all missing data codes and formatting date variables or numerical numbers will also remove any future discrepancies.

In Python development, we can take support from built-in libraries such as Pandas and NumPy to classify datasets and make separate groups. Data which is collected randomly features different categorical values and we need to label each variable before making it a part of training data. Based on the knowledge of business analytics goal and results of different data cleansing strategies, we can arrange the relevant data into a usable format without any hassle.

Underfitting and Overfitting

Underfitting and overfitting are two of the major issues which arise when building machine learning models and need to be overcome when handling input data. Underfitting occurs whenever a model is unable to detect relationships from data and it also indicates the essential variables to be included. On the other hand, overfitting begins whenever a machine learning model includes data having no predictive power and is only suitable for the given dataset.

Furthermore, if the machine learning algorithm or a statistical model captures vulnerable data it is known to be affected with overfitting. As a result, the algorithm shows high variance and low bias which in return affects its overall predictive powers. Overfitting and underfitting result in poor predictions on new data sets and greatly affect the performance of machine learning models. Nonetheless, we have to focus on validation and cross validation when building machine learning models to avoid overfitting and underfitting in each case.

Datasets which are used for the training of machine learning models are featured with multiple predictors. This helps businesses to avail accurate predictions and data insights in the long run from machine learning models.

Generalization

Machine learning models are known to learn from training data. The learning of target function from training data in the model is referred to as inductive learning because the aim of machine learning models is to apply specific rules and scenarios while generating outcomes. Generalization tells us how well the machine learning models have adapted the rules and information from training data and allows the model to make accurate predictions for the future. Overfitting and underfitting can surely make a machine learning model useless because they make it impossible for the models to learn from given datasets.

Generalization is also used to describe the ability of a model to react to new data and it usually happens when a model is being trained on a specific training dataset. If a model is trained well and accurately on training data, it will be unable to generalize the data and will make relevant predictions in future. Supervised machine learning models also make predictions based on the training data for which the outcome is already known. Predictions and outcomes from the model are then compared with the actual data and the model's parameters are changed to achieve desired results.

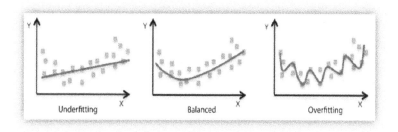

The above figure demonstrates underfitting, balanced, and overfitting graphs for a machine learning model. Based on the training data, the model notes that there is not a specific trend in data to capture relevant information, and because of this it is unable to make accurate predictions for new training data. This concept is known as underfitting and is illustrated by a straight blue line. In the middle, the line is representing a balanced model and shows the trend in data that could be easily generalized. Furthermore, on the right the line showcases a model which is too specific and inaccurately models the training data. This concept is also known as overfitting.

Chapter 4: Building Machine Learning Models

Interpreting machine learning and deep learning models is a complex task for which in depth understanding regarding data handling and ML algorithms is necessary. Nowadays, most of the businesses are relying on deep learning and AI models to drive their strategy and achieve best outcomes. Modern day examples of machine learning models are face recognition systems, self-driving vehicles and voice recognition systems such as Siri and Alexa. In-depth knowledge about statistics and linear recognition models is mandatory to design and build efficient machine learning models by using Python modules including Matplotlib, Pandas, and NumPy.

Data Science

Data science is a source of finding certain patterns in datasets and training data which are utilized by machine learning models to make accurate predictions. Initially, activities to build machine learning algorithms such as data mining were performed through basic statistical methods, but with the evolution of programming languages and modules, Python and R deliver support to different computing packages that are based on statistics-focused approaches.

There are different steps involved in the collection of data. At first, data is collected from various sources and is then classified into structured and unstructured data categories. Next, the derived data is explored and transformed to remove any discrepancies. Aggregation and labeling of data are usually performed by a data scientist for which various machine learning and artificial intelligence algorithms are implemented. Once the goal is clear, we can set an evaluation protocol and decide how the ongoing progress will be measured. This will also help in determining the performance and capability of the machine learning model.

The process of training a machine learning model through data science techniques involves the selection of ML algorithms. There are different ways to deploy machine learning models for which we can make use of data modeling techniques.

Acquisition and Data Gathering

Before the training model is loaded with the annotated data, we must focus on predictive maintenance approaches. These approaches also help in upgrading performance of ML models and also improve their efficiency with time. With the availability of new data, we are given opportunities to make better decisions and consider best suitable variables for predictive maintenance.

Failure of machine learning models can also be minimized through root cause analysis. Predictive maintenance is generally performed through root cause analysis for which machine learning engineers have to determine the likelihood and occurrence of events. To get started with predictive maintenance, we need to feed high quality data into machine learning models and get the required insights as well. If there is a lot of usage information such as maintenance logs, it is compulsory that correct identifiers and variables are used to identify connectivity between the data sets.

DataRobot is a highly efficient automated machine learning platform that allows researchers and machine learning engineers to develop models that deliver accurate predictions and long-term insights. Furthermore, it also streamlines the data science process so that users get high quality predictions within a short period of time.

Data Pipelines

A machine learning system undergoes an extensive number of data processing workflows and has to perform multiple operations like cleaning and ingesting data. The process of developing and deploying continuously can lead to complications which need to be handled immediately to avoid any kind of unwanted scenarios. Machine learning pipelines have different parts and steps which are used to train the model. These models are cyclical and iterative because each step is directly linked with the other one. One after another, each process is repeated and to build better machine learning models, we need to derive scalable and accurate development techniques.

Data that is extracted from large datasets is also known as Big Data and is responsible for actionable insights in future. New connections and precise predictions can be performed with the support of data pipelines and it is not all about storing data, but we need to focus on achieving better outcomes. Today, most of the machine learning models are trained through neural networks and have the capability to perform a specific task in multiple ways. Machine learning deployment and development pipelines are separate from each other for which the data is supposed to be retrained or upgraded.

Furthermore, the pipeline approach also helps in releasing new versions and upgradations of machine learning models for which real time data is utilized. There are several tools, libraries and frameworks available for data scientists to work with pipeline methods. After the data has been collected and processed through data pipelines, the next step is to filter, aggregate and consolidate it before transferring the dataset to a permanent data store. Databases like SQL Azure and SQL Server are best suitable for handling machine learning data. Moreover, a machine learning pipeline helps to automate machine learning workflows and improves performance of models as well.

Challenges for Machine Learning Pipelines

Developing machine learning pipelines requires the data scientists to perform extensive research and evaluation. Generally, the process is divided into three sub categories which are data quality, data accessibility, and data reliability. Each of these categories is responsible for the performance, efficiency, and management of machine learning pipelines. Machine learning models need to be fed with accurate and complete training data so that they deliver the best suitable outcomes. The greater the availability of high-quality training data, the more accurate and reliable outcomes are achieved.

When it comes to data reliability, data scientists are supposed to determine the reliability of data and analyze its accessibility and source of generation as well. In most cases, implementation of a repository for data outcomes which serves as a single source of truth is necessary. Moreover, single source repositories allow machine learning models to run from multiple locations through a data center. Data reliability also helps in avoiding varying and duplicate versions of data so that analytical teams are always provided accurate and reliable data.

One of the major challenges that is being faced by data

scientists for building machine learning model pipelines is data accessibility. Before the model is implemented into the system for commercial use, it undergoes deep cleaning and cleansing. This activity is performed to remove redundant and irrelevant data during the pre-analysis stage. In the development of machine learning model pipelines, feature extraction approach allows the developers to extract existing features along with their associated transformations into the latest formats to describe variances between data. Once the data is cleansed, it can easily be aggregated and combined with other cleansed data.

Object Storage in Machine Learning Pipelines

Machine learning pipelines tend to get better with time. True value occurs when more data points are collected along with different data assets which are collected from multiple sources. The activity of correlating new data formats into the data center is a complex task and various sets of applications are required to handle massive data load. In machine learning model development, cloud storage and object storage systems play a vital role because they serve a great purpose and support custom data formats as well.

Data analysts and scientists also consider mapping of statistical methods to solve key problems for object storage in machine learning models. For quick business implementation, data scientists prefer to store everything locally and not in a public cloud because it takes more time and effort to extract information when needed. There is an abundance of machine learning content and immediate access is mandatory to maintain the performance and efficiency of machine learning models. Furthermore, each step in the process is iterative and cyclical which makes it convenient to upgrade and manage the algorithms.

Architecture of Machine Learning Pipelines

Machine learning pipelines are designed and architected through a predefined model. As it involves batch processing and handling of data to perform different operations, a machine learning pipeline has special features which allow it to make accurate predictions and insights. A pipeline is comprised of different stages and each stage is fed with processed data from its preceding stage. In the preprocessing stage, scientists use data mining techniques for data preprocessing which also involves transferring raw data into an understandable format. Data taken from external resources in often inconsistent and incomplete for which various treatment procedures are applied to remove the inaccuracies.

Constructing pipelines gives several advantages and makes it easier to implement machine learning models. The units of computation for ML pipelines are quite easy to replace and are highly flexible as well. Upgrading or changing a single part of the system can be done without dismantling the entire system. Every part of computation can be controlled through a common interface and if any part is not performing up to the mark, engineers can scale that component independently as well. Furthermore, the functionality and performance of machine learning pipelines can be increased by adding extensions into the system.

Pipelines are based on the approach of overnight batch processing which includes collection of data, sending of data, and processing it through multiple channels to feed the machine learning models. Predictions and features in pipelines are highly time sensitive because its performance is directly dependent on online model analytics and offline data recovery. Online model analytics represents the operational component of the system and is generally applied for real-time decision-making approaches. On the other hand, the offline data recovery method represents the learning component of ML pipelines and utilizes the historical data to create machine learning models through batch processing.

Online and Offline Layers

Gathering and funneling the incoming data into storage is the first step of creating any kind of machine learning workflow. Without undertaking any transformation, we can have an immutable record of original dataset for which the data can be fed from multiple sources or obtained from other services as well. Generally, data scientists use NoSQL document databases to store large volumes of constantly changing structured and unstructured data.

Online ingestion service is the gateway to streaming architecture in machine learning pipelines because it decouples and completely manages the workflow as well. The information from data sources is processed and transferred to storage components for which the system ensures better reliability, low latency, and high throughput. Offline layers in the machine learning pipelines utilize ingestion services to confirm data flows into the raw data store. To perform this activity, a repository pattern is used to interact with a data service and also with the data store. As soon as the data is received and saved in the data store, it is automatically assigned a batch ID which allows efficient querying and traceability.

Ingestion distribution in machine learning pipelines ensures that there is a separate pipeline for each dataset and all of them are processed and managed independently. Furthermore, the data is partitioned within each pipeline to take benefit of multiple server cores and processors in the system. Furthermore, spreading the data preparation through multiple pipelines horizontally and vertically also reduces the overall time to complete the workflow.

For example:

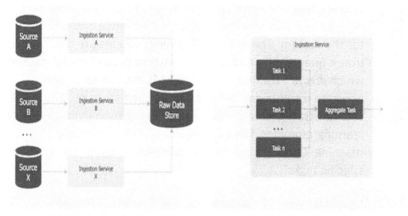

Dedicated pipeline for each dataset   Within each pipeline: distribution into parallel tasks

Source: https://towardsdatascience.com/architecting-a-machine-learning-pipeline-a847f094d1c7

As briefed in the diagram above, we can notice that ingestion services operate regularly on a predefined schedule or depend on a trigger. As it is supposed to fetch data from thousands of sources each day, the producer system automatically releases a message to the broker so that the embedded notification service gives prompt response to the subscription.

In both of these layers, we can see that a distributed pipeline is developed which examines the condition of data and searches for various trends, formats, differences and skewed data. Furthermore, it is mandatory that the correct design pattern is chosen before developing machine learning pipelines in order to ensure consistency and better outputs from training data.

Data Segregation

Data segregation splits the subsets of the given data in order to train machine learning models. Apart from training, data segregation also analyzes model performance and efficiency for the system. The machine learning systems are designed to utilize quality data and perform pattern prediction for data on which it is not trained. This allows ML models to deliver accurate insights and predictions on each scenario. There are several strategies to perform data segregation in machine learning pipelines. Data segregation is not separately a machine learning pipeline and is known as an API to facilitate specific tasks.

Model training of machine learning pipelines is usually performed offline because the schedule is strictly dependent upon the criticality of application. Moreover, service and maintenance time can also affect learning of a machine learning pipeline for which schedulers can be implemented.

Parallelization

Machine learning models have a dedicated pipeline which allows all of the models to run concurrently. To apply the parallelization technique, we are required to parallelize all of the training data which is partitioned. Each of the partitions has a copy of the original model and it is preferred that all of the fields of instance perform computation on their own. Furthermore, a machine learning model can also be parallelized by itself for which the model is completely partitioned. Each partition is responsible for handling and updating each portion of parameters. This approach is best suitable for Linear machine learning models such as SVM and LR.

Training of machine learning pipelines is implemented with slight error tolerance. The model training service is supposed to get training configuration parameters and hyper-parameters from configuration services. This approach allows the model to utilize the configuration service and fetch the training dataset from Data Segregation API. As a result, the dataset which is sent to all of the other models is complete and is based on the original configuration.

In machine learning model pipelines, the Model Evaluation Service is applied to request evaluation dataset from Data Segregation API. This activity is done for each model which is directly sourced from the model candidate repository and also applies relevant evaluators as well. As a result, the evaluation is saved back to the repository and becomes a part of the hyperparameter and iterative process techniques.

Importance of Metadata

Python programming language is best suited for the development of machine learning models and pipelines. Data scientists and analysts who are determined to achieve the best predictions and efficiency from ML models get support from Python libraries and functions. One of the major tasks for developing machine learning models is the extraction of metadata. Once a pipeline or model is trained sufficiently, it can be made operational for industries, businesses, and brands to yield accurate data insights.

Traditionally, file-based network attached storage (NAS)

architecture was used to figure out data which had to be traversed with each operation. With thousands of directories waiting to be processed, the activity took a lot of time and effort. As a solution, object storage and ML training approaches were implemented in the architecture of artificial intelligence and deep learning models. In an object storage platform, data including text documents, files, or videos can be stored as a single object. To make things manageable, metadata is attached with the files which provides descriptive information regarding the captured data.

Model Evaluation

Evaluating a machine learning model is a crucial step of the development procedure. Although ML models yield satisfying results when trained on proper data sets, we are required to evaluate the performance, efficiency, and reliability to achieve best results in future. There are several evaluation metrics defined to examine the accuracy and response of machine learning models. We can see how the model generalizes and forecasts on unseen data as it directly affects the performance of machine learning pipelines as well. To evaluate the aspects in a better way, we need to understand how the model actually works and whether we can trust its predictions or not.

Generally, the methods for evaluating the performance of machine learning models are separated into two categories, namely cross validation and holdout. Both of these methods utilize a test data to evaluate model performance and it is never feasible to use the data which we used to build the model to examine it in future.

The following techniques are the best source of measuring performance and evaluating the efficiency of machine learning models:

Confusion Matrix

Confusion matrix is an approach which provides a complete detail of correct and incorrect classifications. For a confusion matrix, we need to remember a few key points so that the efficiency can be calculated properly. Accuracy is the part of the total number of correct predictions made by the model, whereas the positive predictive value is considered as the part of positive cases identified correctly. Negative prediction value in machine learning models is the part of negative cases which were identified correctly, whereas specificity identifies the proportion of actual negative cases that are identified correctly.

At first, we can take an N x N matrix and consider N as the number of classes for prediction as follows:

	Class1 Predicted	Class 2 Predicted
Class 1 actual	TP	FN
Class 2 actual	FP	TN

A confusion matrix can be examined through the following important terms:

1. True Positives - Occurs for cases in which Yes was

predicted whereas the actual output is also the same.

2.   True Negatives - Occurs for the cases in which NO was predicted whereas the actual output is also the same.

3.   False Positives - Occurs for the cases in which Yes was predicted whereas the real output is NO.

4.   False Negatives - Occurs for the cases in which No was predicted whereas the real output is YES.

Classification rate or accuracy for a machine learning model can be calculated from the equation below:

$$\text{Accuracy} = \frac{TP + TN}{TP + TN + FP + FN}$$

Taking the example of a cancer detection model, we can consider that the actual chances of having cancer are quite low for which a probability of 10 out of 100 is possible. We will never want to miss any patient in this case who has cancer but remains undetected. In this case, detecting every patient as not having cancer yields an accuracy of 90% for which the machine learning model can be held accountable.

F1 Score

The F1 score in machine learning and data analytics models is known as the harmonic mean of recall and precision. The score utilizes the contribution of precision and recall calculations to analyze the performance of a machine learning model. Moreover, if the model performs well in F1 score, it will have a higher ratio of making accurate predictions as compared to the model which has a lower F1 score.

Formula to calculate F1 score:

$$F_1 = \left(\frac{\text{recall}^{-1} + \text{precision}^{-1}}{2} \right)^{-1} = 2 \cdot \frac{\text{precision} \cdot \text{recall}}{\text{precision} + \text{recall}}$$

Logarithmic Loss

Logarithmic loss approach is used to evaluate the performance of a classification model. To evaluate logarithmic loss through mathematical calculation, we need take prediction input probability ranging from 0 to 1. With the increase of logarithmic log or log loss, the predicted probability changes from the actual label to minimize the end value.

PR Curve

Precision and Recall curve are the best way to represent properties of a classifier. PR curve is the curved formed between recall and precision for different threshold values. For example:

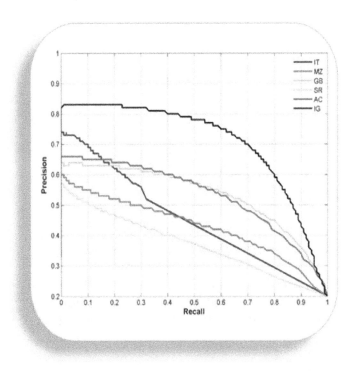

Source: https://github.com/MenuPolis/MLT/wiki/PR-Curve

From the above graph, we can notice that precision is represented by the fraction of blue circle or retrieved documents that are used as TP. Upon a low precision value, the system will have to search through different irrelevant searches to find the required value. Furthermore, we can repeat the search by eliminating an unwanted meaning of the searched word. For machine learning models, precision is considered as a measure of usefulness whereas recall is known as a measure of completeness.

Chapter 5: Machine Learning Algorithms

Before starting a data science or machine learning project in Python programming language, understanding the ideas, concepts, and functionality of ML models is compulsory. Whether you want to load data into the model or evaluate its performance, the parameters set in machine learning algorithms can help in achieving the best outcomes. As discussed earlier, data can be extracted, uploaded, and managed through Python libraries like NumPy and Pandas. In machine learning, the most commonly used format for data is known as Comma-Separated Values or CSV format, which is also applicable for storing and handling files.

Introduction to Model Handling

With the increasing demand in big data analytics and deep learning, machine learning has become a popular approach for solving real life and business problems. The approach is widely used in system development for various fields including health care, computational finance, computer vision, image processing, and computational biology. Furthermore, data science plays a vital role in automotive, energy production, and natural language processing systems.

The models are programmed to find natural patterns in data and generate insight for making accurate predictions in the future. Basically, machine learning models are divided into two major categories called supervised learning and unsupervised learning. Because machine learning models have the capability to find non linear dependencies between input data, we need to check before making any changes in our data because it can create cascading effects on downstream systems and model accuracy.

Linear Regression in Python

Artificial Intelligence and machine learning systems have the capability to handle large amounts of data which makes them best suited for powerful computers. Linear regression is one of the major parts of machine learning and deep learning algorithms because it is based upon the fundamentals of statistics and mathematics.

Regression

The term "Regression" refers to the search for relationships amongst variables in datasets. It is considered as a statistical measurement to determine the strength of a relationship between an independent variable, and the approach is widely implemented in the finance industry. Regression analysis is one popular technique used by researchers and data scientists to understand the phenomenon of interest and findings of different observations.

To implement regression in machine learning models, we are required to find a function that maps variables and features to others in an effective way. Dependent features are also known as dependent responses, outputs, or variables, whereas the independent features can be referred to as independent predictors, inputs, or variables in machine learning. Generally, regression problems result due to unbounded and continuous dependent variables for which the data needs to be handled with different techniques.

Why is Regression Important?

Regression is a useful approach to forecast a response by the support of new predictors and datasets. For machine learning models and deep learning analytics, linear regression is a widely used regression technique because it delivers great ease of comparing and interpreting results. Furthermore, implementation of linear regression in machine learning models is now possible with Python libraries and functions.

The below graph represents linear regression in machine learning models:

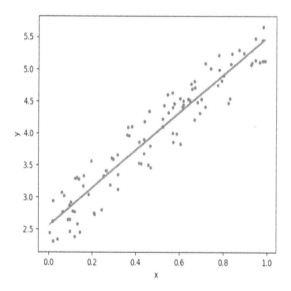

Equation to represent linear regression model:

$$Y = \theta_0 + \theta_1 x_1 + \theta_2 x_2 + \ldots + \theta_n x_n$$

Python implementation for creating random dataset to train machine learning models:

```
import numpy as np

import matplotlib.pyplot as plt

# generate random data-set

np.random.seed(0)

x = np.random.rand(100, 1)

y = 2 + 3 * x + np.random.rand(100, 1)

# plot

plt.scatter(x,y,s=10)

plt.xlabel('x')

plt.ylabel('y')

plt.show()
```

Source: https://towardsdatascience.com/linear-regression-using-python-b136c91bf0a2

In linear regression model graphs, we can notice the error line between the observed and predicted values which is also known as regression line or the line of best fit.

Types of Linear Regression Models

Linear relationship

It is the linear relationship between feature variables and response in a machine learning model. Linear relationship can be described by the following graphs:

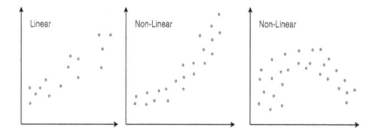

Homoscedasticity

Homoscedasticity is known as an error term that occurs as a result of a random disturbance between the dependent and independent variables.

Multiple Linear Regression

Multiple linear regression occurs in an event of linear regression between two or more independent variables in a machine learning model. The estimated regression function for two independent variables can be represented through the equation $f(x_1, x_2) = b_0 + b_1x_1 + b_2x_2$. If there are more than two independent variables, we can determine the value of estimated regression function through the equation $f(x_1, ..., x_r) = b_0 + b_1x_1 + \cdots + b_rx_r$.

Polynomial Regression

Polynomial Regression is an essential part of linear regression because the polynomial dependence for inputs and outputs is considered as the polynomial estimated regression function. The equation to calculate polynomial regression is $f(x) = b_0 + b_1x + b_2x^2$.

Implementation

On a given dataset, we can use different Python libraries to implement linear regression. Here is the program to import all of the required libraries and read the dataset in Python:

```
import numpy as np

import pandas as pd

import seaborn as sns

import matplotlib.pyplot as plt

from sklearn import preprocessing, svm

from sklearn.model_selection import train_test_split

from sklearn.linear_model import LinearRegression

df = pd.read_csv('sample.csv')

df_binary = df[['Python',]]

df_binary.columns = ['Age', 'Year']

df_binayr.head()
```

Syntax for data cleaning:

```
Df_binary.fillna(method = 'fill', inplace = True)
```

Scikit Learn

Scikit-Learn is a built-in Python library which is exclusively designed for the development of machine learning models. The library provides complete support and execution for major machine learning algorithms including random forest, k-neighbors, and linear regression. Furthermore, libraries such as NumPy and SciPy can also become a part of Scikit-Learn Python library to develop state of the art and high performance machine learning models. Scikit-learning library is designed to make machine learning development easier through Python programming language because of its various data handling and plotting techniques that help to visualize data.

Loading Data Sets

Loading datasets is the first step of developing ML models through Sci-kit learn Python programming technique. Each process and activity in data science starts with loading data, and this approach is more suitable for observed data. Before loading data into the program, make sure it is free of any independencies or mistakes so that accurate data visuals and results could be attained. Furthermore, finding datasets is challenging, for which you can also create your own sets of data to implement within the Sci-kit learn algorithm.

To load data into the program, we are required to import datasets module from sklearn and implement the load_digits() method. Python syntax to load data:

#import datasets from sk-learn

from sklearn import

digits = datasets.load_digits()

print

The dataset's module includes other methods to load and fetch reference datasets and we can also consider this in the case of artificial data generators. Moreover, the dataset can be inherited through the UCI Repository as well.

Exploring Data

After you are done with loading data, the next step is to start exploring the dataset for which Python libraries provide simple methods to be implemented. Scikit-learn library does not provide information related to data and if you are importing data from another source, there is a slight detail given about data which can be used to generate insights during model development.

If you are using the read_csv() module to import data, you can have a dataframe which contains just the data. No information related to the dataset is given in this case, but you will implement head() and tails() methods to inspect data. Data exploration is an essential step in the development of machine learning or data science projects. Even a quick evaluation for data can give true insights related to quality and reliability of the datasets.

Predicting and Learning

Datasets including numbers, images, or text files can be examined through sklearn.svm.SVC estimator class. The estimator class in Python can be set by using the following syntax:

from sklearn import svm

clf = svm.SVC(gamma= 0.005, C =50)

In Scikit-learn library, the estimator for classification can also be implemented through fit(x,y) and predict(T) methods. For classifier, we can use the clf estimator which must learn from the model. Furthermore, the method is completed by passing the training set to the fit method in the Scikit-learn library and for the training set, we can use all images or text from our dataset.

How to Split Data into Training and Test Sets Through Scikit-learn

To assess a machine learning model's performance, we can divide the data set into two parts which can also be named as a test set and a training set. Training set is used to train the system whereas the test set is implemented to evaluate the trained or learned system. In Scikit-learn, we can apply train_test_split() method along with the random_state argument to split data sets in the program. For example:

from sklearn.cross_validation import

X_train, X_test, y_train, y_test, images_train,

images_test = train_test_split(data, digits.target, digits.images, test_size=0.25, random_state=42)

Creating a DataFrame

Before splitting, we are required to create a DataFrame for which importing Pandas library is mandatory. Python syntax for creating a DataFrame is defined as follows:

import numpy as np

from sklearn.preprocessing import MinMaxScaler

sampleData – np.random.randint(50, 100)

sampleData

scalar_model = MinMaxScalar()

feature_data = scalar_model.fit_transform(sampleData)

feature_data

Output for the above program:

```
In [22]: scalar_model = MinMaxScaler()
         feature_data = scalar_model.fit_transform(demoData)
         feature_data

         /anaconda3/lib/python3.6/site-packages/sklearn/utils/validation.py:475: DataConversionWarning: Data with input dtype
         int64 was converted to float64 by MinMaxScaler.
         warnings.warn(msg, DataConversionWarning)

Out[22]: array([[0.        , 0.27602906, 0.13174946, 0.17372881],
                 [0.95081967, 0.75302663, 0.42548596, 0.05508475],
                 [0.8989071 , 0.31234867, 0.32613391, 0.77118644],
                 [0.38251366, 0.49394673, 0.        , 0.31144068],
                 [0.7704918 , 0.22760291, 0.83585313, 0.875     ],
                 [0.43169399, 0.52542373, 0.26131909, 1.        ],
                 [0.20491803, 0.07021792, 0.31317493, 0.74788136],
                 [0.81040109, 0.57869249, 0.16844652, 0.52118644],
                 [0.98907104, 0.3220339 , 0.20086393, 0.15466102],
                 [0.13934426, 0.        , 0.3650108 , 0.        ],
                 [0.38251366, 0.58595642, 0.35205184, 0.56367797],
                 [1.        , 1.        , 0.23326134, 0.20762712],
                 [0.24590164, 0.62227603, 0.09071274, 0.53813559],
                 [0.86338798, 0.7748184 , 0.15982721, 0.72669492],
                 [0.1147541 , 0.63196126, 0.47732181, 0.87711864],
                 [0.85519126, 0.95883777, 0.80345572, 0.59322034],
                 [0.54644809, 0.93220339, 0.82289427, 0.70127119],
                 [0.05464481, 0.1622276 , 0.91144708, 0.81355932],
                 [0.40928962, 0.09232446, 1.        , 0.53601695],
                 [0.46994536, 0.07263923, 0.75593952, 0.68008475]])
```

Splitting data into train and test:

from sklearn.model_selection import train_test_split

X_train, X_test, y_train, y_test = train_test_split(X,y, test_size = 0.50, random_state = 50)

Source: https://www.dataquest.io/blog/sci-kit-learn-tutorial/

Splitting and scaling are the most crucial steps in machine learning model development for which scikit-learn approach gives the best suitable methods to handle data sets.

Building Pipeline

Pipelines are the best source for feeding data to machine learning models. Raw data is entered into the pipeline to perform various operations for which we are required to standardize categorical data and continuous variables. The Python syntax to implement pipeline in a machine learning model is defined as follows:

from sklearn.preprocessing import StandardScaler, OneHotEncoder, LabelEncoder

from sklearn.compose import ColumnTransformer, make_column_transformer

from sklearn.pipeline import make_pipeline

from sklearn.linear_model import LogisticRegression

Scikit-learn also provides different functions to run cross validation and parameter tuning. In cross validation, the training set is run multiple times to evaluate the performance and efficiency of models, whereas the grid search approach includes various hyperparameters to check the machine learning model. Logistic classifier is one of the best sources to tune an ML model and can also be used to speed up training.

Effective Data Visualization

Data visualization is one of the major aspects of machine learning and data science. To begin with construction of ML models through Python programming language, we need to understand each of the underlying dataset and explore variables in great depth. Effective data visualization is the core tool for designing and developing machine learning models with high performance and great efficiency. Python data visualization is done through Seaborn, Pandas, and Numpy libraries.

Three important considerations for data visualization are accuracy, clarity, and efficiency. Efficiency makes use of efficient visualization approaches to highlight specific data points, whereas accuracy makes sure that only appropriate graphical representation is taken to deliver the message. Furthermore, clarity portion makes sure that the given dataset is relevant and complete. This allows data scientists to study new patterns which are derived from data in specific places from the graph.

To install Seaborn, we can use the following syntax:

pip install seaborn

Types of Data Visualizations

Scatter Plot

Python programming can be used to design and create graphs of different categories. Scatter plots are the same as line graphs and we can utilize both vertical and horizontal axes to visualize the data points. As they are comprised of a large body of data, a straight line is formed because of the closer data points. Note that a stronger correlation between two variables yields a completely straight-line graph.

Details of Line Properties

Property	Value Type

Animated	True/False
Alpha	Float
Clip box	A matplotlib.transform.Bbox instance
Clip path	Patch
Linewidth	Float value in points

Implementation for Scatter Plot in Python:

```python
import matplotlib.pyplot as plt
import pandas as pd
import seaborn as sns
import warnings

warnings.filterwarnings('ignore')

fig = plt.figure(figsize=(5, 10))
```

```
df = pd.read_csv('SampleData')

ax = sns.regplot(x="wt", y="mpg", data=df)
```

Histogram Plot

Histograms are the graphical representations for a probability distribution and can be created through matplotlib and bar chart function in Python. For example:

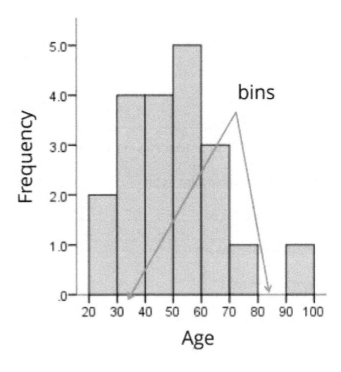

Python implementation:

```
import pandas as pd
```

```
import seaborn as sns


df = pd.read_csv('SampleData')


fig = plt.figure(figsize=(5, 100))

sns.distplot(df.Temp, kde=False)
```

Bar Plots

In Python, we can also create bar graphs or bar plots to display and compare the frequency or number of data. Remember that the data can be of different discrete categories because bar plots have more frequency as compared to other types of graphs. Bar plots can be implemented through Python with Pandas barplot method. For example:

```
import pandas as pd

import seaborn as sns


df = pd.read_csv('SampleData', index_col=0)


df_grpd = df.groupby("cyl").count().reset_index()

fig = plt.figure(figsize=(12, 8))

sns.barplot(x="cyl", y="mpg", data=df_grpd)
```

Source: https://pythonspot.com/matplotlib-bar-chart/

Pie Chart and Error Bars

Pie charts are created to show proportional data or percentage. Through pie charts, we can summarize huge datasets in visual form and display the relative proportion of different classes of data. On the other hand, error bars are used to show the graphical representation of variability of data and is mainly used to point out errors in data. This approach is also best suited for performing data analysis by overviewing statistical differences between the two groups of data.

Error bars demonstrate how a model and function are used in data analysis. It shows us the variability in data and also indicates any possible errors. To implement these graphs, we can take support from Seaborn Python visualization library. Seaborn provides high level interface for creating attractive statistical graphics and is widely used for visualizing data and plotting. Furthermore, Seaborn provides built in themes for better visualizations and includes built in statistical functions.

Naïve Bayes Model

Naïve Bayes classification theorem is implanted to calculate the probability of data belonging to a specific class. Classification is done by overviewing the previous knowledge about data and is used to solve both binary and multiclass classification problems. Naïve Bayes is a fast and straightforward classification algorithm which is best suitable for large volumes of data. The algorithm has the capability to perform different activities such as text classification, recommender systems, and spam filtering which makes it one of the greatest algorithms used in developing machine learning models.

How is Classification Performed?

To perform classification, data scientists need to understand the given problem and identify datasets to make specific labels. These attributes can also be considered as features of data which are directly affected by labels. Classification is divided into two phases known as evaluation phase and learning phase. In the evaluation phase, the model tests classifier performance on the basis of different parameters including recall, precision, accuracy, and error. For the learning phase, the classifier trains the model on the provided dataset so that it can deliver the best results when implemented in the machine learning system. Computation through Naïve Bayes theorem can be performed by the following equation:

$$P(h|D) = \frac{P(D|h)P(h)}{P(D)}$$

P(h) is the probability of hypothesis h and is also named as the prior probability of h, whereas P(d) is known as the probability of data or prior probability regardless of the hypothesis. P(h|D) is the probability of hypothesis h for given data D and is also named as posterior probability. P(D|h) represents the probability of data d in case of true h hypotheses and is also named as posterior probability.

Naïve Bayes Classified Development in Scikit-Learn

In the below example, we will define the best methods to define dataset, encode features and generate a machine learning model through Python programming language.

Defining the Dataset and Encoding Features to the Data

Basic syntax:

weather=['Sunny','Sunny','Overcast','Rainy','Rainy','Rainy','Ov ercast','Sunny','Sunny',

'Rainy','Sunny','Overcast','Overcast','Rainy']

temp=['Hot','Hot','Hot','Mild','Cool','Cool','Cool','Mild','Cool',' Mild','Mild','Mild','Hot','Mild']

play=['No','No','Yes','Yes','Yes','No','Yes','No','Yes','Yes','Yes','Y es','Yes','No']

from sklearn import preprocessing

#creating labelEncoder

le = preprocessing.LabelEncoder()

weather_encoded=le.fit_transform(wheather)

print weather_encoded

Generating model and loading data

from sklearn.naive_bayes import GaussianNB

```
#Create a Gaussian Classifier

model = GaussianNB()

# Train the model using the training sets

model.fit(features,label)

#Predict Output

predicted= model.predict([[0,2]]) # 0:Overcast, 2:Mild

print "Predicted Value:", predicted

#load Data

from sklearn import datasets

wine = datasets.load_wine()


Implementation of Split() function

# Import train_test_split function

from sklearn.cross_validation import train_test_split


# Split dataset into training set and test set

X_train, X_test, y_train, y_test = train_test_split(wine.data,
wine.target, test_size=0.3,random_state=109)
```

Source: https://machinelearningmastery.com/naive-bayes-
classifier-scratch-python/

Evaluating Accuracy of the Model

from sklearn import metrics

print("Accuracy:", metrics.accuracy_score(y_test, y_pred))

Source:
https://www.datacamp.com/community/tutorials/naive-bayes-scikit-learn

Advantages of Naïve Bayes

Naïve Bayes is a fast approach to obtain accurate model predictions with low computation cost. Furthermore, this theorem can work efficiently on large datasets and performs ideally in case of discrete response variable as compared to continuous variable. As compared to other machine learning models such as logistic regression, Naïve Bayes yields better results in cases of independence holds as well.

K-Means Clustering

The K-Means clustering algorithm is a major part of machine learning algorithms which is based upon three important steps. These steps are named as Initialization, Assignment, and Update. K-Means clustering algorithm is used to partition n observations into k clusters for managing datasets and making accurate predictions in machine learning models.

In the Initialization step, the k means or centroids are generated at random, whereas the Assignment portion allows the creation of k clusters by associating each observation with another nearest centroid. The Update portion allows the centroid of clusters to become new mean and Update and

Assignment portions are repeated iteratively until the desired outcome is achieved. As a result, the sum of squared errors is reduced between centroids and their respective points.

To implement K-Means algorithm in Python, we are required to import the following modules at first:

import pandas as pd

import numpy as np

import matplotlib.pyplot as plt

import random

from sklearn import preprocessing

Syntax to read data:

data = pd.read_csv('Sample.csv')

data = data[:30]

max_clusters = 5

data['Age'].fillna(np.mean(data['Age']), inplace = True)

data['Fare'].fillna(np.mean(data['Price']), inplace = True)

data['Age'] = preprocessing.scale(data['Age'])

data['Fare'] = preprocessing.scale(data['Price'])

Expectation-Minimization Algorithm

Expectation-Minimization is an essential part of the K-Means algorithm and it plays a vital role in machine learning model development. This algorithm has the capability to guess cluster centers and repeat the process until the model is fully converged. E-step is used to assign points for nearest cluster center, whereas the M-step is considered to set the clusters to mean. E-step is also known as expectation step because it involves updating of expectations which is used to study point location for each cluster.

Furthermore, the M-step is named as maximization step and it involves maximization of fitness function and is best suited to define the location of cluster centers. In Python programming, there are predefined syntax and libraries to implement K-means algorithm for achieving different outcomes from the machine learning model. K-Means cluster algorithm is limited to linear cluster boundaries which are always linear. In particular, K-means can be implemented in Scikit-Learn through SpectralClustering estimation method for which the following syntax can be used:

```
from sklearn.cluster import SpectralClustering

model = SpectralClustering(n_clusters=2,
affinity='nearest_neighbors',

                assign_labels='kmeans')

labels = model.fit_predict(X)

plt.scatter(X[:, 0], X[:, 1], c=labels,

        s=50, cmap='viridis');
```

Graphical Output:

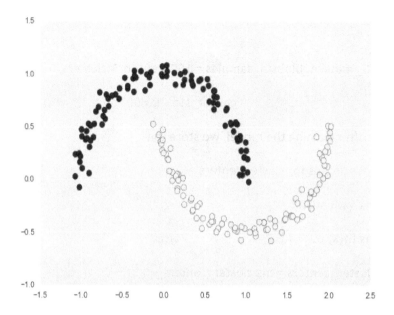

Mean Shift Algorithm

Mean shift algorithm has the capability to assign and outline data points to clusters by turning points towards the mode. This is a hierarchical clustering algorithm based on unsupervised learning techniques and is also named as Mode-seeding algorithm. To apply Mean shift algorithm in Python programming language, we need to perform kernel density estimation and represent the data in mathematical format. This makes it easier for the model to process data and use it for delivering accurate insights and predictions.

Kernel is also known as a function to perform convolution in datasets and is suitable for developing high performing machine learning models. Here is a simple program in Python to demonstrate how Mean shift algorithm works:

clusters = [[2, 2, 2], [7, 7, 7], [5, 13, 13]]

```
X, _ = make_blobs(n_samples = 150, centers = clusters,

                  cluster_std = 0.60)
# After training the model, we store the

coordinates for cluster centers

ms = MeanShift()

ms.fit(X)

cluster_centers = ms.cluster_centers_


# Plot the data points and centroids in 3D graph

fig = plt.figure()

ax = fig.add_subplot(111, projection ='3d')

ax.scatter(X[:, 0], X[:, 1], X[:, 2], marker ='o')

ax.scatter(cluster_centers[:, 0], cluster_centers[:, 1],

           cluster_centers[:, 2], marker ='x', color ='red',

           s = 300, linewidth = 5, zorder = 10)
plt.show()
```

Output:

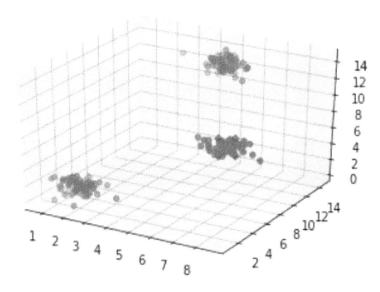

Source: https://www.geeksforgeeks.org/ml-mean-shift-clustering/

There are several advantages of using Mean shift algorithm in machine learning models. The algorithm is good for finding a variable number of modes and is an application independent tool. Furthermore, the model does not assume any prior shape on data clusters like elliptical or spherical.

Chapter 6: Deep Learning and Artificial Intelligence

Machine learning is a branch of computer science which is based on the study of algorithms having the capability to learn and predict on their own. Each algorithm is based on a predefined set of rules and procedures that are used to perform specific operations in machine learning models. These algorithms are also known as Artificial Neural Networks (ANN) in deep learning which is also a subfield of machine learning. Python provides simple and easy to implement approaches for developers and data scientists to program machine learning models and enhance their performance as well.

To develop, maintain, and evaluate deep learning models, we can take help from Python libraries such as Pandas, TensorFlow, and Keras. As they are based on efficient numerical modules, you can get started with deep neural networks and utilize built-in modules to develop high performing machine learning models.

Introduction to Artificial Neural Networks

It is important to learn the basics and functionality of artificial neural networks before starting with deep learning in Python. Neural networks are based on the perception of neurons in the human brain and how they work to perform specific operations. The human brain is the greatest example to be inspired from because it is composed of millions of neurons working together to control different operations in the human body. The brain is capable of performing complex computations within seconds, which is surely the biggest inspiration for artificial neural networks.

Understanding Data

Before developing neural networks or deep learning models, getting information about data and its qualities can deliver long term advantages. At first, check the description folder to overview variables of datasets and learn about details and other vital information as well. Generally, a neural network is comprised of an input layer which is your actual data and is present in numerical form. There are various hidden layers in neural networks which are present between input and output layers. With a single layer, the model is capable of handling linear relationships, whereas in the case of hidden layers, the model can handle non-linear relationships as well.

TensorFlow and Keran are best suited for building multiple layers in a neural network. Here is the syntax to implement these libraries in Python:

pip install tensorflow

import tensorflow.keras as keras

import tensorflow as tf

Once we are done with importing TensorFlow, we can start to prepare our data and make it ready for training in machine learning models. The syntax is defined as follows:

mnist = tf.keras.datasets.mnist

(x_train, y_train),(x_test, y_test) = mnist.load_data()

Keras

To implement Keras, you are required to install and configure Python 2 or 3 along with SciPy and NumPy libraries. TensorFlow and Keras can be installed and configured without complex coding because there are predefined Python modules which you can easily add in your program.

Starting with the first step, we need to load our dataset for which the following two classes form Keras library can be implemented to define the model:

from numpy import loadtxt

from keras.models import sequential

from keras.layers import Dense

Source: https://machinelearningmastery.com/keras-functional-api-deep-learning/

Defining Keras Model

To define Keras model, we need to develop a sequential model and add layers until the required network architecture is complete. There are specific heuristics to determine the best network structure for which data scientists implement the process of trial and error experimentation. A fully connected layer can be defined by Dense class and we can also specify the number of nodes or neurons present in the layer by the help of activation argument. Python syntax to define Keras model is defined as follows:

model = Sequential()

model.add(Dense(10, input_dim=5, activation= 'relu'))

model.compile(loss- 'binary_crossentropy' , optimizer = 'adam', metrics= ['accuracy'])

Evaluation and Prediction

For evaluating Keras model, we can use the evaluate() function on the model and pass the same input and output for training as well. Moreover, this activity will also generate a prediction for every input and output including the average loss or accuracy metrics. Implementation in Python for evaluating the model and predicting values in Keras is defined as follows:

accuracy = model.evaluate(X, y)

print('Accuracy: %.2f %(accuracy*100))

predictions = model.predict(X)

predictions = model.predict_classes(X)

Machine Learning

Machine learning is a branch of Artificial Intelligence which is based on statistical methods and cognitive behavior. The concept also allows computers to learn on their own without being programmed repeatedly whenever the system is exposed to new data. The process of prediction and training is based on specialized algorithms which are developed to perform specific tasks in machine learning models. For developing machine learning systems in Python programming language, major libraries including SciPy, NumPy, Matplotlib, Pandas, Keran and Scikit-learn need to be installed and configured at first.

For efficient learning and accurate predictions, machine learning models should be fed with data having certain attributes and variables during training. Majorly, machine learning tasks are categorized as predictive modeling, clustering, and concept learning whereas the ultimate goal of developing ML models is to take decisions without human intervention.

Categories of Machine Learning

Machine learning is divided into three main sections: Supervised learning, Unsupervised learning, and Reinforcement learning. Supervised learning is the most used paradigm for building machine learning models because it is absolutely easy to understand and implement. With the passage of time, ML models become capable of learning the relationship between examples and their labels until they become fully trained to make accurate predictions.

Supervised and Unsupervised Learning

Supervised learning algorithms have the power to model relationships and dependencies to achieve specific target prediction output. Common algorithms for implementing supervised learning are Nearest neighbor, Decision Trees, Naïve Bayes, and Neural networks. Unsupervised learning is based on machine learning models that are trained with unlabeled data. The models are not given any supporting training datasets and they have to learn through patterns and attributes in data. Common algorithms for developing unsupervised machine learning models are K-Means clustering and Association Rules. Unsupervised learning algorithms are mainly used in the development of descriptive modeling and pattern detection systems because there are no labels or output categories defined.

Another major category of machine learning is named as Semi-supervising learning. For supervised and unsupervised machine learning models, there are labels for data given in some cases whereas in other scenarios, there are no labels for observation in datasets. Categories and techniques of machine learning are selected after complete observation and evaluation of external factors such as cost, security, reliability, and maintenance. These factors play a vital role in machine learning model development as well.

Reinforcement Learning

The reinforcement learning method has a capability to utilize observations from interaction with external factors and environments to make specific decisions in a machine learning model. Agents in reinforcement learning models consistently learn from the environment and repeatedly try for exploring a new range of possible states. Being an important part of machine learning and artificial intelligence, reinforcement learning allows systems and software agents to automatically determine ideal behavior within a certain context to boost performance.

There are several algorithms to implement the reinforcement learning model in Python. Usually, reinforcement learning models are created for a specific problem and all of the solutions are given by the model itself. Common algorithms for reinforcement learning are Q-Learning, Deep Adversarial Networks, and Temporal Difference.

Deep Neural Networks

What are Neural Networks?

Deep neural networks are comprised of various algorithms which are modeled according to the functionality and connectivity of the human brain to recognize specific patterns. The human brain has the capability to predict, analyze, and make decisions overviewing any given scenarios and perform tasks successfully. Neural networks classify and cluster data and utilize the given variables and attributes to make relevant predictions and perform certain tasks as well. A deep neural network is actually a neural network with a certain level of complexity because it is based on more than two layers.

By using mathematical modeling, neural networks process data in different ways because they are designed to simulate the activity of the human brain. Furthermore, the model performs specific types of ordering and sorting by utilizing artificial intelligence and machine learning approaches. Patterns recognized by neural networks are numerical and include vectors through which any real-world data such as sound, time series, or text could be translated. Moreover, they also group unlabeled data as per its similarities when provided a labeled dataset.

Neural networks are comprised of various components. These include an input layer, an output layer, and some hidden layers as well. To complete the network architecture, we can select an activation function for each hidden layer along with a set of biases and weights between the layers. We can easily create a neural network in Python through the following syntax:

```
class NeuralNetwork:

    def __init__(self, x, y):

    self.input    = x

    self.weights1  = np.random.rand(self.input.shape[2],8)

    self.weights2  = np.random.rand(4,1)

    self.y         = y

    self.output    = np.zeros(y.shape)
```

Generally, the values for biases and weights determine the strength and effectiveness of predictions. Training of neural networks involves fine tuning of biases and weights from input data for which we are required to perform different iterations. Each iteration of training involves the calculation of feed forward and updating of biases and weights through back propagation approach.

Recurrent Neural Networks

Recurrent Neural Networks are also known as RNNs and are basically used in the implementation of Natural Language Processing or language modeling because they allow data to flow in any direction. As they can repeat the same task for each element of the sequence, the output is usually dependent on the previous computations and RNNs are known to have built-in memory that records the previously calculated information.

Training Neural Networks

Training neural networks is an essential part of machine learning model development. As we are required to find the most suitable values of weights and bias of a neural network to achieve the desired output, the training must be performed by using effective techniques such as the iterative gradient descent method. Once random initialization is complete, we can make predictions on subset of data through forward propagation process and update each weight by an amount proportional to dC/dq or the derivative of cost functions with respect to the weight. The calculation can also be referred to as the learning rate and implemented through a computational graph as well. Gradients can be calculated through back-propagation algorithm for which we can implement chain rule of differentiation as well.

Back propagation algorithm is implemented by analyzing data through a computational graph which has each neuron expanded to several nodes. The computational graph does not have any kind of bias or weights on the edges, so weights become their own nodes.

Gradient Descent

Gradient descent optimization technique is used to find out which weight produces the fewest errors and is used to translate signals from input data into a correct classification. A neural network learns and adjusts to several weights so that it can map signal meaning in the best suitable manner. Furthermore, each weight factor in deep network is based on several transforms because the signal of weight has to pass through different sums and activation over the layers. The idea behind deep learning is to adjust a model's weight and increase its performance and capability to make accurate predictions.

Deep learning can process millions of images and classify them as per their similarities. As it performs automatic feature extraction, we can perform complex tasks without human intervention even by training machine learning models on unlabeled data. During processing, neural networks try to learn and recognize correlations between the features and optimal results. This activity is done by drawing specific connections between feature signals and labeled data.

Optimization

The training process of deep learning neural networks is dependent upon input data, labels, and attributes. As they learn to map inputs and outputs over a training dataset of examples, the process is usually iterative and involves finding a set of weights that are best suited for the network. An iterative training process for neural networks is best for solving optimization problem and searches for model weights that yield minimum loss or error when evaluation examples in training datasets. Remember that optimization is a search procedure and can become challenging when implemented in deep neural network models.

To perform optimization and training for deep learning neural networks, the best method is back propagation of the error algorithm. Generally, we can handle the difficulty in terms of features of error surface or landscape which the algorithm has undergone changes so that it can navigate on its own and select the right path as well.

Artificial Neural Networks

The Artificial Neural Networks are based on the working and functionality of biological neural networks and are capable of modeling non linear relationships between inputs and outputs. Being statistical models, Artificial neural networks are widely implemented in machine learning systems because they are based on the approach of learning and observing datasets. Optimization techniques such as cost function allow ANN's to determine best values of each tunable model parameter and improve the learning rate as well. Furthermore, these optimization techniques allow developers and data scientists to develop state of the art machine learning models which are capable of making accurate predictions and insights.

Machine learning models are complex because of the increased abstraction and higher problem-solving capabilities. Due to the increased number of hidden layers, the number of paths between each neuron and given layer increases which in return makes the ANN system more complex. Tuning and model architecture are major components of Artificial Neural Networks. Each of these characteristics allow ANN to make a significant impact on the reliability and performance of the deep learning model.

Remember the fact that Artificial Neural Networks are extremely powerful and they can often become complex. Furthermore, they are also named as black box algorithms as their actual working and functionality is impossible to understand. In contrast with deep learning algorithms, these models are also dependent on optimal model selection and model tuning approach for maximizing performance and output. Furthermore, statistical techniques and deep learning leverage concepts are a major part of Artificial Neural Networks.

How Do They Work?

Artificial Neural Networks have the capability to make decisions and calculations on their own. As the model works as a supervised learning approach, it is fed with enough examples and similar scenarios which allow ANN's to make accurate predictions on their own. This process is usually done through back propagation approach because Artificial Neural Networks are represented as weighted directed graphs. In these graphs, node is designed by artificial neurons for which the connection between neuron inputs and neuron outputs is represented through directed edges and weights.

Each given input is multiplied with its corresponding weights and the output is directly dependent upon the details and labels of the weight for solving a specific problem. Furthermore, the weights are represented through the strength of interconnection in between neurons of the artificial neural network. In case the weighted sum is zero, we can add a bias to make output non-zero or update the system to meet the model's requirements. Weights of inputs can range from zero to positive infinity and to keep the response according to the limits of desired values, we can create a specific threshold value as well.

Furthermore, activation functions can also be implemented in artificial neural networks which comprise of a set of functions implemented to achieve a desired value. Some of the common activation functions are named as Sigmoidal, Tan hyperbolic sigmoidal, and binary.

Architecture of ANN's

Artificial Neural Networks or ANN's contain a huge number of artificial neurons, and this is the main reason they are named as artificial neural networks. The architecture is comprised of an Input layer, an Output layer, and a Hidden layer. The input layer has artificial neurons which are subject to receive input from external resources and are responsible for learning and recognition as well. For the output layer, the information that is fed into the system is analyzed and recognized before it is sent for further processing. Moreover, the output layer also accepts or rejects the training data by overviewing the labels and attributes to make sure that the information is best suited for the artificial neural network. The illustration below will better help you in understanding the architecture of artificial neural networks:

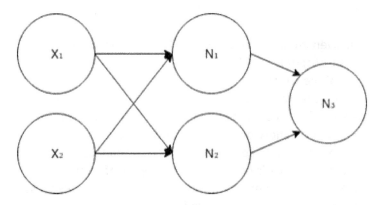

Hidden layers are present between input layers and output layers. Their job is to transform the input into meaningful data so that the output layer can utilize it in the best manner. Each of the artificial neural networks is interconnected and the hidden layers cover each portion of data present in the system. This makes it easier to complete the learning process and allows the system to make relevant updates without any hassle.

Advantages

Artificial neural networks have several key advantages that make them ideal for solving complex problems in machine learning and artificial intelligence. Having the capability to model non-linear relationships, ANNs can solve real life problems by defining relationships between inputs and outputs from non linear data as well. Furthermore, artificial neural networks can learn from initial inputs and generalize relationships to predict unseen data and make the model capable of performing complex operations without any hassle. Unlike other prediction models, artificial neural networks never impose any restrictions over input variables which allows researchers to train the model through different techniques.

Applications of ANNs

Character recognition and image processing are the greatest applications of artificial neural networks. As this network has the power to process large sets of input data, it can also define non-linear relationships and help in the development of character and image recognition applications. Artificial neural network models are widely implemented in fraud detection and security systems because they have the capability to perform facial recognition in real time.

Moreover, artificial neural networks also serve as a useful tool for food quality and safety analysis. This covers the development of microbial growth models through which prediction of food safety and interpretation of spectroscopic data is performed.

Chapter 7: Data Science in Real World

Data science is a combination of statistics, mathematics, and programming. In order to develop data science and machine learning models, we are required to have in depth knowledge and information regarding the subject so that accurate training data can be fed into the system. On the other hand, business thinking and domain knowledge are also essential for developing high performing machine learning models and data science projects.

Python is a completely suitable programming language for developing machine learning and data science models because it is absolutely easy to learn and implement. Furthermore, we can perform specific tasks and operations by utilizing built-in Python libraries such as Pandas, NumPy and Scikit-Learn.

How Can We Implement Data Science in Real Life Scenarios?

Most industries and businesses are now using systems that are based on the latest machine learning and data science models. This helps in automating processes and allows businesses to make accurate predictions for the future to increase sales and boost profits. Traditional information systems are not capable of bringing long term benefits to companies and businesses because of outdated technology. To make things better, data scientists and machine learning experts have utilized the concepts of computer science, mathematics, and statistics to develop systems which are capable of making accurate predictions and learn from the training datasets as well.

There are several key advantages of data science in business and real life for humans. An experienced data scientist can also serve as a trusted advisor and strategic partner to the company by providing accurate data insights and predictions for the future. This activity is done through measuring performance across the entire organization and recording performance metrics. Furthermore, data scientists perform different tests to determine the status of an organization's current analytics system to bring further improvements.

Data Science Applications

Most of the advanced applications and systems developed nowadays are based on machine learning and data science models. The impact and performance of machine learning systems is a lot better as compared to traditional computing systems which is the main reason why machine learning and artificial intelligence are widely being researched. By using data science, companies and businesses have become intelligent enough to sell products and promote their services in a shorter time frame.

Here are a few major applications of Data Science:

Image recognition

You might have noticed that once you have uploaded any image with your friends on Facebook, you start to get suggestions for adding tags. This feature of automatic suggestion is based on an image recognition algorithm which has the capability to detect specific patterns and yield outcomes with matching data. Furthermore, image recognition systems are widely being used by security agencies and financial institutes to detect people involved in fraudulent activities in real time.

Speech Recognition

Speech recognition systems allow users to perform different tasks by communicating with their devices such as smartphones or computers. Google Voice, Cortana, and Siri are the finest implementations of speech recognition systems that were originally designed with machine learning and data science models.

Virtual Assistants

Chatbots from different websites and applications are the finest implementation of deep learning and artificial intelligence. Virtual assistance is now available in mobile applications through which patients can avail healthcare guidance and basic support without any hassle. Furthermore, you can book appointments and make schedules with chatbots through virtual assistants and receive vital information as well.

Risk and Fraud Detection

Financial institutions such as banks are the biggest users of automated fraud detection and risk management systems. Banks can now analyze user data and information to check credit history for thousands of people instead of checking for everyone individually. Furthermore, companies can avoid bad debts and losses by overviewing and managing transactions in real time.

Data Analytics in Detail

Data analytics is an approach which is used to analyze data sets and draw conclusions regarding the available data. To tackle the increasing demand and requirements of businesses and companies, research for specialized software and systems is being performed by data scientists and machine learning engineers to improve scientific models and theories. Online analytical processing and business intelligence are the major forms of advanced analytics. Data analytics systems can make businesses improve operational efficiency and increase revenue by meeting customer demands and increasing sales.

Process and Working

Analyzing and evaluating data are the basic concepts of data analytics. Most of the work in the development of data analytics systems includes collection, integration, and preparation of data which has to be used for model training. The models are then tested and upgraded to produce accurate results. For development of data analytics models, the first step is data collection for which scientists take support from particular analytics applications and work with data engineers to implement the information in the best possible manner.

Data combined from different sources needs to be refined with data integration tools so that it can be transformed into a common format. Once the labels and format are properly analyzed, we can load the data into an analytics system such as Datawarehouse or Hadoop cluster for fast processing. Moreover, data scientists have to find and solve data quality problems so that the accuracy of analytics applications is never compromised. Furthermore, data cleansing and data profiling techniques can be used to make sure that the data set is consistent and free of mistakes. This will help in achieving accurate insights and predictions in future.

Analytical models are built by taking support from predictive modeling tools and programming languages such as Python or Scala. Once the model is developed, it undergoes proper testing for which different types of test training datasets are used. The process is repeated until the model completely learns and adapts characteristics from training data so that it can make accurate predictions when implemented into the system. Furthermore, the model is also run in production mode for which full datasets are used and if any problem arises, it is solved immediately to ensure reliability and performance of the analytics model.

Types and Categories of Data Analytics

Generally, data analytics is divided into four major categories which are predictive, prescriptive, diagnostic, and descriptive analysis. Each of the categories has unique characteristics and is capable of performing various operations for business analytic models. Starting with predictive analysis, the category is best for gaining insights and predictions for the future. This approach uses historical data to identify the given records and trends which are likely to occur. Furthermore, predictive analysis tools also provide valuable insights for scenarios which might happen in the future if they are likely to occur. To implement predictive analysis, we can use machine learning techniques including decision trees, regression, and neural networks.

Prescriptive analysis approach gives us ideas for activities that could be performed to avail best outcomes. The technique uses insights from predictive analysis to make reliable data driven decisions. Furthermore, businesses can get help from predictive analysis to determine the likelihood of events and outcomes because this approach has the capability to detect patterns in large datasets. Diagnostic analytics can be helpful for obtaining reasons related to the happening of certain aspects in an analytics model. The technique takes points from descriptive analysis and works deeper to find the root cause of each event.

Moreover, diagnostic analysis also includes performance indicators which help to discover the main reason which might have affected the performance or reliability of the analytics system. Diagnostic analysis is used to identify and outline anomalies in data and information related to each anomaly is also collected. At the end, data scientists implement statistical techniques to find trends and relationships to outline the root causes of these anomalies. The fourth category of data analytics is named as descriptive analysis which summarizes large datasets into separate portions for describing outcomes in a better way.

Descriptive analysis can be considered as a way of analyzing the main reason why a specific scenario happened for which data scientists implement key performance indicators (KPI) to develop analytics models. Furthermore, other metrics like return on investment (ROI) are also based on descriptive analysis because they are implemented in systems for large scale businesses and industries to gain performance and sales insights.

Importance of Data Analytics

Analyzing big data is an essential part of machine learning model development. There is a wide range of applications of data analytics that have greatly improved the performance of business systems and have allowed companies to compete in today's world. Talking about the earliest adopters of data analytics tools, the financial sector has widely implemented machine learning and data analytics systems to secure transactions and avoid fraudulent activities. Furthermore, data analytics can also be used to detect fraud in real time and take certain actions to stop all kinds of fraudulent activities.

Data analytic also provides vital information for healthcare, environment protection, and crime prevention. These applications bring long term advantages and support for people as they can protect themselves from fraudulent activities and get medical assistance without any hassle. Data analysis, statistics, and mathematics have always been a part of scientific research through which advanced analytic techniques and tools are designed. The Internet of Things (IoT) is another great invention made through data analytics methods and its devices are comprised of sensors that collect meaningful data which is then utilized by data analytics models to make predictions and accurate insights. There are endless applications of data analytics and the increasing volume of data being collected each day reveals new pathways for machine learning and deep analytics models to learn effectively.

Data Mining

This is the method of analyzing data from various

perspectives and converting it into useful information. The converted and summarized information is used to make vital decisions and training data. In machine learning models, data mining is considered as a technique of detecting, analyzing, and exploring patterns in large amounts of data and the processed information is then sorted and classified into separate categories. Moreover, classification and data prediction techniques help us in getting accurate insights and prediction results through data mining methods without any hassle.

Logistic regression, classification trees, neural networks, anomaly detection, and clustering techniques such as K-nearest Neighbors are a few examples of data mining. The characteristics of data analysis are dependent upon different aspects such as variety, velocity, and volume. In order to get better results and outcomes from data mining, we are required to address each scenario in-depth and implement the best algorithms to develop data mining models. Furthermore, framing a problem makes data scientist clear about the requirements of systems and helps data scientists to gain accurate insights from the data mining model.

Steps in Data Mining

The first step in data mining is data cleaning, in which we are supposed to check the quality of data and remove any kind of irregularities. Multiple data sources are combined to complete the data integration process so that data could be extracted from the database. Data selection and data transformation approaches are used to perform summary analysis and aggregatory operations over data while doing data mining. In data mining, we have to extract useful information and data from the data source and analyze several patterns as well.

In the final step of knowledge representation, data scientists have to represent knowledge to users in the form of metrics, graphs, trees, and tables. Data mining is widely implemented in the development of fraud detection, risk management, market analysis, and corporate analysis systems to explore and manage data.

Importance of Machine Learning

Machine learning is responsible for transforming operations for each sector including finance, health care, security, information technology, and education. Based on the idea of learning from data, machine learning is a branch of artificial intelligence that automates analytical model building and allows systems to make decisions without human intervention. Because of the ever-increasing advancements and revolutions in computing technologies, businesses can find the best solutions to boost their sales and increase profits.

The aim of machine learning is to understand the structure of data and utilize theoretical models for developing systems which are capable of making accurate predictions and data insights. Data driven decisions always bring positive outcomes for businesses because machine learning models are trained on factual data which delivers the best possible solutions for any problem. In traditional computing systems, data analysis was performed through trial and error-based approach which cannot yield accurate results when implemented over large data sets and heterogeneous data.

Data Science Lifecycle and Model Building

Building data science models by focusing on each important aspect of the data science lifecycle will help you in achieving the best results and outcomes. Discovery, data preparation, model planning, model building, operations, and results analysis are key portions of the data science lifecycle. Starting with the first steps of discovery and data preparation, data scientists need to understand the requirements, specifications, and priorities of the system. Budget and time constraints should also be kept in mind before starting the project, as it will save you from further issues as well.

In the data preparation phase, sufficient training data and information must be discovered so that the data science model is capable of making accurate predictions and evaluations in future. Extract, transform, and load are the major approaches that should be considered while creating datasets for the system. Once the data preparation step is done, the next part is model planning where data scientists have to determine the techniques and methods to draw relationships between variables.

The next phase is known as model building in which data scientists and engineers have to develop datasets for testing and training purposes. Implementing techniques like clustering, association, and classification will make it easier to complete the model building phase. For the operations phase, data scientists are supposed to deliver briefings, technical documents, code, and final reports for the project.

Challenges in Neural Networks and Deep Learning Algorithms

Neural networks and deep learning algorithms are widely used in the development of machine learning and artificial intelligence models. Although the performance and effectiveness of deep learning models is directly dependent upon the quality and reliability of training data, there are several other factors that can be held accountable for the performance of machine learning models. Overfitting and underfitting are two of the major challenges that are faced by ML systems and to prevent further loss, data scientists have to research and implement effective techniques to improve the performance and functionality of machine learning models.

To avoid overfitting, we can apply regularization methods such as data augmentation, drop out, early stopping, and transfer learning during training of deep learning models. This will help in protecting the model from overfitting and also improves rare dependencies. For neural networks, we use the dropout approach which is a popular regularization technique to finish overfitting. Other methods like early stopping, data augmentation, and transfer learning can also be implemented to avoid the challenges that are being faced during the development of deep learning and neural network systems.

Deep Learning Limitations

Although deep learning systems are great performers, there are some external factors which can have a direct impact on their functionality and effectiveness. Usually, artificial intelligence models are given training through a supervised learning approach which includes training data that is completely labeled and classified by humans. Deep learning systems are based on the same approach and require huge training datasets to become properly trained. Complex and large models are difficult to train for which data scientists need to classify and label training data as well.

Improving Data Science Models

Machine learning models developed with the Python programming language can be updated and improved by making simple changes in the code. Although there are different checks to overview the performance and effectiveness of a data science model, we need to focus on some key factors explained below to avail best outcomes:

Determine Problems

For improving results, we need to analyze the problems with our data science model at first. Learning curves are a great source to verify a test set against the provided training data. By analyzing computational graphs, one can easily identify the weaknesses of a data analytics or machine learning model. Furthermore, you can also perform cross validation to overview performance of your model. A large difference between the results and cross validation estimates is a common problem which usually occurs with training data.

Choosing Hyper Parameters

When solving a data science problem, you need to analyze the problem and determine the best metric for getting a long-term solution. Remember that most of the algorithms perform best even with default parameter settings. However, you can optimize the efficiency of machine learning and artificial intelligence models by implementing hyperparameters as well. To perform this activity, you have to design a grid search containing possible values supported by your parameters and start to evaluate the results through a score metric.

Testing and Evaluation

Testing and evaluation will help you in determining the quality of predictions and data insights delivered by a deep analytics model. In some cases, bias can affect the performance of the model for which you can implement various techniques such as automatic feature creation and support vectors to achieve a better solution. Although these techniques will make the model perform slightly better, your understanding and expertise regarding the machine learning model are the best source to examine, test, and improve the overall performance and efficiency.

Search for More Data

No matter what amount of training data you have used, there is always room for improvement because machine learning and deep learning models always improve when a new data set is fed into the system. Increasing the size of the training set is also a vital approach to be considered. In case you have been training your model with simple data, you can feed complex or unlabeled data so that the model is capable of learning and making better decisions on its own.

Chapter 8: Deep Learning and Business

Business processes nowadays are completely transformed due to the involvement of artificial intelligence, deep learning, and machine learning systems. They are key aspects of enacting digital transformation and development of computational systems. There are several forms of prescriptive analysis that can help businesses in achieving desired outcomes within a short period of time. These procedures include automated stock transactions, intelligent traffic flow pattern optimization, autonomous data center functions, and autonomous cars. The basic fundamentals behind each of these technologies are deep learning and major concepts of artificial intelligence.

Actually, artificial intelligence is an approach to mimic human intelligence process through the application of mathematical and statistical algorithms. Machine learning is actually a subset of artificial intelligence and is a major field of computer science that focuses on interpreting structures and patterns in data.

How Does Deep Learning Work?

Deep learning is an approach based on the construct of human neural networks and is also a subfield of machine learning and artificial intelligence. The approach has the capability to learn from both structured and unstructured data to initiate automated learning from training data. In order to improve accuracy of deep learning models, data scientists need to remove weak correlations and assumptions in data. The presence of reliable and high-quality data is the key aspect to building accurate machine learning models.

For extracting more information from existing data, we can follow the feature engineering approach in deep learning. This method is used to extract new facilities and features from data and allows the deep learning model to understand variance in data as well. As a result, data scientists are able to develop models with improved accuracy and better prediction capabilities. Feature engineering is based on a hypothesis generation approach which is divided into feature transformation and feature creation methods.

In feature transformation, the algorithms work with normally distributed data. Methods such as inverse, square root, or log of the values are implemented to remove skewness from data and this approach is also known as data normalization. Numeric data can also be created by adding discrete values into the deep learning model. On the other hand, feature creation method derives new variables from existing variables and helps to uncover hidden relationships between datasets. Moreover, data scientists also take support from the feature selection process to find out the best subset of attributes to explain the relationship of independent variables with the available target variable.

Feature selection is based on major machine learning model development metrics like domain knowledge and visualization. Through domain knowledge, we can select features which might yield a higher impact on target variable whereas the visualization approach helps to visualize the relationship between multiple variables. In return, this approach makes variable selection processes easier and more effective. To enhance performance and reliability of the model, we can also consider working on statistical parameters like p-values and other modules to select the right features.

Algorithm Tuning and Method Ensemble

The performance of machine learning algorithms is dependent upon parameters and variables in the dataset. The parameters can influence the efficiency and outcome of the learning process for which data scientists follow the approach of algorithm tuning. This approach is used to figure out the best value for each parameter which in return improves the accuracy of the model. To tune the parameters, you should have in-depth knowledge about the machine learning model and datasets in advance. Furthermore, the process can be repeated multiple times until the desired outcome is achieved.

Ensemble methods are commonly used in the development and maintenance of machine learning and deep learning models. This technique combines outcomes of weak models and performs operations to produce a model with better results. Bagging and boosting are two major techniques used to implement ensemble methods on machine learning models.

Model Interpretability

Businesses and industries require information systems that have the capability to deliver accurate data insights and predictions that bring long term benefits to the organization. To deliver the best machine learning models in industry, we need to interpret and analyze the effectiveness and performance of deep learning and artificial intelligence models before starting with the implementation process. Model interpretability in machine learning is an approach which is used to assess how easy it is for humans to evaluate and understand the working process of a machine learning model.

Models such as logistic regression are ideal for use in the development of business AI models because you can add extra features and implement deep learning methods to meet system requirements. Model interpretability is immensely important because algorithm outcomes are responsible for making high stakes decisions and it is mandatory to know which features to add and which need to be removed. Additionally, in case the model is not interpretable, the company might not be legally permitted to make changes to processes by using insights.

Model interpretability can be performed with the help of DataRobot. DataRobot features several components that yield fully human-interpretable models because of the model blueprint and feature explanation techniques. Model blueprint provides insights related to the preprocessing steps on which each model is based to achieve a desired outcome. Furthermore, it also helps data scientists to justify the models and explain regulatory details if needed.

On the other hand, prediction explanations reveal the top variables that can make an impact on the model's outcome. This allows users to explain how the model has derived a specific outcome and the steps involved in deriving accurate predictions and data insights.

Deep Learning in Business Systems

Pioneers in deep learning system development have been using artificial intelligence and deep learning to advance machine learning model capabilities. These advancements have deployed at scale in order to achieve greater efficiency and speed for which a wide range of new training data is used in model training. Business systems now require deep learning models that are capable of making real time decisions and deliver outcomes that bring long term benefits to the business. The process of scoring predictive models and processing of decision requests in real time have added great value to machine learning models.

Technologies today have advanced to a point where machine learning models can be implemented and deployed at a scale to achieve better performance, reliability, and effectiveness. These advances are unleashing new pathways of data science capabilities such as the acceptance of real time decision requests from various channels and processing of decision requests in real time according to the given business rules. To handle thousands of requests per second, machine learning engineers have to design and control processes through multiple model recalibration methods.

Usage of Deep Learning in Businesses and Industries

Marketing, Sales, and Finance industries are the biggest users of deep learning models and machine learning algorithms. Modern day marketing models and approaches are designed to attract customers and improve sales by showcasing services of a company in unique ways. To make this happen, marketing departments work to find large datasets which are then implemented in deep learning models to understand customer purchase decisions and recommendations. Deep learning has the power to replace traditional heuristics-based lead scoring because it can determine relationships between data and generate useful insights as well. On the other hand, sales teams can also get support from deep learning models to analyze customer predictions.

Generally, companies and businesses get unstructured data from a variety of sources and sales teams are unable to understand purchasing trends of customers. With the help of deep learning models, businesses are now able to predict insights, deal cycles, and deal sizes which can yield the highest return on investment and sales ratio. Evaluating customer and sales interactions that are likely to yield best outcomes can deliver long term benefits to business for which deep learning models are ideal and best performing.

In the finance sector, we can see deep learning and artificial intelligence systems that are used to perform certain tasks to avoid fraud and analyze credit history of customers. Banks can now overview credit history for thousands of customers within seconds and make major decisions such as loan approval with the help of automated machine learning systems. Furthermore, machine learning systems have also eliminated the need to perform manual data entry for which predictive modeling algorithms and machine learning methods are used.

Applications

Here are some examples of the best deep learning applications that have brought significant benefits and ease to humans.

Language Recognition

Language recognition systems are based on deep learning models which allows them to differentiate dialects of any language. The dialects are determined by artificial intelligence models and can be differentiated in real time without human involvement. Language recognition and translation systems are some of the best implementations of deep learning algorithms as they can perform translation from images and text in real time as well.

Autonomous Vehicles

The biggest revolution in our transport system is the addition of self-driving or autonomous vehicles. Artificial intelligence and machine learning models in self-driving vehicles have the capability to detect patterns, humans, and other traffic for making accurate decisions.

Computer Vision and Text Generation

The deep learning approach has provided best models for image classification, image segmentation, and object detection systems. Computer vision and text generation methods are widely used in education systems because they have the capability to automate tasks and perform required text generation without any hassle.

Limitations of Machine Learning Models

Machine learning models developed with Python and R programming languages are capable of automating processing and deliver accurate insights when trained through high quality training datasets. It is simple to understand the value of ML and the great advantages it has brought in today's world. Although technology has greatly revolutionized how different tasks and processes are done, there are still a lot of limitations and consequences of automating tasks which need to be overlooked by human beings.

Information explosion has now resulted in the collection of massive amounts of data, and this amount of data is engaged with rapid development of computer parallelization and processor power. The concept of trusting machine learning models has its own advantages and disadvantages. When trained with high quality training data, artificial intelligence and machine learning systems can generate 100 percent accurate predictions and complete the given tasks without failure. Although machines can never achieve the level of human intelligence, they have significantly improved with time to bring positive outcomes.

Machine learning models can never tell us about the normative values which need to be accepted and answers to questions like how we should act in certain scenarios. The approach is extremely powerful for sensors and can be used to design and calibrate systems for delivering accurate outcomes.

Finding Useful Data

The most vital part of developing and training a deep learning model is to find accurate and high-quality data. If you feed a model with poor or unstructured data, it will surely provide inaccurate results in future. Finding quality data is difficult for which data scientists need to verify the resources and include information that is completely reliable and authentic. Furthermore, most of the machine learning models require huge amounts of data to be trained perfectly. The larger the architecture, the greater the size of data needed to produce viable results.

Reusing data in machine learning models is surely a bad approach. In case you are not able to find data in bulk, try to train your model with labeled and structured data so that it can learn within a short period of time. Whenever fake data is fed into a machine learning model, it will start to train by itself and when tested on an unseen data set, it might not deliver accurate prediction results. Like quality of training data, features also play a vital role in the predictions made by machine learning models.

Chapter 9: Advanced Python Data Science

Data is the core part of the machine learning model development process. Traditional data and Big Data are major types of data that are used to train machine learning models. It has become mandatory to build new platforms to meet the ever-increasing demand of organizations. There are several challenges and difficulties faced by traditional data because it requires collaborative efforts of people to be managed and utilizes a lot of resources and time as well.

What is Big Data?

Big data is known as the collection of large amounts of information which is processed and manipulated for analytics. This approach is divided into three major portions which are volume, velocity, and variety. In the volume section, organizations have to collect information and data from different sources including social media, industrial equipment, Internet, and business transactions. Storage mediums like Hadoop and Data lakes are widely used to store and process information in big data.

To deal with millions of transactions each minute, big data systems have built in velocity handling modules. Moreover, data streams and tons of information from the Internet can now be processed through big data algorithms without any hassle. Data is present in different formats; it can be either structured or unstructured for which the variety properties in big data are used to handle database operations.

Importance of Big Data

Big data systems can change the way we handle information. When it comes to handling large volumes of data, we need to select the most suitable tools and models to manage the available information. With the implementation of big data, companies can take data from any source and manipulate it to get accurate insights. Tools such as in-memory analytics and Hadoop can identify new sources of data and reduce the time needed to process the information. Furthermore, these tools are cost saving and can help companies in processing large volumes of data without any hassle.

There is no business that claims success without having the need to develop strong customer relations. Customers are the most vital asset for any business and if the company is not able to deliver quality services, losing potential customers becomes inevitable. The use of big data systems allows businesses to analyze customer behavior and purchase decisions by overviewing the trends and patterns in data.

Organizational Benefits

Advanced Python data science applications are designed to bring long term benefit to large scale industries and businesses. Big data systems help businesses to understand market trends, evaluate product effectiveness, and gain information regarding customer behavior. Furthermore, the approach also promotes cost saving measures and delivers high returns and meaningful insights within a short period of time. Machine learning and artificial intelligence systems have to handle big data regularly for which the model is programmed to learn and gain insights from high quality data. In return, this approach brings long term benefit to companies and businesses.

Modern day computing systems provide the power, flexibility, and speed needed to access huge amounts of big data. Furthermore, companies need new methods with reliable access and storage facilities in order to store and manage huge volumes of data. High performance tools such as in-memory analytics and grid computing have greatly increased reliability and efficiency of big data systems.

Python Machine Learning Limitations

Python is the finest general purpose and high-level programming language which is widely being used by developers to create state of the art machine learning and artificial intelligence models. Compilation of a Python program is not similar to a conventional C or C++ program because its execution occurs with the support of an interpreter. For other languages, the compiler is responsible for executing and running the program. This makes Python execution slower as compared to the execution of other programming languages. Furthermore, memory consumption of Python is higher because of the complexity of data types and implementation of libraries.

There are specific limitations of Python programming language which make it difficult for beginners to develop machine learning models through Python. Numerous kinds of runtime errors occur during the development of Python programs which need to be addressed sequentially to avoid any future problems. Moreover, Python features and extensions can be customized to make programming easier, as this is not the case with other programming languages such as C, C++ and R.

Reasons to select Python in Data Science

Python programming language allows programmers to express logical concepts and libraries without writing long lines of code. There are no extra steps to compile and execute steps as we can directly run the program through source code. Furthermore, Python has the capability to convert the source code into bytecodes so that it can be easily translated into the native language of the computer. Developers can load and link libraries directly without adding any type of additional lines of code or functions.

Memory management and exception handling approaches make Python suitable for developing data analytics and machine learning models. Python standard libraries including Pandas, NumPy, and Matplotlib are the ultimate sources to design, develop and test machine learning models. Libraries provide pre-written piece of code which can be enhanced by the developers to meet the requirements of the machine learning model. As machine learning requires continuous data processing, Python libraries can be used to access, handle, and transform data without any hassle.

For handling basic machine learning algorithms such as linear regression, clustering and classification, we can use Scikit-Learn library whereas Pandas library is best for handling high level data structures. Pandas allows data scientists to gather data from external sources and also performs filtration of information to create high quality training datasets. Moreover, Pandas also provides extra facilities such as data extraction from external resources such as Excel.

578

Is Machine Learning Perfect?

Despite its amazing advantages and facilities in the real world, machine learning models cannot be considered one hundred percent perfect and ideal. Although data scientists and machine learning engineers are researching to make AI models work accurately and perform near to human intelligence, there is still a lot of room for improvement. Machine learning models require loads of training datasets, and these should be of high quality as well. Data is not always available which makes the training process difficult and machine learning models start to make predictions that might not be suitable for human beings.

Machine learning requires a lot of resources and time to develop algorithms and complete the training process. As we can achieve a considerable amount of relevance and accuracy, there are several other functions and external resources required to avail maximum outcome from the machine learning models. Furthermore, interpretation of results might not be accurate in all cases, as humans are not completely aware of the functionality of machine learning models and how they are yielding predictions.

Machine Learning vs Data Science

Artificial intelligence and data science are major technologies in today's world. Although artificial intelligence is involved in data science operations, it definitely does not completely represent artificial intelligence. Data science involves various underlying data operations and supports both structured and unstructured data. In artificial intelligence, there is a limited implementation of machine learning algorithms and we are required to use vectors and embeddings.

Generally, data science is widely used in advertising, Internet search engines, and marketing industries whereas artificial intelligence models are more focused on manufacturing, healthcare, transportation, and robotics projects. Artificial intelligence and data science models can also be combined together for boosting the performance of machine learning systems. Data has become an essential factor for each industry and business for which companies are focused on developing secure storage systems as well.

Data science covers various fields such as programming, mathematics, and statistics. For data scientists to develop the best performing data science models though Python programming, getting information and accurate training datasets is immensely important. Moreover, other steps involved in data science including maintenance, visualization, manipulation, and extraction of data to forecast predictions, and occurrence of future events is also a major part of data science model development approach.

Most of the traditional artificial intelligence and machine learning algorithms were provided with goals in advance. With the evolution and development of the deep learning approach, data scientists have been able to understand the patterns and get valuable insights from data in a better way.

Differences and Constraints

There are considerable differences between artificial intelligence and machine learning. Computer systems still do not have consciousness and full autonomy like human beings which makes it difficult for data scientists to achieve one hundred percent accurate results from machine learning systems. Instead, the models only perform tasks for which they are trained, whether they are for the benefit of humans or not. Data science is the study and analysis of data, and a data scientist is responsible for outcomes the model will be delivering in the industry.

Moreover, the main requirement of data science models is to process data and complete other activities like transformation and cleaning. Artificial intelligence is a tool for data scientists and it is the best available approach to analyze data. On the other hand, data scientists are also held accountable for reviewing patterns in data by applying predictive modeling techniques. Depending on the requirements, the limitations and constraints of data science models can be managed to achieve accurate data insights and analytics in the future.

Different statistical techniques are used in data science models whereas in artificial intelligence, we take support from computer algorithms. Data science is all about finding hidden patterns in data, whereas artificial intelligence concepts are based on the autonomy and performance of machine learning models.

Useful Deep Learning Methods and Techniques

Learning about the advantages of transfer learning and latent features of pre-trained architecture can help you gain better insights and predictions from deep learning models. Remember that pre-trained weights are a good option to be considered as compared to the randomly initialized weights because they can be easily modified. Furthermore, we can also limit weight sizes and absolute value of weights to generalize the machine learning model. In this way, you can achieve maximum output and performance from your training data as well.

Moreover, you can also change the output layer and replace model defaults with a specific output size and activation function which is best suited for your domain. Make sure that you do not remove the first layers of a neural network because they are responsible for interpreting features and performing interactions throughout the domain as well.

Quality Assurance

Optimizing deep learning and machine learning models is quite simple if you are well aware of the design, algorithms, and functionality of the model. Hyperparameter settings and optimization algorithms make it easier to check the performance of a machine learning model and are ideal for conducting quality assurance checks as well. Each model is based on a specific set of hyperparameters which include number of hidden layers, number of neurons, activation functions, and optimization algorithm. Moreover, other factors such as learning rate, regularization hyperparameters, and regularization techniques are best for conducting in-depth quality checks for a machine learning model.

Most of the time, quality assurance mechanisms are not recognized by some artificial intelligence and machine learning systems. To avoid such problems, we are required to research and select the best approaches to test each machine learning model separately. Using training data to overview the performance and prediction capabilities of a machine learning model is absolutely not recommended because it might not yield accurate results in each case. Understanding statistical techniques for data such as mean, median, and mode will be helpful in reviewing data relationships at a high level.

As the machine learning model gets trained, it is likely to

make accurate predictions and data insights for any scenario. Model testing is mandatory because machine learning systems are implemented in information systems of businesses and companies of each category. As they are subject to handle critical data, we have to make sure the information is never compromised or mishandled by the machine learning model. Although machine learning systems are not 100 percent accurate, we can surely improve the performance, safety, and reliability by regularly conducting quality checks.

Advanced AI

An artificial intelligence system can become super intelligent and perform activities for positive development in today's world. Powerful programming languages such as Python and R can be used to develop high end machine learning and artificial intelligence models which are capable of completing complex tasks without any hassle. Although advanced artificial intelligence can unleash the potential of machine learning systems, there are several consequences that need to be focused. As we all know, intelligent systems are given training through specific datasets and they might not make suitable predictions in each scenario, which in return can become harmful for humans.

Things to Remember

An efficient machine learning model has the capability to adapt unseen and new data. This approach can be done by generalizing the machine learning model development process for which you have to follow some specific rules and techniques. The model will better generalize if the data contains a wide spectrum of observations and is reliable by all means. To predict an accurate outcome, a machine learning model utilizes training data at first whereas the testing data is used afterwards.

Remember that machine learning, artificial intelligence, and deep learning will never take over a human level of intelligence and decision-making capabilities. In fact, the models are vulnerable to human mistakes and whenever an error is found in a machine learning system, the model is completely held accountable for the mistake. Most of the hard work for developing machine learning model lies upon data transformation.

Most of the effort and time is spent on feature engineering and data cleansing methods. These methods allow data scientists to uncover the hidden features in the training data sets so that a relationship can be developed between the layers, variables, and attributes within the machine learning model. Deep learning has achieved great acceptance in the real world because the models developed from deep learning can be implemented in a broad range of applications and fields.

Today, the use of machine learning and deep analytics has reached a new level of success and acceptance. Due to the consistent improvement and development in hardware systems, the performance, reliability, and security of machine learning models is also increasing which brings long term benefits to companies and businesses.

We should try to focus on the outcomes and predictions of machine learning models which are directly associated with human beings. Taking the example of a healthcare system, there is absolutely no room for errors or mistakes because the patient who is following instructions from the machine learning model is absolutely unaware about the negative effects in case the model delivers misleading information. Such is the case with the machine learning and artificial intelligence models that are implemented in autonomous vehicles or financial systems.

Although machine learning, deep learning, and artificial intelligence models are reliable, they might never meet the level of human intelligence because computer systems are absolutely unaware about external factors associated with humans such as ethics or relationships. If a model is programmed to perform a specific task, it will keep on learning and developing predictions to achieve best outcomes even if it is bringing loss for humans. Machine learning algorithms provide intelligent services and products which have delivered great advantages to humans.

Data analytics and deep learning are key factors that can directly affect the prediction capabilities of a model. To implement these strategies into a business model, we need to understand the core requirements of the business and implement the techniques and machine learning algorithms that can help in achieving the highest return on investment. Deep learning algorithms can bring long term advantages to businesses and humans in real life as well. Through accurate predictions and data insights, machine learning models serve as a best source for automating processes and tasks that were previously done through traditional computer systems. To achieve desired results, data scientists always focus on the maintenance and training of machine learning systems.

Conclusion

Python Data Analytics: How to learn python data science and use python machine learning. Introduction to deep learning to master python for beginners is a comprehensive guide for learning Python for machine learning and artificial intelligence. The concepts and methodologies explained in this book can be adopted to understand how data science actually works and why Python is the best programming language to develop high performing machine learning and data analytics models. Designed for beginners, we have explained each aspect and portion of Python programming language with code samples which will greatly help our readers in developing machine learning models.

Machine learning has revolutionized business processes and the way we are performing routine activities. By learning the basics and findings of data science, researchers can understand the functionality of machine learning systems and implement their Python programming skills to develop high end data science models. *Python Data Analytics: How to learn python data science and use python machine learning. Introduction to deep learning to master python for beginners* is absolutely easy to understand as it is intended to help beginners in learning core concepts of Python machine learning, data analytics, and data science with the support of examples and real-life scenarios.

References

(2019). What is Data Analytics?. Retrieved from
https://www.mastersindatascience.org/resources/what-is-data-analytics/

Assessing Data and Creating a dataset, (2017). Retrieved from
https://wp.wwu.edu/machinelearning/2017/01/29/accessing-data-and-creating-a-dataset/

Chris, N. (2019) A Beginner's Guide to Neural Networks and Deep Learning. Retrieved from
https://skymind.ai/wiki/neural-network

James, W. (2028). Big Data VS Traditional Data. Retrieved from http://customerthink.com/big-data-vs-traditional-data-what-to-know-when-it-comes-to-defines-big-data/

Jason, B. (2018). Your First Deep Learning Project in Python with Keras Step-By-Step. Retrieved from
https://machinelearningmastery.com/tutorial-first-neural-network-python-keras/

Machine Learning Algorithms. Retrieved from
https://www.datarobot.com/wiki/algorithm/

Moussa, T. (2018). Lessons Learned from Building Scalable Machine Learning Pipelines. Retrieved from
https://techblog.appnexus.com/lessons-learned-from-building-scalable-machine-learning-pipelines-822acb3412ad

Victor, R. (2019). How To Develop a Machine Learning Model From Scratch. Retrieved from
https://towardsdatascience.com/machine-learning-general-process-8f1b510bd8af

Python for data science

circumstances is the author responsible for any losses, direct or indirect, that are incurred as a result of the use of information contained within this document, including, but not limited to, errors, omissions, or inaccuracies.

Introduction

You have taken the first step on your path to learning data science by purchasing *Python for Data Science: The ultimate python guide for beginners. Python machine learning tools, concepts and introduction. Python programming crash course.* Allow yourself to be guided in the field of data science step by step from the very beginning with the help of this book. The purpose of *Python for Data Science* is to educate the complete beginner on the fundamental topics of data science.

Studying this field can be exhausting, difficult and even intimidating to some, especially those with limited programming knowledge. Fortunately, the step by step approach of this book will teach you the theory as well as the practical skills you need to implement learning algorithms and techniques on your own in no time. All you need is a desire to learn and a good instruction manual with a practical approach towards study.

This book includes the following topics:

- In the first chapter you learn how to setup your Python work environment by creating a virtual environment where you will install a scientific distribution that includes all of the tools you need. Keep in mind that you will be working only with free tools and open source datasets, so you won't have to pay a dime.
- Once your toolkit is ready, the next two chapters will teach you about the importance of data pre-processing and exploration. Do not rush through these sections because the more time and effort you invest in preparing your data, the better results you will obtain.
- Once your data is prepared, you will begin exploring a variety of supervised and unsupervised learning

algorithms and techniques. You will learn about linear regression, the Naïve Bayes classifier, the K-nearest neighbor algorithm, support vector machines, decision trees, K-means clustering and more.

- After learning the fundamental learning techniques you will start exploring the power of neural networks. These structures are some of the most powerful data analysis techniques in data science, and this chapter will introduce you to the most popular ones. You will learn about a variety of neural networks such as the single layer and multilayer perceptron, as well as the Restricted Boltzmann Machine.

- Finally, you will also be introduced to the field of Big Data, which is a subfield of data science that processes vast volumes of data. You will learn why this subfield is the future and what real world applications exist for it. Furthermore, you will gain an idea about which supervised and unsupervised learning algorithms can be used when handling Big Data.

Take note that in order to learn fast and benefit from this guide, you need to practice along with it. It is very tempting to start reading and not let go of the book, however, doing things that way means you won't learn much. The book is divided in such a way that it allows you to go section by section, bit by bit, and make your way up the ladder until you understand the fundamentals of data science. And make sure to practice every concept and technique!

Chapter 1: Getting Started

Data science is a relatively new discipline that has entered the market only recently. Even though this field has existed for decades, it was only studied and researched mostly on a theoretical level by mathematicians and specialists from various technical fields. Data science includes a number of components that can be studied individually as well, such as machine learning, computational linguistics, data analysis, linear algebra and many more. From these elements alone we can conclude that data science is in fact a seemingly chaotic mixture of mathematics, programming, and data communication. However, this combination is one of the main reasons why data science is so widely used for a variety of purposes. It is a versatile field. This versatility, however, leads to a number of different specialties destined for certain areas of expertise within data science.

But before we discuss what data science is in detail, you should understand what it isn't. Many beginners get the wrong idea about this field and they end up making mistakes that can set them back on their journey.

First of all, know that data science is not equal to software development or engineering. Your job as a future data scientist will not be developing products, systems, or features. Secondly, data science is not about graphical work, or visualization. You will not develop tools focusing on cool visuals or graphical elements. Thirdly, data science does not involve scientific work in the sense of academia. The field is determined by what the industry or market requires from the data scientist. Finally, there is a false image of data science involving mostly statistics. The field of statistical analysis and anything related to that subject can be part of data science and having that kind of knowledge can prove to be useful, however, there is far more to it than that. Statistical knowledge alone will not qualify you to become a data scientist.

With that in mind, let's now discuss what data science actually is. This field involves programming skills, statistical understanding, visualization concepts, and finally a business sense. This last component may often be harder to acquire, however, it is just as important as the others, if not more so. When we refer to a business sense we are discussing the ability to answer any possible business questions with all the available data you are provided with. You need to be capable of connecting the dots by using only the carefully selected data from a world full of data. Essentially, the data scientist is the one who connects the world of business with the technical world of data.

To keep it simple for now, data science can be compared to cooking. You start preparing your ingredients first by cleaning the vegetables, the meat, and chop everything to the desired size. In the same way you start the data science process through data munging, which involves data cleansing, debugging, extraction, loading and so on. Once this step is completed, you start cooking your ingredients, step by step, timing every process until the raw food can be eaten. This step corresponds to data exploration and various processes such as feature reduction or construction. Now the meal is ready to be served and you arrange it nicely on your plate in order for it to be nice and presentable, and you serve everything in a specific sequence. In data science this final step is the part where you display your data mining results, perhaps with the aid of graphical visualization in order to make it easy for your business users to understand the data reports.

Now that you have an idea about the ingredients behind the cooking process, you need to obtain the right set of tools. Developing a professional toolkit from the beginning is a crucial step. In the field of data science you will always be learning new techniques and add to your toolkit. However, there is one tool that serves as the foundation for everything else, and that is Python.

Python is one of the best multi-purpose tools in data science, as well as other technical specializations. In this case, it is particularly powerful when it comes to data munging, as well as data mining, especially with the help of packages and libraries such as Scikit-learn. However, it's worth mentioning that sometimes R is used as the alternative, however, it is somewhat lacking when it comes to data munging. It is often used as a way to prototype your data science problem because of its usefulness when undergoing data exploration or testing algorithms under different conditions.

In this book, we are going to focus on Python due to its simplicity, power, versatility and ability to be extended with a variety of open source libraries and packages. This programming language is used in many fields, as it's becoming increasingly impossible to work with computers without hearing about Python. Some people consider it nothing but a trend for beginners, however, that's not the case as it is used in everything from software development to machine learning and data science by everyone whether a complete novice or professional.

Python's humble beginnings are found in 1991 when Guido van Rossum, a big fan of the famous Monty Python comedy group, designed it. Speaking of comedy, if you are a fan yourself, keep your eyes open as you go through the documentation for this language and you'll find several fun Easter eggs. With that bit of trivia out of the way, here are some of the main characteristics that make Python the optimal choice for studying data science:

1. Python is powerful: This programming language can

equip you with every tool you need for every step you need to perform and it won't cost you a thing. Being an open source product has its advantages. Developers from around the world continue to improve and refine the language, especially with the addition of various packages, libraries, and modules. Python is more powerful than ever before because of how much its usability can be extended.

2. Python is versatile and user friendly: This feature is tied to the first one in many ways. First of all, Python is one of the most beginner-friendly programming languages you can learn and that is why it is often recommended for aspiring data scientists and machine learners. All you need is a basic grasp on the language and then you can focus on the data science concepts and techniques. Secondly, the ability to extend the language makes it easier for you to work with algorithms, especially if you are a complete beginner.

3. Python is easy to integrate: Many other tools and even programming languages can be used in combination with Python. For instance, if you know how to code in C or C++, you can use that language for the bulk of your programming tasks and then use Python as the central hub which connects all your tools to your code.

4. Python is compatible with many platforms: Portability is sometimes a problem, especially when you work on one system to achieve your goals and then you have to move your entire work to a different system. This is where Python excels. The code and the tools you work with using Python will automatically run on any operating system, whether it's Windows, Linux or Mac.

To summarize, Python is powerful, easy to learn and even master, and can be integrated with a variety of tools, programming languages as well as operating systems. With that being said, let's dive in and start installing Python, as well as all the other tools we will need.

Python Setup

In this section we are going to discuss the installation process for Python, as well as a number of its extensions. If you are already familiar with the programming language, you can skip the setup and continue reading about libraries and scientific distributions. If this is the first time you are installing it, however, you should know that Python comes in two different versions. You have the option to install Python 2 or Python 3. As you can probably tell, version 2 is the older one, however, it is still in use and many data scientists choose to stick with it for the time being. Read up on the documentation and perhaps check what the online Python community has to say as well and then decide which version to use. Some tools and extensions work only with Python 2, so keep that in mind as well.

In this book we are going to focus on the up to date Python 3 because this version is the future and it will continue receiving support for quite some time. Whatever your decision is, please stick to one of them all the way in order to avoid any compatibility issues. If you write your code in Python 2 and then you execute it in a system that runs with Python 3, you might encounter serious errors.

With that in mind, head to Python's official webpage at www.python.org and download your chosen version of Python for the operating system your computer is using. Keep in mind that for the purpose of data science, installing Python alone is not enough. Therefore, you have two options. You can either install everything manually and select each element and tool as needed, or install a Python scientific distribution, which essentially is a package that contains everything you need. Nonetheless, we are going to discuss both methods because having full control over what is needed for your project is important.

Once you downloaded Python, simply follow the instructions to perform the basic setup. Now, you need to also install a variety of packages, otherwise the language alone with its base components isn't that useful for data science. To perform this step manually, you need to use a package manager. Fortunately, Python comes with one already installed and it's called "pip". Open you command terminal and type pip in order to launch the manager. This package manager will allow you to install and uninstall any component whenever you wish. You can even perform updates to every single package, or only to certain ones. You even have the option of rolling back to a different version if the update causes some kind of conflicts within your project. With that being said, let's install a package by typing this command:

pip install < myPackage >

That's it! You only need to know the name of the package you want to install and use its name as a keyword. Updating and removing the packages is done the same way. Simply replace the "install" keyword with the appropriate one for each command.

Now that you have an idea about the basic installation process, let's discuss scientific distributions. Installing and maintaining dozens of packages and modules by hand can be quite tedious, so let's automate it.

Python Scientific Distributions

Creating your Python working environment can be time consuming and can lead to compatibility errors if you go through the process manually. Some tools don't work well together, or they require the installation of certain dependencies you aren't aware of. It is good to be able to customize your Python installation, however, as a beginner you might want to stick to a Python distribution instead.

Save your time and effort to practice data science and machine learning concepts and techniques instead of fiddling with various packages. A scientific distribution will allow you to automate the entire installation process, finish it within minutes and then jump straight into practical data science. There are different scientific distributions out there and they each contain a certain set of tools designed for various types of projects. However, they all have in common the fact that they contain a number of powerful Python libraries, specifically designed with data science in mind, as well as an Integrated Development Environment and other tools to get you started as soon as possible. With that being said, let's discuss the most important distributions that you should download and explore.

Anaconda

One of the most popular scientific distributions you can find is Anaconda. In a way it completes Python by extending it with around 200 pre-installed packages that include the ones data scientists use the most, such as NumPy, Pandas, Matplotlib and Scikit-learn. Furthermore, Anaconda can run on any computer no matter which operating system and version you're running and can even be installed next to other distributions without causing any conflicts.

This scientific distribution contains everything you need, especially in the beginning of your journey. It offers you all the tools needed to perform data analyses and explorations, as well as mass data processing and computing. In addition, it comes with its own package manager, which allows you to tweak the packages yourself or maintain them manually if you prefer. However, the most attractive part about using

601

Anaconda is the fact that it offers you all of that for free, while other distributions might involve certain fees.

If you decided to go with Anaconda, you will need to get accustomed to its internal package manager which is accessed with the keyword "conda". The manager works just like pip and is used to install, delete, or update any or all of your packages. Furthermore, it can also be used to setup a virtual environment (we'll discuss it soon). Now, let's check to see if we are running the most recent version of conda before we do anything else. Perform the verification and update by simply using the update keyword like so:

conda update conda

Now, in order to manually install certain packages, because the distribution might not contain quite everything you need, you need to use the install keyword just like you did when testing out the pip package manager. You can even install several packages at the same time by simply listing them all in a sequence. Here's how that looks like in the command console:

conda install < package1> < package2 > < package3 > < package100 >

Next, you can update the packages with the update function. The easiest way to do this is to simply update everything at once by adding the "—all" keyword. Here's how:

conda update –all

Lastly, you might want to remove some of the packages you don't need, or if you installed one that causes some kind of conflicts with another package. Simply use the "remove" keyword to instruct the manager to remove the desired package. It's that simple.

Conda is a very intuitive package manager and it is easy to use. If you discover that you prefer it over other managers like pip, then you can even install it separately to use it with any other scientific distributions.

Now, let's explore another scientific distribution called Canopy.

Canopy

This distribution is a popular alternative to Anaconda because its aim is to provide data scientists and analysts with all the tools they need to do their job. It also contains approximately 200 packages, including Pandas and Matplotlib. Make sure to check the distribution's documentation to see all the other packages it contains because they are too numerous to list here.

In many ways Canopy is similar to Anaconda. They both have many packages in common, however, without paying a fee you will only have basic access to Canopy. For starters that's enough, however, if you ever need its advanced features you need to install the main version of the distribution.

WinPython

This distribution is aimed at Windows users, as the name suggests. Essentially, it offers you the same features as Anaconda and Canopy, however, while the others have paid versions with more advanced features, this distribution is entirely community driven and therefore free. WinPython is an open source tool that you are free to use however you want and you can even modify it yourself if you have the required skills to do so.

The main drawback of course is the fact that it can be installed only on a Windows machine, but if you do use one, you should consider it because it even allows you to install several versions of it on the same computer. In addition it also offers you a free IDE.

Virtual Environments

Now that you have an idea about scientific distributions, let's take a sidestep and discuss the power of virtual environments before exploring various Python libraries and other tools you need.

Virtual environments are one of the most useful tools when practicing something new, or when you want to be able to perform multiple tasks in different environments. Keep in mind that you are normally restricted by your operating system or by the version of Python which you currently installed on your system. No matter the chosen installation method, it is difficult to install different versions of the same tools without risking potential software conflicts and errors. However, if you take the virtual environment route, you will have a number of advantages and no significant disadvantages.

One of the biggest benefits of working through a virtual environment is the fact that it can be your testing ground. This means that you can dedicate an area of your system to experimentation and learning without any consequences. You can try any variety of libraries, modules, different versions of your tools and so on. Furthermore, you can learn and practice data science concepts and techniques without being worried that you will damage your system in some way. Eliminate the stress of having to reinstall your operating system or fix complicated errors by learning to work through a virtual environment. The worst case involves resetting the environment, which means you don't need to Google obscure error codes or try to fix your operating system because you messed something up.

Studying aside, another reason why so many choose to work through a virtual environment is because it allows them to have multiple Python and data science distributions installed at the same time. In addition, you can also install multiple versions of your operating system to see how your project behaves. You can even install different operating systems altogether on the same machine without affecting your main system. Some of the packages and modules work only with certain versions of Python for instance. Therefore you can use a virtual environment for Python version 2 and another one for Python version 3. Create unique virtual environments that suit your needs precisely.

Finally, a virtual environment will help you verify the replicability of your project. Sometimes you need to make sure that whatever task you performed or project you worked on can be replicated on a different operating system or with a different Python version. By installing different versions of your tools or the operating system in separate virtual environments you can test your prototype and see how it performs.

Now that you understand what virtual environments are for, let's install one with pip:

pip install virtualenv

Installation is quite straightforward, however, you will need to make some considerations at the end of the setup. For instance, you will need to decide which version of Python your virtual environment should use. The default version is the one from which virtualenv is installed. Next, you need to consider your packages. With each virtual environment installation, all of the packages will also be installed. This is a good thing because it's one less task you need to perform, however, when you setup multiple virtual environments each one of them will install the same packages once again. This is a waste of system resources, as well as time. There is no need to install the same thing more than once, therefore you need to issue a command for the virtual environment to use the files it already has access to instead of installing a new set. Finally, you need to consider whether you need the option to relocate your virtual environment to a different system that perhaps even uses a different version of Python. To make your virtual environment relocation-friendly, you need to specify that you want the scripts to work no matter the path.

Once you choose the correct options for your situation, you can finally create and launch the environment. Type this line to generate the new environment:

virtualenv myEnv

A new virtual environment will be created together with a directory named "myEnv" where it will reside. Now let's launch the environment with these commands:

cd myEnv

activate

The environment is now ready and we can install all of the tools we need as before. The environment acts exactly the same as your system so everything you did so far you can do in any virtual environment you create.

Data Science Packages

So far we kept mentioning how powerful Python is because of the wide variety of packages, libraries, and extensions that we have access to specifically for data science and analytics. As a beginner data scientist you will need to understand these packages because they represent your toolkit without which your knowledge can't be easily applied.

In this section we are going to briefly explore the most important Python packages and tools you will be working with throughout this book. Keep in mind that these tools have been selected because they are industry standard, polished, and frequently updated, and most importantly well-documented.

1. Scikit-learn: This is one of the most important tools used by data scientists, analysts, machine learners, and software engineers. This is a free Python library that contains some of the algorithms that you will frequently use, such as classification, clustering, and regression algorithms. They include k-means clustering, support vector machines, random forests, gradient boosting and many more. Furthermore, this library is designed to be used with other libraries, such as the Python numerical library known as NumPy and the scientific library known as SciPy. In order to install the library, simply type *pip install scikit-learn*. Remember to replace pip with the keyword for your chosen package manager, if you prefer a different one.

2. NumPy: This library goes hand in hand with Scikit-learn due to the support it offers for multi-dimensional arrays. This includes various algorithms that operate purely on these arrays which are used for data storage and certain matrix operations. The reason why we need this Python extension is because the

programming language wasn't initially designed for numerical computing operations. Since complex mathematical operations are part of any data scientist's daily work, NumPy is a must-have.

3. SciPy: NumPy and SciPy are frequently used together because they fill each other's weak points. This open source library is used for technical and scientific computing processes. It adds modules to Python that are used for optimization, interpolation, linear algebra, image processing and much more. The reason why SciPy compliments NumPy is because it builds on the array object that is part of the NumPy library. Furthermore, it also expands on other libraries and tools such as Matplotlit and Pandas.

4. Pandas: This Python library was created mainly for manipulating data as well as analyzing it. Its most important features include data structures and operations that are needed to manipulate tables, as well as time series. Take note that Pandas is also free software and that it has nothing to do with pandas. The name of the library refers to "panel data", which describes data sets that involve a set of observations over a number of recorded time periods.

5. Matplotlib: Sometimes you might want to sit back and visualize your data without looking at confusing numbers to form a conclusion. Sometimes you have to present your findings to those who are not technically inclined and do not understand raw numbers. In either case you would benefit from using plots to build a graphical representation of your findings. This is what Matplotlib is for. It allows you to build plots by using an array and then visualize the data, including interactively. In case you don't know what a plot is, it is a graph that is often used in statistical analysis in order to demonstrate a connection between certain variables.

6. Jupyter: Finally, we have Jupyter which will act as your

data science IDE. It is often used by machine learners and data scientists because of how user-friendly it is and because it works with any programming language. However, the most important aspect is the fact that it allows you to visualize your data straight in the environment instead of opening new windows or panels and being forced to switch them. You write your code, your algorithms, and look at your data. In addition, Jupyter also provides you with the ability to directly communicate with other users and collaborate with them by sharing project files. We will discuss Jupyter in a bit more detail soon.

These Python tools should be more than enough for a beginner data scientist. You may feel overwhelmed, especially when you consider there are hundreds of packages and libraries that you will eventually use. However, for now, you should stick to the tools that form the foundation of nearly every project.

Before moving on, let's discuss one more component which we mentioned only briefly, namely Jupyter. This tool forms your development environment and you will use it for every project. If you are used to the usual IDE's that are designed with programming and software development in mind, like Atom and Visual Studio, you will notice that Jupyter is quite different and you might even feel a bit lost. Therefore, let's take a moment to discuss using this environment.

Jupyter

All the concepts and techniques you will practice with the help of this book will be done using Jupyter. In order to install it, all you need to do is download it and use the install command with your chosen package manager. The setup itself is very easy to follow, so just perform every step as requested by the installer. If you encounter any errors, then you probably downloaded the wrong installer, so make sure you choose the correct one based on your operating system and its version. Once the installation is complete, fire up the program with the following command:

jupyter notebook

You will notice that the tool isn't opened inside an application window, but in your browser instead. The next step is to press the "New" button in order to tell Jupyter which version of Python you are using. Keep in mind that in this book the chosen version is Python 3. Next, you should see a blank window which is your environment and interface.

The first thing you will notice with this particular environment is that you aren't dealing with a typical text editor. Instead, the code is organized in cell blocks that are executed one cell at a time. This design gives you the advantage of testing and verifying your code one small block at a time. Furthermore, you will notice that you have an input where you type your code and an output where the result is displayed. Now, let's type something to see how it all works:

In: print ("I'm testing Jupyter!")

In order to execute this line of code you should click on the play button. You can find it beneath the Cell tab. The result of the code will be displayed inside the output cell, followed by a blank input cell where you can continue typing. You will also notice a small plus symbol which is used to create more cells.

Summary

In this chapter you learned what it takes to set up your work environment in order to get started. You learned step by step how to install Python and the various options you have. You explored the option of using a scientific distribution instead of a manual installation and you learned how to setup a virtual environment. Remember that if you are the type of person always worrying about messing up, especially when working with code and terminal instructions, then you should use a virtual environment and eliminate all of your fears and doubts with one swift blow.

Furthermore, you explored a number of Python libraries, packages, and extensions which make data science a much more approachable field. All of these tools are free to download and install and they offer you a great deal of benefits. Keep in mind that this book relies on some of these libraries for the practical implementations. For instance, Scikit-learn is used throughout the book because it contains all the algorithms we are going to use, as well as all of the datasets. This way all you need to do is type a command to import them, instead of manually downloading them and setting them up.

Chapter 2: Data Munging with Pandas

Now that you're set up with all the tools you need and with a clean environment, it's time to begin with the data science process known as data munging. Sometimes known as data wrangling, this step is one of the most important ones in the entire data science pipeline. The basic concept behind it is that you need to process a set of data in order to be able to use it together with another set of data, or to analyze it. Essentially, you will make enough changes to an original dataset in order to make it more useful for your specific goals. This is a pre-processing step.

In order to understand this idea better, imagine that you have a set of data on which you need to apply a classification algorithm. However, you realize that you can't perform this step just yet because the dataset is a combination of continuous and categorical variables. This means that you have to modify some of these variables to match the correct format. The challenge here is that you are dealing with raw data and you cannot analyze it just yet. First you need to clean the data with various data munging techniques and tools.

In most real world scenarios you will be dealing with a great deal of data that is raw and cannot be analyzed just yet, unlike the datasets used for study and practice. This is why you need to clean the data and it can actually take you a great deal of time. In fact, many data scientists spend more time preparing the data instead of coding or running various algorithms. So how do we prepare our data? One of the most popular methods includes using the Pandas library which is used for data analysis and manipulation, as mentioned earlier. The purpose of this library in this case is to allow you to analyze raw, real world data a lot faster.

Keep in mind that the purpose of data munging is to gather enough information in order to be able to detect the pattern within it. Furthermore, data needs to be accurate in order to be useful to a data scientist or analyst in order to cut down on the time and resources needed to come up with meaningful results. With that in mind, the first step you need to take involves acquiring the data. After all, without data you can't do anything. However, before you gain access to it you need to understand that all data items are different and are not created equally. You will often have issues recognizing authentic data with an identified source. The second step is about joining the data once it has been extracted from every source. At this stage, the data needs to be modified and then combined in order to proceed at a later time with the analysis. Finally, we have the last step that involves cleaning the data. This stage is the main one. You will need to modify the data in order to obtain a format you can use. You might also have to perform optional steps like correcting noisy data or bad data that can negatively influence the results.

As you can already see, this step is essential although tedious and time consuming. However, you sometimes cannot avoid it. You will have to make sure that you have relevant, up to data information that doesn't contain any null values in order to select only the data you are interested in for analysis. Fortunately, Python together with Pandas are some of the most powerful tools you can use to aid you in data munging.

The Process

As already mentioned, even if data science projects are unique, the workflow is generally the same. It all begins with the acquisition of data. You can gather data in many ways.

You can extract it from a database, from images, from spreadsheets and any other digital source that holds information. This is your raw data, however. You cannot use it for a proper analysis because among all that data you also have missing information and corrupted data. You need to first bring order to chaos by using Python data structures to turn the raw information into an organized data set made out of properly formatted variables. This dataset is then processed with the help of various algorithms.

Next, you can examine your data in order to come up with an early observation that you will later test. You will obtain new variables by processing the ones you currently have and move up the data science pipeline with the various techniques such as graph analysis and reveal the most valuable variables. You will now be able to create the first data model, however, your testing phase will tell you that you will have to apply a number of corrections to your data and therefore return to the data munging processes to rework each step. Keep in mind that in most cases the output you expect will not reflect the real output that you will receive. Theory doesn't always lead you in the direction you expect and that is why you need to process a number of different scenario and test to see what works.

Importing Datasets

Before we can do anything we need the actual data. In order to import a dataset we are going to use Pandas to access tabular information from various databases or spreadsheets. Essentially, this tool will build a data structure in which each row of the tabular file will be indexed, while also separating the variables so that we can manipulate the data. With that being said, we will work in Jupyter and type the following command to import Pandas into our environment and access a CSV file:

In: import pandas as pd

iris_filename = 'datasets-ucl-iris.csv'

iris = pd.read_csv(iris_filename, sep=',', decimal='.', header=None,

names= ['sepal_length', 'sepal_width', 'petal_length', 'petal_width',   'target'])

(Source: The Iris Dataset https://scikitlearn.org/stable/auto_examples/datasets/plot_ir is_dataset.html retrieved in October 2019)

As you can see, the first step of this process is to import the tool we are going to use. Whether you are going to use Pandas or Scikit-learn, it is not enough to just have it installed on your system. You need to import it into your project in order to have access to its functions and features. Next, we created a new file and named it, while also defining the character that will act as a separator and a decimal. In this example the new file will contain an open source dataset that has been used to teach new data scientists and machine learners for years. The dataset is called Iris and it contains 50 samples of three different species of Iris flowers. We also mentioned that we don't want to define a header because it is not needed in our example. What we did so far was create a new data item named iris, which is in fact a data frame when we discuss it in the context of working with Pandas. In this case a data frame is actually the same as a Python list or dictionary, but with a set of added features. Next, we want to explore what the data item contains by typing:

In: iris.head()

This is a simple instruction without any parameters. By

default if we don't specify we are going to access the first five rows from the file. If you want more, then you simply need to mention the number of rows you want to access by typing it as an argument between the parentheses of the function. Next, we want to read the names of the columns to see what kind of information they contain:

In: iris.columns

Out: Index(['sepal_length', 'sepal_width', 'petal_length',

'petal_width', 'target'], dtype='object')

As you can see in the output, what we have for now is an index of each column name. The structure of the output looks like a list. Now, let's obtain the target column:

In: Y = iris['target']

Y

This is what you should see as the output.

Out:

0   Iris-setosa

1   Iris -setosa

2   Iris -setosa

3   Iris -setosa

...

149   Iris-virginica

Name: target, dtype: object

The "Y" in this result is a series typical of Pandas. What you should know is that it is nearly identical to an array, however, it is only unidirectional. Furthermore, you will notice that the index class is the same as the one for a dictionary. Next, we are going to make a request to extract the list of columns by using the index:

In: X = iris[['sepal_length', 'sepal_width']]

Now we have the data frame, which is a matrix instead of a unidimensional series. The reason why it is a matrix is that we asked to extract several columns at once and therefore we essentially obtained an array that is structured in columns and rows. Now let's also obtain all of the dimensions.

In: print (X.shape)

Out: (150, 2)

In: print (Y.shape)

Out: (150)

The result is now a tuple and we can analyze the size of the array in either dimension. These are the bare bones basics of manipulating a new dataset and performing some basic exploration. Let's move on to the next step and preprocess the data so that we can actually use it.

Data Preprocessing

Now that you know how to load a dataset, let's explore the procedures you need to take in order to preprocess all the information within it. First, we are going to assume that we need to perform a certain action on a number of rows. In order to use any function, we first need to setup a mask. Take note that in this case a mask is in fact a collection of Boolean values that determine the selected line. The practical example will clear up this notion, so let's get to it:

In: mask_feature = iris['sepal_length'] > 7.0

In: mask_feature

0   False

1   False

...

146   True

147   True

148   True

149   False

As you can see we have chosen only the lines which contain a sepal length value that is greater than seven. These observations are declared with a Boolean value. Next, we are going to apply a mask in order to modify the iris virginica target and create a new label for it:

In: mask_target = iris['target'] == 'Iris-virginica'

In: iris.loc[mask_target, 'target'] = 'MyLabel'

Wherever the old iris virginica label appeared it will now be replaced with "MyLabel" as the new label. Take note that for this operation we need to use the "loc" function in order to gain access to the data with the help of the indexes. Now let's take the next step and see the labels that are contained by the target column:

In: iris['target'].unique()

Out: array(['Iris-setosa', 'Iris-versicolor', 'New label'], dtype=object)

Now let's group all of the columns together:

In: grouped_targets_mean = iris.groupby(['target']).mean()

grouped_targets_mean

Out:

In: grouped_targets_var = iris.groupby(['target']).var()

grouped_targets_var

With this step we have grouped the columns together by using the groupby function. Take note that this is similar to the "group by" command that you have in SQL. In the next input line we have also applied the mean function which of course calculates the mean value. Keep in mind that we can apply this method either to a single column or multiple columns at the same time. Furthermore, we can use the variance, count, or sum functions in order to gain different values. Take note that the end result you obtain is also a Pandas data frame, which means you can connect all of these operations together. In this example we are grouping all of our data observations by labels in order to be able to analyze the difference between all the values inside the groups. But what if we also have time series to deal with?

In case you aren't familiar with time series, you should know that they imply the analysis of a collection of data entries that appear in an order. This order is determined chronologically. In essence, you are dealing with a group of points that are distributed in time with an equal space dividing each one of them. You will frequently encounter time series because they are used in many fields, usually regarding statistical analysis. For instance, when you have to work with weather data you will find time series regarding the forecasting or the detection of sunspots.

The next challenge, however, is dealing with data entries that contain noise. Keep in mind that while these training datasets have been documented and processed for years, they tend to be very clean and in fact they require very little preprocessing and cleaning. However, in the real world, you will frequently deal with noisy data. In that case, the first thing we can do is use a rolling function, which looks like this:

In: smooth_time_series = pd.rolling_mean(time_series, 5)

For this process we are applying the mean function once more. Keep in mind that you don't necessarily have to use the mean. You can also go with the median value instead. In addition, you will notice that we request to only access five samples. Next, we are going to use the apply function to perform a number of operations on our columns and rows. This is a function that can be used for multiple purposes, so let's start by determining how many non-zero items we have per line:

In: iris.apply (np.count_nonzero, axis=1).head()

Out: 0   5

1   5

2   5

3   5

4   5

dtype: int64

Finally, the applymap function is then used to perform operations on the elements themselves. Let's say that we need to obtain the value of the length for every single string representation inside every cell:

In: iris.applymap (lambda el:len(str(el))).head()

In order to obtain these values, the cells are casted to a string and then we can determine the length.

Now that you have an idea about using Pandas for data preprocessing, let's also discuss the topic of data selection with the help of the same tool.

Data Selection

What do we mean when we are referring to data selection? Let's assume that you have a dataset with an index column which you need to access in order to modify it and work with it. For the sake of this example, we are going to presume that the index starts from 100, like so:

n,val1,val2,val3

100,10,10,C

101,10,20,C

102,10,30,B

103,10,40,B

104,10,50,A

As you can see, the first row is row number 0 and its index value is 100. Once you import the file, you will see an index column as usual, however, there's the possibility of changing it or using it by mistake. Therefore, it would be a good idea to split the column from the rest of the data in order to avoid making any mistakes when you are running low on coffee. We are going to use Pandas to select the column and break it apart from the rest:

In: dataset = pd.read_csv('a_selection_example_1.csv',

index_col=0) dataset

That's it! Now you can manipulate the values as usual, whether you select the values by index, column, or line locations. For instance, you can access the fourth value from the fifth line which in our example has an index value equal to 105. Here's how the selection looks:

In: dataset['val4'][105]

You might be tempted to consider this to be a matrix, however, it isn't, so make sure not to make the confusion. In addition, you should always determine the column you want to access before you specify the row. This way you won't make any mistakes when looking to gain access to a certain cell's value.

Preparing your data and learning some surface information about it can greatly help you along the line, so make sure to always dedicate some time for data munging and preprocessing. In the next chapter, we are going to continue going deeper in order to gain further insight about the data exploration and data science pipeline as a whole.

Summary

In this chapter you learned the most elementary steps you

need to take before starting to explore and analyze the data. You learned about data munging, which involves the preparation of data and how to work with a real dataset. You imported a real dataset and performed a number of basic operations on it with the purpose of preparing it for analysis. Now you know how to find out some basic information about your data, and therefore have a much easier time exploring it further. Keep in mind that while these steps may feel boring, they will make your job far easier down the line. In addition, you will gain much better results if you pre-process and explore your data as much as possible before you start implementing various learning algorithms and techniques.

Chapter 3: The Data Science Pipeline

So far we have imported a dataset and performed a few preprocessing operations with a series of Pandas function. The next step is to dive into the data science workflow. Preprocessing is a useful step, however, it is only the beginning, or the pre-beginning in fact.

In this section we are going to go through a series of somewhat challenging phases, so make sure to research and read the documentation of every tool we are going to use. We are going to discuss certain aspects about data science, such as creating new data features, performing dimensionality reduction, running performance tests and much more. All of this can be challenging and even overwhelming to a beginner, so make sure to read up on everything line by line and continue practicing the operations.

Exploring Data

The first phase within the data science workflow is performing the exploratory analysis. You need to gain a more detailed understanding of the data you are going to work with. This implies learning about the dataset's features, the shape of the elements, and using everything in order to form your hypothesis so that you can continue with the next steps. In this section we are going to continue working with the Iris dataset because it is very beginner-friendly and you are already somewhat familiar with it. So start by importing the dataset once more and create a new file like you did in the previous section. Once you've performed that step we can start exploring and go where no aspiring data scientist has gone before. Puns aside, we are going to use the describe function first in order to learn a bit more about our dataset:

In: iris.describe()

Now you should have access to various features such as deviation, minimum and maximum values, and so on. We need to take this basic data and analyze it at a deeper level, so let's start by exploring a graphical representation of it. For now we are going to use the simple "boxplot" function to create the plot, and not bother with Matplotlib just yet.

In: boxes = iris.boxplot(return_type='axes')

Keep in mind that you don't have to perform this step. Visualization is actually optional, unless you have to present your findings to someone who isn't very mathematically inclined but he or she can understand charts and plots much easier. For the same reason, as a beginner you should visualize your data so that you can place your focus elsewhere. Now, let's observe the relation between our features. For this step we are going to use a similarity matrix like this:

In: pd.crosstab(iris['petal_length'] > 3.758667, iris['petal_width'] > 1.198667)

You will notice that we are simply calculating the number of times the petal length appears when compared to the petal width. We are making this comparison with the crosstab function. If you look at the results you will see these features are well-related to each other. You can observe this even better by creating a scatterplot like so:

In: scatterplot = iris.plot(kind='scatter', x='petal_width',

y='petal_length', s=64, c='blue', edgecolors='white')

The scatterplot makes it easy to see that the petal width is connected to the length. When exploring data this way you can also use a different kind of graph, namely a histogram. In our case we are going to use one in order to see a display of the distribution of the values.

In: distr = iris.petal_width.plot(kind='hist', alpha=0.5, bins=20)

In this case we have selected twenty bins. If you aren't familiar with histograms you should know that bins refer to a variable's intervals. This is calculated by determining the square root of the total count of observations. That value represents the total number of bins.

New Features

Unfortunately, we are rarely so lucky to discover a close connection between certain features like we did in our basic example. That's when we need to apply a series of transformations. Let's say that you are trying to determine the value of a house. All you know for certain is the size of each room. You can use this information to create a new feature that represents the construction's volume. This transformation needs to be applied because we cannot observe the volume, however, we can observe features like length, width and height and then use these features to calculate the volume. Here's how all of this can be applied with code:

In: import numpy as np

from sklearn import datasets

from sklearn.cross_validation import train_test_split

from sklearn.metrics import mean_squared_error

```
cali = datasets.california_housing.fetch_california_housing()

X = cali['data']

Y = cali['target']

X_train, X_test, Y_train, Y_test = train_test_split(X, Y,
train_size=0.8)
```

(Source: California Housing dataset

https://scikitlearn.org/stable/modules/generated/sklearn.dat asets.fetch_california_housing.html retrieved in October 2019)

This time we imported a new dataset called California housing, which contains a great deal of data on the Californian housing market. In this example we are going to implement a regressor together with a mean absolute error with a value of 1.1575. If the code is difficult to understand and you don't know what a regressor is, don't worry about it at this time, we will discuss this later. All you need to understand for now is the concept we're discussing.

```
In: from sklearn.neighbors import KNeighborsRegressor

regressor = KNeighborsRegressor()

regressor.fit(X_train, Y_train)

Y_est = regressor.predict(X_test)

print ("MAE=", mean_squared_error(Y_test, Y_est))

Out: MAE= 1.15752795578
```

Now we need to try and reduce the value of the mean absolute error by implementing Z scores. This way we can perform the regression comparison and feature normalization. This process is also known as Z normalization because it seeks to map all of the original features to the new features we created. Let's continue:

In: from sklearn.preprocessing import StandardScaler

scaler = StandardScaler()

X_train_scaled = scaler.fit_transform(X_train)

X_test_scaled = scaler.transform(X_test)

regressor = KNeighborsRegressor()

regressor.fit(X_train_scaled, Y_train)

Y_est = regressor.predict(X_test_scaled)

print ("MAE=", mean_squared_error(Y_test, Y_est))

Out: MAE= 0.432334179429

The value of the mean absolute error has now been reduced from the previous value of approximately 1.15 to nearly 0.4, which is quite a great result. There are other methods that can be employed in order to minimize this value, however, the transformations required would be too complicated to implement at this state. What you should gain from this example is the fact that basic transformations can be easily applied and they can make your exploratory analysis much easier to conduct.

Dimensionality Reduction

In the real world you will often work with datasets that

contain tens of thousands of data items, if not hundreds of thousands. Such datasets tend to also contain a large number of features, which means there will be some of them that you will not need. Just because the information exists, that doesn't mean it's useful. In some cases features are simply irrelevant and they just contribute to the noise. Noise is one of the elements which reduce the accuracy of your analysis and anything you can do to reduce it translates to an accuracy boost. When noise is caused by irrelevant features, your best option is to use dimensionality reduction methods.

As the name suggests, dimensionality reduction is all about reducing useless features and cutting back on the time it takes to process your data. In this section we are going to discuss a couple of techniques and algorithms you can use to eliminate the features you don't need.

Covariance Matrix

As mentioned earlier, you need to compare all of your features, or collections of features, in order to determine whether a relationship exists between them. You don't want to eliminate useful features. The covariance matrix is one of the techniques you'll be using to achieve this.

Dimensionality reduction implies the detection of relevant features, as well as the removal of the rest. Once you detect the ones that don't offer much, you can eliminate them. To demonstrate this concept, we are going to once again import the Iris dataset. Remember that this dataset contains four features for each observation, therefore a correlation matrix will yield some useful results.

In: from sklearn import datasets

import numpy as np

```
iris = datasets.load_iris()

cov_data = np.corrcoef(iris.data.T)

print (iris.feature_names)

print (cov_data)
```

And this is how your output should look as a result.

['sepal length (cm)', 'sepal width (cm)', 'petal length (cm)',

'petal width (cm)']

[[1. -0.10936925 0.87175416 0.81795363]

[-0.10936925 1. -0.4205161 -0.35654409]

[0.87175416 -0.4205161 1. 0.9627571]

[0.81795363 -0.35654409 0.9627571 1.]]

With the covariance matrix in place, let's create a visual representation of our results in order to have an easier time drawing conclusions. As a beginner, you should always use visualization methods because they are so much easier to read than pure numbers. This time we are going to import Matplotlib to draw the plot for us:

```
In: import matplotlib.pyplot as plt

img = plt.matshow(cov_data, cmap=plt.cm.rainbow)

plt.colorbar(img, ticks=[-1, 0, 1], fraction=0.045)

for x in range(cov_data.shape[0]):

for y in range(cov_data.shape[1]):
```

```
plt.text(x, y, "%0.2f" % cov_data[x,y],

size=12, color='black', ha="center", va="center")

plt.show()
```

You will notice that this time we haven't used a scatterplot or a histogram. In fact, we created a heat map. Take note of the most important value, which is 1. Every feature covariance has been normalized to a value of one in order to help us see the powerful connection between a number of features. By analyzing the heat map, you will notice that feature one has a strong relation to feature three, as well as four. The third feature is also strongly connected to the fourth feature. Finally, we have feature two which seems to have no relation to any of the other features. It is completely independent. Now that you know which features are useful and which one is irrelevant, you can cut some of the useless information.

Principal Component Analysis

The next step is to use an algorithm like the principal component analysis in order to define smaller features from their parent features. The new ones will be linear, however. This means that the output's first factor will have most of the variance. The second vector will have the most of the left over variance, and so on. The information will be aggregated to a new set of vectors that are formed after employing a principal component analysis.

The implementation relies on the fact that the vectors contain the data that comes from the input, and everything else is just noise. All you need to do in this case is to decide the number of vectors to have. The decision is made based on the variance, however. Let's take a look at the practical approach to this algorithm:

```
In: from sklearn.decomposition import PCA

pca_2c = PCA(n_components=2)

X_pca_2c = pca_2c.fit_transform(iris.data)

X_pca_2c.shape

Out: (150, 2)

In: plt.scatter(X_pca_2c[:,0], X_pca_2c[:,1], c = iris.target,

alpha=0.8, s=60, marker='o', edgecolors='white')

plt.show()

pca_2c.explained_variance_ratio_.sum()

Out:

0.97763177502480336
```

(Adapted from: https://educationalresearchtechniques.com/2018/10/24/fact or-analysis-in-python/)

After the implementation, you will see that we only have two features in our output. The principal component analysis object is represented by the "n_components" object and its value is equal to two, which translates to what we just discussed.

We aren't going to dig deeper into the principal component analysis algorithm because it would just add an additional layer of confusion. For now, as a beginner, you should understand the concept of dimensionality reduction and not the inner workings of the algorithm. However, if you wish, you are encouraged to explore further. For now, we are going to move on to discussing another dimensionality reduction technique, namely the latent factor analysis.

Latent Factor Analysis

This concept is similar to the principal component analysis. The main idea here is that a latent factor always exists somewhere. Take note that a latent factor is just a variable, which cannot be observed through direct methods. We can only assume that our features are affected by a latent variable. This type of variable contains a specific kind of noise known as an arbitrary waveform generator. With that being said, let's see how this methodology is used for dimensionality reduction.

In: from sklearn.decomposition import FactorAnalysis

fact_2c = FactorAnalysis(n_components=2)

X_factor = fact_2c.fit_transform(iris.data)

plt.scatter(X_factor[:,0], X_factor[:,1], c=iris.target,

alpha=0.8, s=60, marker='o', edgecolors='white')

plt.show()

(Adapted from: https://educationalresearchtechniques.com/2018/10/24/factor-analysis-in-python/)

The difference in this case is that we establish the covariance between the variables in the output.

Outlier Detection

This next stage is one of the most important ones. Determining outliers is important because if we have any kind of erroneous information in our dataset, or partially incomplete data, adapting any new data will be extremely problematic. In turn, this issue can lead to algorithms that process faulty data and create inaccurate results.

So what is an outlier in this case? When we detect that a data point deviated from other data points we can compare them and establish that it is in fact an outlier. Let's discuss several cases where we have a different outlier in order to gain a better understanding of how to detect them and treat them.

Mainly there are three situations and each one is handled differently. Firstly, we will presume that the outlier is an infrequent appearance in whatever dataset we are working with. In this scenario, the information is based on another set of data from which it was extracted. Here we have a data sample which contains an outlier that is flagged as one because of its assumed rarity. This type of outlier is dealt with through a basic removal process.

In the second example, we have an outlier that frequently manifests itself. In this case it appears frequently. Whenever you experience similar occurrences, there's a sizable chance of encountering an error that affects the data sample generation. The problem here is that the algorithm's priority isn't the generalization, instead it focuses on learning the non-focused distribution. The outlier has to be eliminated.

The third situation involves a data point which is easy to conclude that it is in fact an error. Datasets often contain faulty data entries and they can easily cause inconsistencies in your data whenever you modify or manipulate the value. All you need to do in this case is delete the value and instruct the model to presume that it is a random loss. Another option is calculating and using an average value instead of the erroneous one. This is a preferable solution, however, if you find it difficult to implement it then simply delete the outlier.

Knowing these scenarios will help you understand which one you are experiencing, thus allowing you to have an easier time detecting the outlier and removing it. The first phase is to determine every single outlier and locate it. You can use two techniques to do this, though they are similar. You can either examine all separated variables individually, or all of them at once. These techniques are called the univariate and multivariate analysis.

You already had a brief introduction to the univariate method because you already worked with it unknowingly. If you recall, you created a graphical representation using a boxplot earlier. When this technique is used, you can determine which variable is in fact an outlier because you will see them as extremes. For instance, let's say you are observing the data description. If this observation is beneath the 25% ration or greater than 75%, you are probably looking at an outlier which can easily be seen in a box plot. The same applies if you are making Z-score observations, except in this case you are looking for a value above three. This method is one of the most efficient at detecting outliers, however, not all of them can be exposed with just one technique. This way you will only identify the extreme variables and others will escape undetected. In this case you should also consider the multivariate option, however, for now it's enough to stick to the basics and eliminate the most obvious outliers.

Summary

In this chapter you learned how to prepare your data for

analysis and how to explore it. Once you imported your dataset you need to go through a series of preparation techniques in order to increase your chances of reaching an accurate result. Data exploration is crucial to the preparation of data, as well as various techniques such as dimensionality reduction. Furthermore, you learned how to apply these dimensionality reduction techniques in practice by implementing a covariance matrix and a principal component analysis algorithm.

In addition, you also learned about the importance of finding outliers within your data. Depending on the type of outliers and the learning algorithms you are using, they can severely impact the training process and the accuracy of the final result. In this chapter you learned about situations where they occur and why they should be eliminated.

Chapter 4: Supervised Learning Algorithms

Now that you understand the fundamentals of data preparation and manipulation we can start with the main course.

The algorithms used in data science can be divided into several categories, mainly supervised learning, unsupervised learning, and to some degree semi-supervised learning.

As the name suggests, supervised learning is aided by human interaction as the data scientist is required to provide the input and output in order to obtain a result from the predictions that are performed during the training process. Once the training is complete, the algorithm will use what it learned to apply on new, but similar data.

The idea of supervised learning can be compared to the way humans learn. As a student you are guided by a professor with examples. You work through those examples with his or her help until you are finally able to work on your own.

In this chapter we are going to focus on this type of learning algorithm. However, take note that their purpose is divided based on the problems they need to solve. Mainly there are two distinct categories, namely regression and classification. In the case of regression problems, your target is a numeric value, while in classification it is a class or a label. To make things clearer, an example of a regression task is determining the average value of houses in a given city. A classification task, on the other hand, is supposed to take certain data like the petal and sepal length, and based on that information determine which is the species of a flower.

With that in mind, let's start the chapter by discussing regression algorithms and how to work with them.

Regression

In data science, many tasks are resolved with the help of regression techniques. However, regression can also be categorized in two different branches, which are linear regression and logistic regression. Each one of them is used to solve different problems, however both of them are a perfect choice for prediction analyses because of the high accuracy of the results.

The purpose of linear regression is to shape a prediction value out of a set of unrelated variables. This means that if you need to discover the relation between a number of variables you can apply a linear regression algorithm to do the work for you. However, this isn't its main use. Linear regression algorithms are used for regression tasks. Keep in mind that logistic regression is not used to solve regression problems like the name suggests. Instead, it is used for classification tasks.

With that being said, we are going to start by implementing a linear regression algorithm on the Boston housing dataset, which is freely available and even included in the Scikit-learn library. This dataset contains 506 samples, with 13 features and a numerical type target. Unlike in our previous examples, this time the dataset will not be used as a whole. We are going to break it into two sections, a training and a testing set. There are no rules set in stone regarding the ratio of the split, however, it is generally accepted that it is best to keep the training set with a 70%-80% data distribution, and then save 20%-30% for the testing process.

Linear Regression

For this example we are going to use the Scikit-learn library because it contains the Boston dataset, therefore you don't have to download anything. Let's start the process by importing the dataset and splitting our data into two sets:

In: from sklearn.datasets import load_boston

boston = load_boston()

from sklearn.cross_validation import train_test_split

X_train, X_test, Y_train, Y_test = train_test_split(boston.data,

boston.target, test_size=0.2, random_state=0)

Pay attention to the train_test_split function because it is used to split the dataset into a training and a testing set. Keep in mind that it is also part of the Scikit-learn library, another reason why we are using this amazing tool. Furthermore, you will notice that the data is not randomly categorized. We need to specify certain parameters. In this case, by declaring the size of the test set to be equal to a value of 0.2 we also automatically declare that the training set should be 80% of the total data. You don't have to declare both parameters. In addition, we also have a random state parameter. Its purpose is to generate random numbers during the split.

Now, let's add in the regressor in order to predict the target value of the testing set. In addition, we will also measure the resulting accuracy and make sure there isn't too much noise influencing the result in a negative way.

```
In: from sklearn.linear_model import LinearRegression

regression = LinearRegression()

regression.fit(X_train, Y_train)

Y_pred = regression.predict(X_test)

from sklearn.metrics import mean_absolute_error

print ("MAE", mean_absolute_error(Y_test, Y_pred))

Out: MAE 3.82230762633
```

That's it! The result isn't the best and improvements can certainly be made. However, the purpose of this demonstration is to get you started with linear regression. For now you should focus on correct implementation. As you progress, you will learn more about optimization and fine tuning. Furthermore, you will also see that these algorithms involve two important factors, namely processing speed and prediction accuracy. Your choice is determining the balance between the two.

Logistic Regression

We will not focus on logistic regression in this chapter, however, you should understand what makes it different from linear regression and what defines it. The most important aspect you should always keep in mind is that there is no regressor involved, therefore it is usually implemented to solve classification problems, specifically those of a binary nature. Binary classification refers to performing a classification task when you only have two classes, in other words Boolean labels. The main goal of the Booleans labels is to offer us a true or false result so that we can conclude whether a result has been predicted or not.

Logistic regression may not be quite as popular as its regression solving brother, however, it has started being applied more and more in the medical field nowadays. However, a more popular method of solving binary classification problems is with the use of a Naive Bayse classifier, which we are going to discuss in the next section.

Naive Bayes Classifier

As mentioned, a popular algorithm for classification tasks is the Naive Bayes classifier. Take note that this algorithm can also be used to solve multiclass classification problems as well.

This classifier is a fairly old one, before data science entered the mainstream and everyone talked about Python. However, this doesn't mean that it's obsolete and no longer in use. On the contrary, it is highly popular when performing the categorization of textual information. In plain English, this means that the algorithm can process a number of documents and then categorize them appropriately based on the content. For instance, the classifier can determine which emails belong in your spam box. In other cases, this algorithm is also used in combination with support vector machines (we will discuss this soon) in order to process massive amounts of data with a greater efficiency.

There are three types of classifiers and you will use each one of them under certain circumstances. The first one is known as the Gaussian Naive Bayes, which is an algorithm that automatically presumes which features have a normal distribution and how they are related to each class. The second one is the Multinomial classifier, which is the most popular one when working with model events. This is the algorithm that is used to classify documents based on how often a certain term is found within the content. Lastly we have the Bernoulli classifier, which describes the inputs with binary variables. This algorithm is used for the same purpose as the multinomial classifier.

For the purpose of this beginner's guide to data science, we are not going to apply all three of these algorithms, however, you are free to use the knowledge you gathered so far to use the right tools and put them in application. In this section you will go through the demonstration on how to implement the Gaussian algorithm. This classifier is used more frequently than the other, therefore we will make it a priority.

To demonstrate the application we are going to use the Iris dataset once again:

In: from sklearn import datasets

iris = datasets.load_iris()

from sklearn.cross_validation import train_test_split

X_train, X_test, Y_train, Y_test = train_test_split(iris.data,

iris.target, test_size=0.2, random_state=0)

In: from sklearn.naive_bayes import GaussianNB

clf = GaussianNB()

clf.fit(X_train, Y_train)

Y_pred = clf.predict(X_test)

Just like before, we have divided the dataset into a training set and a testing set with an 80 by 20 division ratio. Then we imported the actual implementation of the algorithm from the Scikit-learn library in order to perform the classification task. The final step is acquiring the classification report so that we can see the data and form our own conclusions. Here's how a typical classification report looks:

In: from sklearn.metrics import classification_report

print (classification_report(Y_test, Y_pred))

Out:

	precision	recall	f1-score	support
0	1.00	1.00	1.00	12
1	0.93	1.00	0.96	11
2	1.00	0.83	0.91	7
avg / total	0.97	0.97	0.97	35

Take note of the four different metrics we have in the report. The first one is the precision metric which shows us the number of labels that are relevant. Next, we have the recall measure that gives us a value which represents the comparison between the relevant results and the labels. The third metric is the f1-score. This one is only important if we are dealing with a dataset that isn't well-balanced. The final metric we are interested in is the support measure that determines how many samples a certain class contains. In conclusion, the results we obtain after implementing the classifier are quite good. Now let's move to an even more powerful classifier that is used to solve complex problems.

K-Nearest Neighbors

This algorithm is one of the easiest ones to work with, however, it can solve some of the most challenging classification problems. The k-nearest neighbor algorithm can be used in various scenarios that require anything from compressing data to processing financial data. It is one of the most commonly used supervised machine learning algorithms and you should do your best to practice your implementation technique.

The basic idea behind the algorithm is the fact that you should explore relation between two different training observations. For instance, we will call them x and y, and if you have the input value of x, you can already predict the value of y. The way this works is by calculating the distance of a data point in relation to other data points. The k-nearest point is selected based on this distance and then it is assigned to a specific class.

To demonstrate how to implement this algorithm we are going to work with a much larger dataset than before, however, we will not use everything in it. Once again, we are going to rely on the Scikit-learn library in order to gain access to a dataset known as the MNIST handwritten digits dataset. This is in fact a database that holds roughly 70,000 images of handwritten digits which are distributed in a training set with 60,000 images and a test set with 10,000 images. However, as already mentioned, we are not going to use the entire dataset because that would take too long for this demonstration. Instead we will limit ourselves to 1000 samples. Let's get started:

```
In: from sklearn.utils import shuffle

from sklearn.datasets import

from sklearn.cross_validation import train_test_split

import pickle

mnist = pickle.load(open( "mnist.pickle", "rb" ))

mnist.data, mnist.target = shuffle(mnist.data, mnist.target)
```

As usual, we first import the dataset and the tools we need. However, you will notice one additional step here, namely object serialization. This means we converted an object to a different format so that it can be used later but also reverted back to its original version if needed. This process is referred to as pickling and that is why we have the seemingly out of place pickle module imported. This will allow us to communicate objects through a network if needed. Now, let's cut through the dataset until we have only 1000 samples:

```
mnist.data = mnist.data[:1000]

mnist.target = mnist.target[:1000]

X_train, X_test, y_train, y_test = train_test_split(mnist.data,

mnist.target, test_size=0.8, random_state=0)

In: from sklearn.neighbors import KNeighborsClassifier

# KNN: K=10, default measure of Euclidean distance

clf = KNeighborsClassifier(3)

clf.fit(X_train, y_train)

y_pred = clf.predict(X_test)
```

Now let's see the report with the accuracy metrics like earlier:

In: from sklearn.metrics import classification_report

print (classification_report(y_test, y_pred))

And here are the results:

Out:

	precision	recall	f1-score	support
0.0	0.68	0.90	0.78	79
1.0	0.66	1.00	0.79	95
2.0	0.83	0.50	0.62	76
3.0	0.59	0.64	0.61	85
4.0	0.65	0.56	0.60	75
5.0	0.76	0.55	0.64	80
6.0	0.89	0.69	0.77	70

7.0 76	0.76	0.83	0.79
8.0 77	0.91	0.56	0.69
9.0 87	0.61	0.75	0.67
avg / total 800	0.73	0.70	0.70

The results aren't the best, however, we have only implemented the "raw" algorithm without performing any kind of preparation operations that would clean and denoise the data. Fortunately the training speed was excellent even at this basic level. Remember, when working with supervised algorithms or any algorithms for that matter, you are always trading accuracy for processing speed or vice versa.

Support Vector Machines

The SVM is one of the most popular supervised learning algorithms due its capability of solving both regression as well as classification problems. In addition, it has the ability to identify outliers as well. This is one all-inclusive data science algorithm that you cannot miss. So what's so special about this algorithm?

First of all, support vector machines don't need much processing power in order to keep up with the prediction accuracy. We discussed several times how you are always dealing with a balancing act between accuracy and speed. This algorithm, however, is in a league of its own and you won't have to worry too much about sacrificing training speed for accuracy or the other way around. Furthermore, support vector machines can be used to eliminate some of the noise as well while performing the regression or classification tasks.

This type of algorithm has many real world applications and that is why it is important for you to understand its implementation. It is used in facial recognition software, text classification, handwriting recognition software and so on. The basic concept behind it, however, simply involves the distance between the nearest points where a hyperplane is selected from the margin between a number of support vectors. Take note that what is known as a hyperplane here is the object that divides the information space for the purpose of classification.

To put all of this theory in application we are going to rely on the Scikit-learn library once again. The algorithm will be implemented in such a way to demonstrate the accuracy of the prediction in the case of identifying real banknotes. We mentioned earlier that support vector machines are effective when it comes to image classification, therefore this algorithm is perfectly suited for our goals. What we need to solve in this example is a simple binary classification problem because we need to train the algorithm to determine whether the banknote is valid or not.

The bill will be described using several attributes. Keep in mind that unlike the other classification algorithms, a support vector machine determines its decision limit by defining the maximum distance between the data points which are nearest to the relevant classes. However, we aren't looking to limit the decision, we just want to find the best one. The nearest points in this best decision are what we refer to as support vectors. With that being said, let's import a new dataset and several tools:

import numpy as np

import pandas as pd

import matplotlib.pyplot as plt

dataset = pd.read_csv ("bank_note.csv")

As usual, the first step is learning more about the data we are working with. Let's learn how many rows and columns we have and then obtain the data from the first five rows only:

print (dataset.shape)

print (dataset.head())

Here's the result:

	Variance Entropy	Skewness Class	Curtosis
0	3.62160 -0.44699	8.6661 0	-2.8073
1	4.454590 1.46210	8.1674 0	-2.4586 -
2	3.86600 0.10645	-2.6383 0	1.9242
3	3.45660 3.59440	9.5228 0	-4.0112 -

4	0.32924	-4.4552	4.5718	-
0.98880	0			

(Source: Based on https://archive.ics.uci.edu/ml/datasets/banknote+authentication retrieved in October 2019)

Now we need to process this information in order to establish the training and testing sets. This means that we need to reduce the data to attributes and labels only:

x = dataset.drop ('Class', axis = 1)

y = dataset ['Class']

The purpose of this code is to store the column data as the x variable and then apply the drop function in order to avoid the class column so that we can store it inside a 'y' variable. By reducing the dataset to a collection of attributes and labels we can start defining the training and testing data sets. Split the data just like we did in all the earlier examples. Next, let's start implementing the algorithm.

We need Scikit-learn for this step because it contains the support vector machine algorithm and therefore we can easily access it without requiring outside sources.

from sklearn.svm import SVC

svc_classifier = SVC (kernel = 'linear')

svc_classifier.fit (x_train, y_train)

pred_y = svc.classifier.predict(x_test)

Finally, we need to check the accuracy of our implementation. For this step we are going to use a confusion matrix which will act as a table that displays the accuracy values of the classification's performance. You will see a number of true positives, true negatives, as well as false positives and false negatives. The accuracy value is then determined from these values. With that being said, let's take a look at the confusion matrix and then print the classification report:

```
from sklearn.metric import confusion_matrix

print (confusion_matrix (y_test, pred_y)
```

This is the output:

```
[[160  1]

 [1      113]]
```

Accuracy Score: 0.99

Now let's see the familiar classification report:

```
from sklearn.metrics import classification_report

print (classification_report(y_test, y_pred))
```

And here are the results of the report:

	precision	recall	f1-score	support
0.0	0.99	0.99	0.99	161
1.0	0.99	0.99	0.99	114
avg / total	0.99	0.99	0.99	

275

Based on all of these metrics, we can determine that we obtained a very high accuracy with our implementation of the support vector machines. A score of 0.99 is almost as good as it can get, however, there is always room for improvement.

Summary

In this chapter we have focused on supervised learning algorithms and techniques. This category of learning techniques contains some of the most beginner-friendly algorithms and methods of exploring and analyzing data. The purpose of this chapter is to offer you a practical introduction to topics such as linear regression, K-nearest neighbors, support vector machines and much more. Each concept is discussed in detail because they will serve as the foundation for any aspiring data scientist and machine learner. Just make sure to go over the code for each algorithm and learning technique and study the tools that we are using for the implementation.

Chapter 5: Decision Trees

Decision trees are built similarly to support vector machines, meaning they are a category of supervised machine learning algorithms that are capable of solving both regression and classification problems. They are powerful and used when working with a great deal of data.

It is important for you to learn beyond the barebones basics so that you can process large and complex datasets. Furthermore, decision trees are used in creating random forests, which is arguably the most powerful learning algorithm. In this chapter we are going to exclusively focus on decision trees explicitly because of their popular use and efficiency.

Implementing Decision Trees

Decision trees are essentially a tool which supports a decision that will influence all the other decisions that will be made. This means that everything from the predicted outcomes to consequences and resource usage will be influenced in some way. Take note that decision trees are usually represented in a graph, which can be described as some kind of chart where the training tests appear as a node. For instance, the node can be the toss of a coin which can have two different results. Furthermore, branches sprout in order to individually represent the results and they also have leaves which are in fact the class labels. Now you see why this algorithm is called a decision tree. The structure resembles an actual tree. As you probably guessed, random forests are exactly what they sound like. They are collections of decision trees, but enough about them.

Decision trees are one of the most powerful supervised learning methods you can use, especially as a beginner. Unlike other more complex algorithms they are fairly easy to implement and they have a lot to offer. A decision tree can perform any common data science task and the results you obtain at the end of the training process are highly accurate. With that in mind, let's analyze a few other advantages, as well as disadvantages, in order to gain a better understanding of their use and implementation.

Let's begin with the positives:

1. Decision trees are simple in design and therefore easy to implement even if you are a beginner without a formal education in data science or machine learning. The concept behind this algorithm can be summarized with a sort of a formula that follows a common type of programming statement: If this, then that, else that. Furthermore, the results you will obtain are very easy to interpret, especially due to the graphic representation.

2. The second advantage is that a decision tree is one of the most efficient methods in exploring and determining the most important variables, as well as discovering the connection between then. In addition, you can build new features easily in order to gain better measurements and predictions. Don't forget that data exploration is one of the most important stages in working with data, especially when there's a large number of variables involved. You need to be able to detect the most valuable ones in order to avoid a time consuming process, and decision trees excel at this.

3. Another benefit of implementing decision trees is the fact that they are excellent at clearing up some of the outliers in your data. Don't forget that outliers are noise that reduces the accuracy of your predictions. In

addition, decision trees aren't that strongly affected by noise. In many cases outliers have such a small impact on this algorithm that you can even choose to ignore them if you don't need to maximize the accuracy scores.

4. Finally, there's the fact that decision trees can work with both numerical as well as categorical variables. Remember that some of the algorithms we already discussed can only be used with one data type or the other. Decision trees, on the other hand, are proven to be versatile and handle a much more varied set of tasks.

As you can see, decision trees are powerful, versatile, and easy to implement, so why should we ever bother using anything else? As usual, nothing is perfect, so let's discuss the negative side of working with this type of algorithm:

1. One of the biggest issues encountered during a decision tree implementation is overfitting. Take note that this algorithm tends to sometimes create very complicated decision trees that will have issues generalizing data due to their own complexity. This is known as overfitting and it is encountered when implementing other learning algorithms as well, however, not to the same degree. Fortunately, this doesn't mean you should stay away from using decision trees. All you need to do is invest some time to implement certain parameter limitations to reduce the impact of overfitting.

2. Decision trees can have issues with continuous variables. When continuous numerical variables are involved, the decision trees lose a certain amount of information. This problem occurs when the variables are categorized. If you aren't familiar with these variables, a continuous variable can be a value that is set to be within a range of numbers. For example, if

people between ages 18 and 26 are considered of student age, then this numerical range becomes a continuous variable because it can hold any value between the declared minimum and maximum.

While there are some disadvantages that can add to additional work in the implementation of decision trees, the advantages still outweigh them by far.

Classification and Regression Trees

We discussed earlier that decision trees are used for both regression tasks as well as classification tasks. However, this doesn't mean you implement the exact same decision trees in both cases. Decision trees need to be divided into classification and regression trees. They handle different problems, however, they are similar in some ways since they are both types of decision trees.

Take note that classification decision trees are implemented when there's a categorical dependent variable. On the other side, a regression tree is only implemented in the case of a continuous dependent variable. Furthermore, in the case of classification tree, the result from the training data is in fact the mode of the total relevant observations. This means that any observations that we cannot define will be predicted based on this value, which represents the observation which we identify most frequently.

Regression trees on the other hand work slightly differently. The value that results from the training stage is not the mode value, but the mean of the total observations. This way the unidentified observations are declared with the mean value which results from the known observations.

Both types of decision trees undergo a binary split however, going from the top to bottom. This means that the observations in one area will spawn two branches that are then divided inside the predictor space. This is also known as a greedy approach because the learning algorithm is seeking the most relevant variable in the split while ignoring the future splits that could lead to the development of an even more powerful and accurate decision tree.

As you can see, there are some differences as well as similarities between the two. However, what you should note from all of this is that the splitting is what has the most effect on the accuracy scores of the decision tree implementation. Decision tree nodes are divided into subnodes, no matter the type of tree. This tree split is performed in order to lead to a more uniform set of nodes.

Now that you understand the fundamentals behind decision trees, let's dig a bit deeper into the problem of overfitting.

The Overfitting Problem

You learned earlier that overfitting is one of the main problems when working with decision trees and sometimes it can have a severe impact on the results. Decision trees can lead to a 100% accuracy score for the training set if we do not impose any limits. However, the major downside here is that overfitting creeps in when the algorithm seeks to eliminate the training errors, but by doing so it actually increases the testing errors. This imbalance, despite the score, leads to terrible prediction accuracy in the end result. Why does this happen? In this case the decision trees grow many branches and that's the cause of overfitting. In order to solve this use, you need to impose limitations to how much the decision tree can develop and how many branches it can spawn. Furthermore, you can also prune the tree to keep it under control, much like how you would do with a real tree in order to make sure it produces plenty of fruit.

In order to limit the size of the decision tree, you need to determine new parameters during the definition of the tree. Let's analyze these parameters:

1. min_samples_split: The first thing you can do is change this parameter to specify how many observations a node will require in order to be able to perform the splitting. You can declare anything with a range of one sample to maximum samples. Just keep in mind that in order to limit the training model from determining the connections that are very common to a particular decision tree you need to increase the value. In other words, you can limit the decision tree with higher values.

2. min_samples_leaf: This is the parameter you need to tweak in order to determine how many observations are required by a node, or in other words a leaf. The overfitting control mechanism works the same way as for the samples split parameter.

3. max_features: Adjust this parameter in order to control the features that are selected randomly. These features are the ones that are used to perform the best split. In order to determine the most efficient value you should calculate the square root of the total features. Just keep in mind that in this case, the higher value tends to lead to the overfitting problem we are trying to fix. Therefore, you should experiment with the value you set. Furthermore, not all cases are the same. Sometimes a higher value will work without resulting in overfitting.

4. max_depth: Finally, we have the depth parameter which consists of the depth value of the decision tree. In order to limit the overfitting problem, however, we are only interested in the maximum depth value. Take note that a high value translates to a high number of

splits, therefore a high amount of information. By tweaking this value you will have control over how the training model learns the connections in a sample.

Modifying these parameters is only one aspect of gaining control of our decision trees in order to reduce overfitting and boost performance and accuracy. The next step after applying these limits is to prune the trees.

Pruning

This technique might sound too silly to be real, however, it is a legitimate machine learning concept that is used to improve your decision tree by nearly eliminating the overfitting issue. As with real trees, what pruning does is reduce the size of the trees in order to focus the resources on providing highly accurate results. However, you should keep in mind that the segments that are pruned are not entirely randomly selected, which is a good thing. The sections that are eliminated are those that don't really help with the classification process and don't lead to any performance boosts. Less complex decision trees lead to a better optimized model.

In order to better understand the difference between an unmodified decision tree and one that was pruned and optimized, you should visualize the following scenario. Let's say that there's a highway that has a lane for vehicles that travel at 80 mph, and a second lane for the slower vehicles that travel at 50 mph. Now let's assume you are on this highway in a red car and you are facing a decision. You have the option to move on the fast lane in order to pass a slow moving car, however, this means that you will have a truck in front of you that can't achieve the high speed he should have in the left lane and therefore you will be stuck on that lane. In this case, the cars that are in the other lane are slowly starting to overpass you because the truck can't keep up. The other option is staying in your lane without attempting to make a pass. The most optimal choice here is the one that allows you to travel a longer distance during a certain amount of time. Therefore if you choose to stay in the slow lane until you gradually pass the truck that is blocking the fast lane, you will eventually be able to switch to that lane and pass all the other vehicles. As you can see, the second option might look slow at the time of consideration, however, in the long run it ends up being the most efficient one. Decision trees are the same. If you apply limits to your trees, they won't get greedy by switching you to the left lane where you will be stuck behind a truck. However, if you prune the decision tree, it will allow you to examine your surroundings in more detail and allow you predict a higher number of options you have in order to be able to make a better choice.

As you can see, performing the pruning process does yield a number of benefits which cannot be ignored. However, the implementation of this technique requires a number of steps and conditions. For instance, for a decision tree to be suitable for pruning, it needs to have a high depth value. Furthermore, the process needs to start at the bottom in order to avoid any negative returns. This issue needs to be avoided because if we have a negative node split at the bottom and another one occurs at the top, we will end up with a decision tree that will stop when the first division occurs. If the tree is pruned, it will not stop there and you will have higher gains.

Visualizing decision trees can sometimes be difficult when all you have is theory, so let's start with a step by step implementation to see them in action.

Decision Tree Implementation

Creating a decision tree starts from the root node. The first step is to select one of the data attributes and set up a logical test based on it. Once you have a set of results you can branch out and create another set of tests, which will you will use to create the subnode. Once we have at least a subnode we can apply a recursive splitting process on it in order to determine that we have clean decision tree leaves. Keep in mind that the level of purity is determined based on the number of cases that sprout from a single class. At this stage you can start pruning the tree in order to eliminate anything that doesn't improve the accuracy of the classification stage. Furthermore, you will also have to evaluate every single split that is performed based on each attribute. This step needs to be performed in order to determine which is the most optimal attribute, as well as split.

But enough theory for now. All you should focus on at this point is the fundamental idea behind decision trees and how to make them efficient. Once you think you grasped the basics, you need to start the implementation.

In the following example we will once again rely on the Iris dataset for the data, and the Scikit-learn library which contains it.

With that being said, let's continue with the practical implementation before the theory becomes too overwhelming. What's important at this stage is to understand the fundamental concepts and more importantly how to apply them in practice. With that being said, let's see what a decision tree looks like in code. Once again, we are going to use the Iris dataset, which is part of the Scikit-learn library. We will use other packages as well, such as Pandas and Numpy, so let's take a look at the code and discuss further:

```
%matplotlib inline

import pandas as pd
```

import numpy as np

import seaborn as sns

import matplotlib.pyplot as plt

from sklearn.model_selection import train_test_split

from sklearn.tree import DecisionTreeClassifier

df = pd.read_csv('Iris.csv')

Once all packages and modules are imported, we need to check the values to see if we have any null values:

df.isnull().any()

Take note that there are no null values in the dataset, however, this check should always be performed just to be certain. Always remember that data exploration is one of the most crucial steps and you should never avoid performing it. Make sure to perform all the other exploration steps we discussed earlier in the book in order to be as familiar with the data as possible. Once you consider you have analyzed and explored the data in enough detail, you can perform the analysis to determine the connection between the data columns. For this purpose in this example we are using the "seaborn" module because it contains the "pairplot" function, which will allow us to visualize all the connections. We will use a certain color for each column and then look for any outliers. Here's how to use this function:

sns.pairplot(df, hue = 'Species')

Take note that we do have a small number of outliers. In this case, they can probably be ignored because they are only a few and they most likely represent data anomalies and incorrect entries. For the purpose of this example we are going to assume they are nearly irrelevant anomalies and not pay them much attention.

The next step is performing the train / test split. Keep in mind that while in all other examples we have used a 80 / 20 ratio, this time we are going to have 30% of the data saved for the test set. Now let's take a look at the code:

```
all_inputs = df [['SepalLengthCm', 'SepalWidthCm',
'PetalLengthCm', 'PetalWidthCm']].values

all_classes = df ['Species'].values

(train_inputs, test_inputs, train_classes, test_classes) =

train_test_split (all_inputs, all_classes, train_size = 0.7,
random_state = 1)
```

Notice that the random state is set to a value of one in order to make sure we always have an identical data split. This is not crucial for our decision tree example, however, if we ever want to recreate the dataset in the exact same way, we need this value.

Now, let's handle the classification process. We can now finally implement the decision tree:

```
dtc = DecisionTreeClassifier()

dtc.fit (train_inputs, train_classes)

dtc.score (test_inputs, test_classes)
```

The result should look something like this:

```
0.955
```

That's it! This is a simple example, but we already managed to achieve 95% accuracy. Now imagine if we would dedicate some time to polishing the decision tree as much as possible. This is why they are so frequently used to solve complex problems. Ultimately, they are easy to implement even if the theory makes it sound difficult, and they offer great results with minimal negative side effects.

Summary

In this chapter you explored decision trees and learned how they are implemented. You studied concepts such as backpropagation and pruning and you learned what advantages and disadvantages you will encounter when working with classification and regression trees. Remember that decision trees are powerful and very useful, however they sometimes need to be used together with other technique in order to enhance some of their characteristics. While they are easy to implement, you should study them in detail because they are often used in data science and Big Data, especially in the form of Random Forests. In this book we aren't going to expand on the concept of Random Forests, however, you should know that they are powerful and versatile in dealing with complex data because they are collections of decision trees. So, make sure you fully understand the concept of decision trees before progressing to more complex topics.

Chapter 6: Unsupervised Learning with K-means Clustering

Unlike supervised learning, this category of algorithms learns only from already established examples without human intervention. These algorithms are often used to process massive datasets that contain only inputs. Their objective is to identify the clusters of data points in order to compare them next to those coming from other datasets.

Unsupervised learning algorithms learn differently from supervised algorithms. They learn from unlabeled data, which hasn't been classified. They seek to define an output based on the common relations found in the inputs. That output is then applied to other datasets as well. Because of their learning mechanism, these algorithms are often used for tasks like explaining data features and statistical density estimations. Unsupervised learning can also be used anywhere where we need to discover what kind of anomalies the input data contains.

Unsupervised learning algorithms are mainly used to learn from complex datasets. Therefore, their top priority is performing an exploratory analysis and identifying important data. One such algorithm is known as the K-means Clustering algorithm and this chapter will focus on it alone. This learning technique is one of the most popular clustering algorithms that is used to discover predictable patterns in large datasets.

K-means Clustering

As mentioned, unsupervised learning methods are ideal for working with unlabeled data. However, to be more specific, one of the best techniques, if not the best, is to use a type of clustering algorithm. The main idea behind this approach is the cluster analysis which involves reducing data observations to clusters, or subdivisions of data, where each cluster contains information that is similar to that of a predefined attribute. Clustering involves a number of techniques that all achieve the same goal because they are all about forming a variety of theories regarding the data structure.

One of the most popular unsupervised learning algorithms and clustering techniques is known as k-means clustering. This concept revolves around building data clusters based on the similarity of the values. The first step is to determine the value of k, which is in fact represented by the total number of clusters we define. These clusters are built as k-many points, which hold the average value that represents the entire cluster. Furthermore, the values are assigned based on the value which is the closest average. Keep in mind that clusters have a core which is defined as an average value which pushes the other averages aside, changing them. After enough iterations, the core value will shift itself to a point where the performance metric is lower. When this stage is reached, we have the solutions because there aren't any observations available to be designated.

If you're confused by now by all this theory, that's ok. You will see that this technique is a lot easier than it sounds. Let's take a look at the practical implementation. In this example we will use the UCI handwritten digits dataset. It is freely available and you don't need to download if you are using Scikit-learn along with the book. With that being said, here's the code:

from time import time

```python
import numpy as np

import matplotlib.pyplot as plt

from sklearn import datasets

np.random.seed()

digits = datasets.load_digits()

data = scale(digits.data)

n_samples, n_features = data.shape

n_digits = len(np.unique(digits.target))

labels = digits.target

sample_size = 300

print("n_digits: %d, \t n_samples %d, \t n_features %d"

% (n_digits, n_samples, n_features))

print(79 * '_')

print('% 9s' % 'init''        time  inertia  homo  compl  v-meas

ARI    AMI  silhouette')

def bench_k_means(estimator, name, data):

t0 = time()

estimator.fit(data)

print('% 9s %.2fs %i %.3f %.3f %.3f %.3f %.3f %.3f'

        % (name, (time() - t0), estimator.inertia_,
```

```
metrics.homogeneity_score(labels,
estimator.labels_),

metrics.completeness_score(labels,
estimator.labels_),

metrics.v_measure_score(labels, estimator.labels_),

metrics.adjusted_rand_score(labels,
estimator.labels_),

metrics.silhouette_score(data, estimator.labels_,

    metric='euclidean',

    sample_size=sample_size)))
```

(Source: K Means clustering – Implementing k Means. Adapted from https://techwithtim.net/tutorials/machine-learning-python/k-means-2/ accessed in October 2019)

If you analyze the code line by line you will notice that the implementation is fairly simple, logical, and easy to understand. In fact, it is somewhat similar in parts to other techniques we used so far. However, there is one major difference that is important to mention, namely the performance measurements we are using in order to accurately interpret the data.

First we have a homogeneity score. This metric can have a value between zero and one. It mainly seeks the clusters that make room only for one class systems. The idea is that if we have a score that is close to the value of one, then the cluster is mostly built from the samples that belong to a single class. On the other hand, if the score is close to zero, then we have achieved a low homogeneity.

Next, we have the completeness score. This metric

compliments the homogeneity measure. Its purpose is to give us information on how the measurements became part of a specific class. The two scores allow us to form the conclusion that we either managed to perform perfect clustering, or we simply failed.

The third metric is known as the V-metric, or sometimes the V-measure. This score is calculated as the harmonic mean of the previous two scores. The V-metric essentially checks on the homogeneity and the completeness score by assigning a zero to one value that verifies the validity.

Next, we have the adjusted Rand index metric. This is a score that is used to verify the similarity of the labeling. Using a value between zero and one, the Rand index simply determines the relation between the distribution sets.

Finally, we have the silhouette metric which is used to verify whether the performance of the clustering is sufficient without having labeled data. The measurement goes from a value of negative one to positive one and it determines whether the clusters are well-structured or not. If the number is anywhere close to negative one then we are dealing with bad clusters. In order to make sure we have dense clusters, we need to achieve a score close to positive one. Keep in mind that in this case we can also have a score that is close to zero. In this case the silhouette measurement tells us that we have clusters which are overlapping each other.

Now that you understand the measurement system, we have to apply one more step to this implementation and make sure that the results are accurate. To verify the clustering scores we can use the bench_k_means function like so:

```
bench_k_means(KMeans(init='k-means++',
n_clusters=n_digits, n_ init=10),

name="k-means++", data=data) print(79 * '_')
```

Now let's see what conclusion we can draw from the scores. Here's how your results should look:

n_digits: 10,   n_samples 1797,
      n_features 64

init	time	inertia	homo	compl
k-means++	0.25s	69517	0.596	0.643

init	v-meas	ARI	AMI	silhouette
k-means++	0.619	0.465	0.592	0.123

As you can see, with a basic k-means implementation we have fairly decent scores, however, there is a lot we could improve. Clustering is sufficient, but we could perfect the scores by implementing other supervised or unsupervised learning techniques. For instance, in this case you might consider using the principal component analysis algorithm as well. Another option would be applying various dimensionality reduction methods. However, for the purpose of learning how to implement the K-means clustering algorithm, these results will suffice. However, you should keep in mind that in the real world of data science you will often implement a number of algorithms and techniques together. You will almost never be able to get useful results with just one algorithm, especially when working with raw datasets instead of the practice ones.

Summary

In this chapter we have focused on learning about unsupervised learning algorithms, namely K-means clustering.

The purpose of this section was to show you a technique that can be used on more complex datasets. Clustering algorithms are the staple of data science and frequently used, especially in combination with other algorithms and learning techniques. Furthermore, as you will learn later, clustering techniques, especially K-means clustering, are highly efficient in dealing with Big Data.

Chapter 7: Neural Networks

Artificial neural networks were designed theoretically in the 1950s, with the purpose of finding a way to copy the human thinking and decision making process. The idea was to create a learning system that would function similarly to the human brain. However, keep in mind that this didn't involve the attempt to replicate the human brain or neural network. What the artificial and the natural systems had in common is only the shallow resemblance. Artificial neural networks were created using the inspiration that came from exploring the human neural network.

Neural networks consist of neurons, or nodes to be more precise. These nodes are in fact just code which seeks to find the solution to a problem through repeated execution. Once an answer is found, it is communicated to the next node which in turn will process that information. These nodes are setup in a system of layers. In other words, there are separate layers that consist of a certain number of nodes and these layers are separate from each other, though they do communicate. First the communication is done only through the nodes of the same layer and only then the information is passed on to the following layer. Based on this simple description, you can already determine that the artificial neural network is nowhere near the human neural net when it comes to capability and processing power. Data travels in a somewhat linear fashion, from node to node and layer to layer. Human processing however is parallel, which means that the data is processed at the same time throughout the vast interconnected network of neurons.

Now that you understand the basic concept behind a neural network we can dive into this chapter and discuss its design and the various types of neural networks that we can implement.

Neural Network Structures

So far you learned that when in a neural network data is explored, classified and then pushed to the next node, ultimately traveling through the whole network. We also mentioned layers, however, take note that there are three different categories of layers. First we have the input layer and the output layer. Between these layers however, we have what is known as a hidden layer. This is where the input layer sends all of the data it analyzes. Keep in mind that neural networks can also function without the hidden layer and only use the two basic input and output layers. On the other end of the spectrum we can also develop networks with hundreds of layers. In this chapter we are going to focus on the more classic design which is based on having the three layers. Generally speaking, if a neural network consists of more than these layers it turns into a deep learning system. This type of network is different and as a beginner there's no need to get into it just yet.

As you may have guessed already, the structure of neural networks is influenced by the way the nodes are arranged inside the network. With each arrangement we end up with a different neural network. The most common arrangements lead to the development of the feedforward neural networks, recurrent neural networks and the Boltzmann machine, just to list a few. Each one of these networks has a different structure and serves a different purpose.

Now let's discuss the structure of a basic network in more detail.

As already discussed, a common network has three layers, but not always. For instance, without any hidden layers, we start working with logistic regression. The input layer is designed to contain an observation matrix that has five units. The output layer, however, has three units. In the case of the output, we need to determine the difference between the three units, or classes, and therefore we have to classify them. In the case of the input, we are dealing with constrained numerical features which need to be turned into categorical features. The hidden layer on the other hand starts with eight units, but this is only the minimum value. There is no actual limitation to how many units there can be, and as already mentioned, there is no limit to the amount of hidden layers we have either. Due the lack of restrictions in this case, the data scientist needs to use his best judgment to make the right decision regarding the type of network he or she implements.

With the fundamentals fresh in your mind, let's discuss the first neural network model, which is the feedforward neural net.

The Feedforward Neural Network

This is the fundamental design of the neural network as it consists of the three basic elements that communicate in a line. The input layer sends data to the hidden layer, which in turn sends it to the output layer. Take note that this type of neural network does not seek to iterate. In other words, the data inside the input layer is processed and the result can be found only in the output layer. In addition, there are two categories of feedforward networks, namely the single layer perceptron and the multilayer perceptron.

The simplest type of neural network you can have is the single layer perceptron. This is a type of feedforward neural network that contains only one node per layer. The node has an input that is directly connected to the node of the next layer because there are no other nodes around it. The second node, however, is in fact the weighted sum of the inputs. The input data is defined by the node and if a certain condition is met, then we gain a result. The single layer perceptron is used only to classify the data into two different parts, therefore it is also known as a linear binary classifier.

Another simplistic neural network is the multilayer perceptron. In this case we have to have at least two layers, however, in a real world implementation we would have quite a few more. The main difference between this model and the single layer perceptron, however, is the fact that the output of one layer turns into the input of the following layer. This architecture is based on a concept called backpropagation (more on this soon). With this design we have to perform a comparison check between the output we assume and the real output. In the event that we find a high inaccuracy level, the data is transmitted once again through the entire network. During the second round of processing the node's weights will be adjusted in order to improve the accuracy level. Keep in mind that this process repeats itself multiple times until the result is accurate. While the single layer perceptron has limited use, as the first type of neural network ever devised, the multilayer perceptron has a wide range of usability because of this efficient structure.

Next up we have the recurrent neural network structures, however before moving on to that topic we should clear up what the concept of backpropagation involves.

Backpropagation

Backpropagation is a concept that appeared in the 70s when neural networks were mostly theoretical. Back then computers were simply not powerful and efficient enough to handle an artificial neural network, therefore, even though this technological advancement was already designed, it could not be applied. Even today working with a neural network requires a great deal of resources from your computer. But let's leave history in the past and see what backpropagation is all about.

This concept is in fact a mathematical concept and therefore we will not dig deep into the subject because we are only interested in the theory and what it means to you as an aspiring data scientist.

Remember that there is always a difference between the imagined output and the actual output. Furthermore, you should focus on the fact that each node has a weight assigned to it, which is adjusted based on the information that arrives from the input. The purpose of backpropagation is to find the off-shoot of this mathematical difference between the two outputs. This result is then applied to the next iteration in order to give the nodes the ability to adjust their weights. This is why every single time the data is processed through the entire network, the inaccuracy level is reduced.

Just in case you are having difficulty with this theory, you should imagine the following scenario. Let's say that you are out playing basketball. You throw the ball to score, but unfortunately it just hits the hoop itself and by doing so the ball just starts going around the ring. With every single pass, the ball will slow down and fall slightly inwards towards the center of the hoop. Eventually, after enough passes the ball will go down through the ring. This is how backpropagation can also be visualized. Every loop the ball completes is in fact an iteration. The more iterations we have, the closer we get to the result, or in our case, the closer the ball gets to the center of the ring. With each pass, the output becomes closer to what we expect.

In data science one of the main goals is to process data automatically with supervised and unsupervised machine learning methods. This same goal applied to artificial neural networks. There is one notable difference, however. The learning algorithms we discussed earlier require already documented information in order to be able to gain experience and learn on their own so that they can make future decisions. Neural networks, on the other hand, are capable of making decisions in the present, which makes them far more powerful and efficient. That is why neural networks are used when dealing with complex data and complicated patterns that require a system strong enough to lead to accurate results.

Recurrent Neural Networks

Now that you have a basic understanding of the simple feedforward neural networks and the concept of backpropagation, we can advance to recurrent neural networks. As you already know, the feedforward network's system works by sending data along a straight line, from node to node and layer to layer. The input is point A and the output is point B. On the other end we have the recurrent neural networks that transmit data both ways. While this is already an important change in the design of the network, it is not what makes it so special.

This type of network has the particular ability to remember all of the states a set of data goes through. After every iteration, the old state of the data will be memorized. Keep in mind that the original neural network design wasn't capable of memorization, meaning that with each iteration the previous data state would be lost. Imagine watching a video and after an ad pops up you forget what you already watched.

The structure of a recurrent neural network can be described as a series of linked nodes that consists of inputs and outputs. This system where an input becomes the output allows for highly accurate results. Now let's discuss one particular recurrent neural network that has been popularized by machine learners and data scientists in the last few years. In the next section we are going to explore the Boltzmann machine and see how to implement it in a real scenario.

The Restricted Boltzmann Machine

This neural network is a special representation of the recurrent network architecture because of the fact that it borrows certain design elements from the multilayer perceptron. For instance, the inputs and the hidden layers structures are the same as those of the perceptron, however, they are also interconnected. Take note that the structure doesn't force the network to communicate data in a particular way, namely linearly, because all elements are connected to each other to a certain degree. This means that the nodes can communicate with each other during every processing cycle, and therefore all the input variables are analyzed and modeled. Other networks only focus on the variables which can be observed. The main benefit of this system is the fact that it makes it possible for the output nodes and layer to advance.

The restricted Boltzmann machine neural network is a model that relies on an energy function. This function is what actually supports the relationship between each value and node configuration. Keep in mind that this energy value is in fact a metric which is determined mathematically and it is used to perform parameter updates. This also means that a free energy value will be present and one of your tasks will be to minimize it in order to create a powerful model.

The reason why we are discussing a restricted Boltzmann machine instead of the fundamental Boltzmann machine is because we don't want to face any scaling problems. With the simple architecture we would have a large number of nodes which would require a lot of computation power and time in order to process the data and reach a satisfactory output. This might not be a problem if we have an adequate amount of resources, however, with the increase in the number of nodes, the value of the free energy would also be higher. This value could become unmanageable, therefore, it is easier to go with a restricted model from the beginning, which implies a change in the structure, as well as the training stage. In order to restrict the network, all we need to do is apply a connectivity limit to all of the network's nodes. In other words, we need to make sure that we restrict the relation between all of the nodes that belong to a certain layer. In addition, we also need to remove the communication line between all the layers that are next to each other. These two limitations are what give this neural network its name.

Keep in mind that these restrictions aren't always the most optimal solution that will solve all of your scaling issues. Another problem we are facing is the time it takes to perform the model training. That is why we also need to implement a machine learning technique known as the Permanent Contrastive Divergence in order to lower the value of the free energy even more.

Now that the theory is out of the way, let's see this popular recurrent neural net in action in the next section and discuss the implementation of the code.

Restricted Boltzmann Machine in Practice

As mentioned, this is one of the most powerful models you can implement, especially as a beginner. You should only use this type of neural network when working with complex datasets that contain a great deal of information. To demonstrate the application of the restricted Boltzmann machine, we are going to use the MNIST handwritten digits dataset. The model will be implemented by first defining an object and its layers, vectors and various functions and attributes that are used to communicate data between the layers. Furthermore, we will apply the contrastive divergence solution in order to improve the time it takes to perform the training process.

```python
class RBM(object):

def __init__(

    self,

    input=None,

    n_visible=784,

    n_hidden=500,

    w=None,

    hbias=None,

    vbias=None,

    numpy_rng=None,

     theano_rng=None

    ):
```

Let's take a break and discuss what we did so far. We have defined a new object that stands for the Boltzmann machine. As you can see there are a number of parameters attributed to this object. They define how many network nodes we have, including those that are visible and invisible, inside the hidden layer. Furthermore we have a few other attributes that are not obligatory, however, they will help in creating a better model.

```
self.n_visible = n_visible

self.n_hidden = n_hidden

if numpy_rng is None:

        numpy_rng = numpy.random.RandomState(1234)

if theano_rng is None:

        theano_rng = RandomStreams(numpy_rng.randint(2
        ** 30))

if W is None:

initial_W = numpy.asarray(

        numpy_rng.uniform(

                low=-4 * numpy.sqrt(6. / (n_hidden +
                n_visible)),

                high=4 * numpy.sqrt(6. / (n_hidden +
                n_visible)),

                size=(n_visible, n_hidden)

        ),

        dtype=theano.config.floatX

)
```

The "w" attribute is used here so that we can enable the use of the GPU. In this example the GPU can handle a great deal more data processing than the CPU. It is one of the simple solutions we can use to speed up the training process. In addition we also allow data sharing between various functions that contain "theano.shared". The next step is to allow this sharing process throughout the network.

```
W = theano.shared(value=initial_W, name='W', borrow=True)

if hbias is None:

hbias = theano.shared(

        value=numpy.zeros(n_hidden,dtype=theano.config.fl
        oatX

        ),

        name='hbias',

        borrow=True

)

if vbias is None:

vbias = theano.shared(

        value=numpy.zeros(n_visible,
        dtype=theano.config.floatX

        ),

        name='vbias',

        borrow=True

)
```

Next, let's setup the input layer.

```python
self.input = input

if not input:

self.input = T.matrix('input')

self.W = W

self.hbias = hbias

self.vbias = vbias

self.theano_rng = theano_rng

self.params = [self.W, self.hbias, self.vbias]

def propup(self, vis):

pre_sigmoid_activation = T.dot(vis, self.W) + self.hbias

return [pre_sigmoid_activation, T.nnet.sigmoid(pre_sigmoid_
activation)]

def propdown(self, hid):

pre_sigmoid_activation = T.dot(hid, self.W.T) + self.vbias

return [pre_sigmoid_activation, T.nnet.sigmoid(pre_sigmoid_
activation)]
```

This part of the code also includes the function which communicates the activation of visible units in an upward direction towards the hidden units. This way the hidden units can determine their activation based on the samples from the visible units. This process is also performed downwards. Next, we are going to transmit the hidden layer's activations as well as the visible layer's activations.

```python
def sample_h_given_v(self, v0_sample):
```

```
pre_sigmoid_h1, h1_mean = self.propup(v0_sample)

h1_sample = self.theano_rng.binomial(size=h1_mean.shape,

n=1, p=h1_mean, dtype=theano.config.floatX)

return [pre_sigmoid_h1, h1_mean, h1_sample]

def sample_v_given_h(self, h0_sample):

pre_sigmoid_v1, v1_mean = self.propdown(h0_sample)

v1_sample = self.theano_rng.binomial(size=v1_mean.shape,

n=1, p=v1_mean, dtype=theano.config.floatX)

return [pre_sigmoid_v1, v1_mean, v1_sample]
```

We have established the connections and therefore we can handle the sampling process.

```
def gibbs_hvh(self, h0_sample):

pre_sigmoid_v1, v1_mean, v1_sample
=self.sample_v_given_h(h0_sample)

pre_sigmoid_h1, h1_mean, h1_sample
=self.sample_h_given_v(v1_sample)

return [pre_sigmoid_v1, v1_mean, v1_sample

        pre_sigmoid_h1, h1_mean, h1_sample]

def gibbs_vhv(self, v0_sample):

        pre_sigmoid_h1, h1_mean, h1_sample =
        self.sample_h_given_v(v0_sample)

        pre_sigmoid_v1, v1_mean, v1_sample =
```

```
self.sample_v_given_h(h1_sample)

return [pre_sigmoid_h1, h1_mean, h1_sample,

pre_sigmoid_v1, v1_mean, v1_sample]
```

As you can see, the implementation of a restricted Boltzmann machine is slightly more complicated than any other models, however, it is also far more powerful. So far we have established all of our layers and neural nodes and we have finished setting up the connection lines. Furthermore, we have taken care of the sampling process. Keep in mind that sampling is used for the implementation of the permanent contrastive divergent concept, which also requires a count parameter. In this phase of the implementation, handling the free energy value is top priority. Once all of this is achieved, all we need to do is check how successful our model is.

```
def free_energy(self, v_sample):

wx_b = T.dot(v_sample, self.W) + self.hbias

vbias_term = T.dot(v_sample, self.vbias)

hidden_term = T.sum(T.log(1 + T.exp(wx_b)), axis=1)

return -hidden_term - vbias_term

def get_cost_updates(self, lr=0.1, persistent = , k=1):

pre_sigmoid_ph, ph_mean, ph_sample = self.sample_h_given_v(self.input)

chain_start = persistent

(

[
```

```
            pre_sigmoid_nvs,

            nv_means,

            nv_samples,

            pre_sigmoid_nhs,

            nh_means,

            nh_samples

            ],

            updates

    ) =      theano.scan(

    self.gibbs_hvh,

    outputs_info=[None, None, None, None, None, chain_start],

    n_steps=k

    )

    chain_end = nv_samples[-1]

    cost = T.mean(self.free_energy(self.input)) -
    T.mean(self.free_energy(chain_end))

    gparams = T.grad(cost, self.params,
    consider_constant=[chain_end])

    for gparam, param in zip(gparams, self.params):

    updates[param] = param - gparam * T.cast(lr,
    dtype=theano.config.floatX)
```

```
updates = nh_samples[-1]
```

```
monitoring_cost = self.get_pseudo_likelihood_cost(updates)
```

```
return monitoring_cost, updates
```

In this section of the code we have defined the permanent contrastive divergence algorithm and we have established the learning rate parameter as well as the k parameter. As it suggests, the learning parameter refers to the speed it takes for the algorithm to learn and it gives us the option to adjust it as needed. The k parameter on the other hand represents the amount of steps which the algorithm has to perform in order to determine the value of the free energy. Now let's write the code to establish the training process.

```
def get_pseudo_likelihood_cost(self, updates):
```

```
bit_i_idx = theano.shared(value=0, name='bit_i_idx') xi =
T.round(self.input)
```

```
fe_xi = self.free_energy(xi)
```

```
xi_flip = T.set_subtensor(xi[:, bit_i_idx], 1 - xi[:, bit_i_idx])
```

```
fe_xi_flip = self.free_energy(xi_flip)
```

```
cost = T.mean(self.n_visible * T.log(T.nnet.sigmoid(fe_xi_flip -
fe_xi)))
```

```
        updates[bit_i_idx] = (bit_i_idx + 1) % self.n_visible
```

```
return cost
```

```
train_rbm = theano.function(
```

```
[index],
```

```
cost,
```

```
updates=updates,

givens={x: train_set_x[index * batch_size: (index + 1)
*batch_size] },

name='train_rbm'

)

plotting_time = 0.

start_time = time.clock()
```

(Source: Adapted from RBM tutorial code

http://deeplearning.net/tutorial/code/deep.py retrieved in October 2019)

That's it! We have successfully implemented a restricted Boltzmann machine. This neural network might be somewhat out of your skill range as a beginner, however, it offers you a glimpse of what's to come. Furthermore, you will see that if you analyze the code line by line and read and reread the theory you will understand that a recurrent neural network such as this isn't that difficult to setup. You can even continue exploring this topic on your own, as our model can be improved and extended. The results we obtained are good, but they can always be better.

Summary

In this chapter you learned about the main types of neural networks and where they fit in the world of data science. The purpose of this section was to educate you on topics such as perceptron and recurrent neural networks. While we mostly focused on beginner-friendly theory so that you can fully understand neural networks, we have also worked with an example of the Restricted Boltzmann Machine. Keep in mind that this topic is somewhat more complex and towards the intermediary level, however, you should understand how neural networks work because they are one of the main structures used to create advanced learning and training models. Just make sure to analyze each line of code because the implementation of the Boltzmann machine can be quite lengthy when compared to basic supervised or unsupervised learning algorithms.

Chapter 8: Big Data

In data science, the purpose of supervised and unsupervised learning algorithms is to provide us with the ability to learn from complicated collections of data. The problem is that the data that is being gathered over the past few years has become massive in size. The integration of technology in every aspect of human life and the use of machine learning algorithms to learn from that data in all industries has led to an exponential increase in data gathering. These vast collections of data are known in data science as Big Data. What's the difference between regular datasets and Big Data? The learning algorithms that have been developed over the decades are often affected by the size and complexity of the data they have to process and learn from. Keep in mind that this type of data no longer measures in gigabytes, but sometimes in petabytes, which is an inconceivable number to some as we're talking about values higher than 1000 terabytes when the common household hard drive holds 1 terabyte of information, or even less.

Keep in mind that the concept of Big Data is not new. In fact, it has been theorized over the past decades as data scientists noticed an upward trend in the development of computer processing power, which is correlated with the amount of data that circulates. In the 70s and 80s when many learning algorithms and neural networks were developed, there were no massive amounts of data to process because the technology back then couldn't handle it. Even today, some of the techniques we discussed will not suffice when processing big data. That is why in this chapter we are going to discuss the growing issue of Big Data in order to understand the future challenges you will face as a data scientist.

The Challenge

Nowadays, the problem of Big Data has grown so much that it has become a specialized subfield of data science. While the previous explanation of Big Data was rudimentary with the purpose of demonstrating the problem we will face, you should know that any data is considered Big Data as long as it is a collection of information that contains a large variety of data that continues to grow at an exponential rate. This means that the data volume grows as such a speed that we can no longer keep up with it in order to process and analyze it.

The issue of Big Data appeared before the age of the Internet and online data gathering, and even if today's computers are so much more powerful than in the pre-Internet era, data is still overwhelming to analyze. Just look around you and really focus on how many aspects of your life involve technology. If you stop to think you will realize that even objects that you never considered as data recorders, save some kind of data. Now this thought might make you paranoid, however, keep in mind that most technology records information regarding its use and the user's habits in order to find better ways to improve the technology. The big problem here is that all of this technology generates too much data at a rapid pace. In addition, think about all the smart tech that's being implemented into everyone's homes in the past years. Think of Amazon's Alexa, "smart" thermostats, smart doorbells, smart everything. All of this records data and transmits it. Because of this, many professional data scientists are saying that the current volume of data is being doubled every two years. However, that's not all. The speed at which this amount of data is generated is also increasing roughly every two years. Big Data can barely be comprehended by most tech users. Just think of the difference between your Internet connection today and just five year ago. Even smartphone connections are now powerful and as easy to use as computers.

Keep in mind that we are dealing with a vicious circle when it comes to Big Data. Larger amounts of data generated at higher speeds mean that new computer hardware and software has to be developed in order to handle the data. The development of computer processing power needs to match the data generation. Essentially, we are dealing with a complex game of cat and mouse. To give you a rough idea about this issue, imagine that back in the mid-80s the entire planet's infrastructure could "only" handle around 290 petabytes of information. In the past 2 years, the world has reached a stage where it generates almost 300 petabytes in a span of 24 hours.

What all that in mind, you should understand that not all data is the same. As you probably already know, information comes in various formats. Everything generates some kind of data. Think of emails, crypto currency exchanges, the stock market, computer games, and websites. All of these create data that needs to be gathered and stored, and all of it ends up in different formats. This means that all of the information needs to be separated and categorized before being able to process it with various data science and machine learning algorithms and techniques. This is yet another Big Data challenge that we are going to continue facing for years to come. Remember that most algorithms need to work with a specific data format, therefore data exploration and analysis becomes a great deal more important and more time consuming.

Another issue is the fact that all the gathered information needs to be valued in some way. Just think of social media networks like Twitter. Imagine having to analyze all of the data ever recorded, all of the tweets that have been written since the conception of the platform. This would be extremely time consuming no matter the processing power of the computers managing it. All of the collected data would have to be pre-processed and analyzed in order to determine which data is valuable and in good condition. Furthermore, Big Data like what we just discussed raises the issue of security. Again, think about social media platforms, which are famous for data gathering. Some of the data includes personal information that belongs to the users and we all know what a disaster a Big Data breach can be. Just think of the recent Cambridge Analytica scandal. Another example is the European Union's reaction to the cybersecurity threats involving Big Data which led to the creation of the General Data Protection Regulation with the purpose of defining a set of rules regarding data gathering. Company data leaks can be damaging, but Big Data leaks lead to international disasters and changes in governments. But enough about the fear and paranoia that surrounds today's Big Data. Let's discuss the quality and accuracy of the information, which is what primarily concerns us.

A Big Data collection never contains a consistent level of quality and value when it comes to information. Massive datasets may contain accurate and valuable data that we can use, however, without a doubt it also involve a number of factors that lead to inaccuracy. One of the first questions you need to ask yourself is regarding those who have recorded the data and prepared the datasets. Have they made some assumptions in order to fill in the blanks? Have they always recorded nothing but facts and accurate data? Furthermore, you need to concern yourself with the type of storage system that was used to hold on to that data and who had access to it. Did someone do anything to change the data? Was the storage system damaged in some way that led to the corruption of a large number of files? In addition, you need to consider the way that data was measured. Imagine four devices being used in the same area to measure the temperature of the air. All of that data was recorded, but every device shows a different value. Which one of them holds the right values? Which one has inaccurate measurements? Did someone make any mistakes during the data gathering process?

Big Data poses many challenges and raises many questions. There are many variables that influence the quality and the value of data and we need to consider them before getting to the actual data. We have to deal with the limitations of technology, the possibility of human error, faulty equipment, badly written algorithms, and so on. This is why Big Data became a specialization of its own. It is highly complex and that is why we are taking this section of the book to discuss the fundamentals of Big Data and challenges you would face as a data scientist if you choose to specialize in it.

Applications in the Real World

Big Data is a component of Data Science, which means that as long as something generates and records data, this field will continue being developed. Therefore if you are still having doubts regarding your newly acquired skill, you should stop. Just think about a market crash. Imagine it as bad as any other financial disasters in the last century. This event would generate a great deal of data, personal, commercial, scientific and so on. Someone will have to process and analyze everything and that would take years no matter how many data scientists you would have available.

However, catastrophes aside, you will still have to rely on a number of pre-processing, processing and analysis in order to work with the data. The only difference is that datasets will continue to grow and in the foreseeable future we will no longer deal with small datasets like the ones we are using in this book for practice. Big Data is the future, and you will have to implement more powerful learning models and even combine them for maximum prediction accuracy. With that being said, let's explore the uses of Big Data in order to understand where you would apply your skills:

1. Maintenance: Sounds boring, but with the automation of everything, massive amounts of data are produced and with it we can determine when a certain hardware component or tool will reach its breaking point. Maintenance is part of every industry whether we're talking about manufacturing steel nails or airplanes. Big Data recorded in such industries will contain data on all the materials that were used and the various attributes that describe them. We can process this information and achieve a result that will immediately tell us when a component or tool should expire or need maintenance. This is a simple example of how Big Data analysis and data science in general can be useful to a business.

2. Sales: Think of all the online platforms and shops that offer products or services. More and more of the turn up every single day. Large businesses are even warring with each other over the acquisition of data so that they can better predict the spending habits of their customers in order to learn how to attract those who aren't interested or how to convince the current ones to make more purchases. Market information is generated at a staggering pace and it allows us to predict certain human behavioral patterns that can generate more business and the improvement of various products and services.

3. Optimization: Big Data is difficult and costly to process and analyze, however, it is more than worth it since corporations are investing more and more into data scientists and machine learners. This kind of data analysis provides them with the much needed information to make their business more efficient and

well-optimized. The larger a company is, the more cracks can be found through which they lose time and money. Predicting various costs and market trends can have a massive impact on a company's or even government's spending habits.

As you can see, analyzing Big Data is one of the next steps in data science as more and more data becomes available. Try to visualize the fact that the global society has generated nearly 90% of all information ever recorded in only two years. Every bit of data is valuable to some degree and you will have to learn all the algorithms and techniques that will help you process Big Data. With that being said, let's take a brief look at some of these techniques that are in use today to explore and process vast amounts of information.

Analyzing Big Data

In the previous chapters we have discussed a number of supervised and unsupervised learning algorithms that are used to explore, process, and analyze data. Additionally, we have also explored neural networks with the purpose of creating powerful models that can deliver accurate results. However, keep in mind that so far we talked about regular datasets. As previously mentioned, Big Data is different. Fortunately, some of the techniques and algorithms you learned can also be used to classify Big Data. In this section we will briefly summarize which methods can be used to process massive volumes of data.

When it comes to supervised learning algorithms you can use support vector machines, the Naïve Bayes algorithm, Boosting algorithm, the Maximum Entropy Method and more. Some of these are beyond a beginner's scope, therefore we did not focus on them in this book. However, you still have some options. Furthermore, you can also use a number of classification techniques such as the K-nearest neighbor algorithm or Decision Trees. Remember that classification simply involves discrete class attributes, while regression involves continuous class attributes. To solve Big Data regression problems you can use both the linear and logistic regression methods.

On the other side we have unsupervised learning algorithms which use unlabeled data in order to classify it by performing a comparison operation on all the data features. In this case you can rely on clustering algorithms, such as the K-means clustering algorithm we discussed earlier. Other techniques you can use are the Adaptive Resonance Theory and the Self Organizing Maps. Feel free to explore these last two on your own. Furthermore, you pursue clustering techniques at a deeper level because they are excellent when working with Big Data. For instance, you can use supervised clustering methods, which involve determining clusters that have a high probability density regarding the individual classes. Ideally, you want to use supervised clustering algorithms only when you have target variables and training sets which included them inside a cluster.

Another option is using unsupervised clustering techniques because they can lower the value of the intercluster similarity and therefore increase it. Keep in mind that these methods are best used on a specific function. K-means clustering is one of these techniques and it remains one of the most popular ones in use even when it comes to Big Data.

Finally, we have semi-supervised clustering algorithms. In this case we have more than just a similarity parameter. This category of clustering methods allows us to make modifications to the domain information. This way clustering can be significantly improved. This information can also act as limitations between the observations variables.

As a beginner, if you attempt working with Big Data, you should focus on using binary classifiers such as the support vector machines you learned about, or data classifiers such as decision trees. Stick to what is familiar for now, however, you should always feel encouraged to experiment on your own. As you can see there are many algorithms and techniques and we can fit only so much in one book. Feel free to use the knowledge you gained so far because it is all you need to get started on your own.

Summary

This chapter was a brief summary of what Big Data involves. You learned the history and fundamentals of this concept, as well as why you should consider focusing more on this topic. Data is generated all around us and soon, smaller datasets will be a thing of the past. Remember that information is generated at an exponential rate and currently our computers and the current number of data scientists and machine learners cannot catch up. There are even Big Data sets that have been gathered over a span of 20 years and they are still waiting to be processed and analyzed. This is a specialization of the future and you should seek to use what you have learned so far on such massive volumes of data. Some of the algorithms you studied can be applied as they are, while some need to be adapted. Use the toolkit you gathered so far and explore how it is to work with Big Data.

Conclusion

Congratulations are in order, as you successfully completed your fundamental training in data science. You came a long way from learning how to install your Python work environment. Sit back and allow time to solidify your knowledge because you have just processed a great deal of information. Data science isn't a light topic, and some of the techniques and algorithms you explored can be challenging.

Now that you have finished learning the basics, you should take the time to go over this book one more time to make sure you didn't overlook anything. It is vital that you understand the theory behind these learning algorithms and analysis techniques before you advance to the next stage. Take what you have learned so far, and make sure to practice every concept on your own with one of the widely available open source datasets. By learning everything in a structured manner and applying it into practice, you will become a data scientist in no time!

Bibliography

Albon, C. (2018). *Machine learning with Python cookbook: practical solutions from preprocessing to deep learning.* Sebastopol, CA: OReilly Media.

Garreta Raúl, & Moncecchi, G. (2013). *Learning scikit-learn: machine learning in Python: experience the benefits of machine learning techniques by applying them to real-world problems using Python and the open source scikit-learn library.* Birmingham, UK: Packt Publishing Ltd.

Géron Aurélien. (2019). *Hands-on machine learning with Scikit-Learn and TensorFlow: concepts, tools, and techniques to build intelligent systems.* Beijing ; Boston ; Farnham ; Sebastopol ; Tokyo: OReilly Media.

Zaccone, G., & Karim, M. R. (2018). *Deep Learning with TensorFlow: Explore neural networks and build intelligent systems with Python, 2nd Edition.* Birmingham: Packt Publishing.

www.ingramcontent.com/pod-product-compliance
Lightning Source LLC
Chambersburg PA
CBHW071057050326
40690CB00008B/1047